THE NO-TILL
ORGANIC VEGETABLE FARM

T0385110

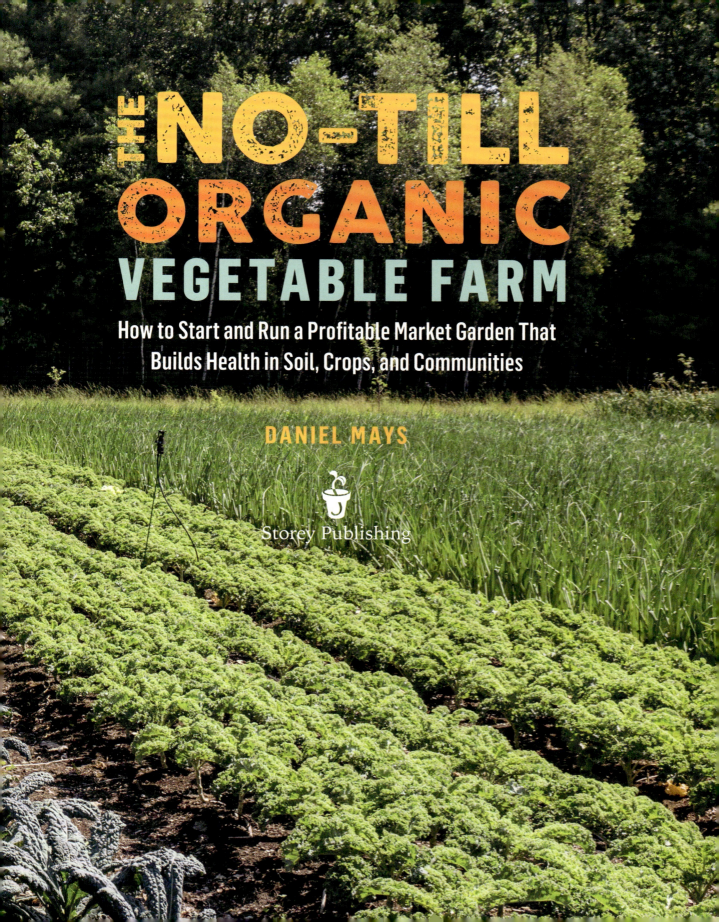

THE NO-TILL ORGANIC VEGETABLE FARM

VEGETABLE FARM

How to Start and Run a Profitable Market Garden That
Builds Health in Soil, Crops, and Communities

DANIEL MAYS

Storey Publishing

The mission of Storey Publishing is to serve our customers by publishing practical information that encourages personal independence in harmony with the environment.

Edited by Deborah Burns
Art direction and book design by Michaela Jebb
Text production by Jennifer Jepson Smith
Indexed by Nancy D. Wood

Cover and interior photography by © John Benford/ johnbenfordphoto.com
Additional photography by Daniel Mays and Sarah Coburn, vii l. & r., 13, 23 r., 24, 25, 29, 30, 38, 40, 56, 58, 59 r., 64, 65, 68, 69 b., 72, 77, 78, 81, 84 t.r., 85, 86 r., 87, 103 b., 109–111, 116, 119, 124, 126 r., 134–136, 137 ex. t.r., 138, 141, 142, 143 r., 147–150, 155, 162 b. (both), 169 r., 170, 172, 175, 181–187, 191, 193–198, 205, 214, 216, 228; Courtesy of Greg and Justina Hamberg, viii, 41, 46; © Mark Brundrett, 20
Illustrations by © Steve Sanford

Storey books are available at special discounts when purchased in bulk for premiums and sales promotions as well as for fund-raising or educational use. Special editions or book excerpts can also be created to specification. For details, please call 800-827-8673, or send an email to sales@storey.com.

Storey Publishing
210 MASS MoCA Way
North Adams, MA 01247
storey.com

Printed in China through World Print
10 9 8 7 6 5 4 3

LIBRARY OF CONGRESS CATALOGING-IN-PUBLICATION DATA

Names: Mays, Daniel (Farmer), author.
Title: The no-till organic vegetable farm / Daniel Mays.
Description: [North Adams, MA] : Storey Publishing, [2020] | Includes bibliographical references and index. | Summary: "Author Daniel Mays outlines the environmental, social, and economic benefits of the no-till farming method"— Provided by publisher.
Identifiers: LCCN 2020022024 (print) | LCCN 2020022025 (ebook) | ISBN 9781635861891 (paperback) | ISBN 9781635861907 (ebook)
Subjects: LCSH: No-tillage. | Vegetables—Organic farming.
Classification: LCC S604 .M347 2020 (print) | LCC S604 (ebook) | DDC 635/.0484—dc23
LC record available at https://lccn.loc.gov/2020022024
LC ebook record available at https://lccn.loc .gov/2020022025

For Stuart and Ellis.
You inspire me to be a better
father and son.

CONTENTS

FROM THE GROUND UP

I started Frith Farm with little experience and no background in agriculture. I had minimal savings and no close farming mentors. I was a classic wannabe: full of energy and enthusiasm but without skills or knowledge. I was determined to make it as a farmer, though, even if that meant making sacrifices and living frugally. And I was privileged to have a network of family and friends who supported me in my brazen ideas for starting a farm.

Nine years later I am managing a farm that has taken on a vibrant life of its own. It is a self-sustaining organism that employs a full-time seasonal crew of nine people, provides food for hundreds of families, earns enough profit to re-invest back into the farm generously each season, and supports an ever-increasing diversity of flourishing life. Nine years ago I never would have dreamed what was possible.

I wrote this book to share the lessons I have learned through my journey from inexperience and depleted soils to a coherent set of no-till practices and a highly productive farm. If I could do it, so can others — and the world needs more farmers.

The planet as we know it is in peril, and agricultural practices are at the root of the problem. Farmers have the unique ability to lead the way to a healthier population, a more sustainable economy, a more just food system, and a more hospitable planet. What an opportunity! What a responsibility. My hope is that this book empowers and encourages more people to take the leap into small-scale regenerative agriculture, and to find success in doing so. The problems of the world are vast, but I believe the solutions begin with the microscopic life below our feet, and the small-time farmers who nurture it to feed their communities.

As anthropologist Margaret Mead said, "Never doubt that a small group of thoughtful, committed citizens can change the world; indeed, it's the only thing that ever has." Let's save the world one earthworm at a time. Let's pull carbon out of the atmosphere and turn it into life-giving soil. Let's build food sovereignty and community health. Let's create local economies. Let's make a good living working intimately with one another and the earth.

1

Growing a Farm

The principles and practices described in this book are based on nine years of starting and managing Frith Farm in Scarborough, Maine. Full of idealism and the energy that graced my mid-twenties, I borrowed money to buy a property with five open acres and a crumbling old house and barn in the fall of 2010. Up to that time, I had volunteered on a number of farms but had yet to work a full season.

The first few years were filled with experimentation, countless mistakes, and the many joys of learning by doing. The 200-year-old farmhouse was in serious disrepair, and it was no small task to gut and renovate (and live in) the house while establishing the farm. The farm would not exist as it does today without the help of friends, family, neighbors, and the stalwart apprentices of those early years.

From the first year growing for 40 community supported agriculture (CSA) families on less than an acre, the farm has expanded to serve a CSA membership of over 150 families as well as four natural food stores, our local farmers' market, and an on-farm store. The operation remains small and intensive, with almost all work done by hand.

While I am wary of undervaluing the farm's growth with financial figures, I recognize that economic viability enables other features of prosperity that cannot be measured in dollars. So here it is: I began the farm with a loan of $180,000 and an interest rate of 3.8 percent. Four years later, the farm grossed over $250,000 in a season. Today, the farm sells about $300,000 of food each year from 2½ acres of vegetables and about the same size of pasture. All profits are reinvested in the farm and its community.

We work hard as a crew for an average of 45 hours a week during the growing season and take off four months, more or less, each winter. The farm has remained my sole source of income from day one and has grown from the dream of an impetuous twenty-six-year-old to a successful business that supports and is supported by a large community of people.

I realize that finances are an important aspect of agricultural sustainability, but I would caution anyone who wants to farm for purely economic reasons. For me, the value of farm life is not measured in dollars but in the smell of the land after a summer rain; the feel of calloused hands, tired muscles, and sun-soaked skin; the community of organisms with whom life is shared; the taste and vitality of the fruits of our labor; and the sense of nourishing something greater than ourselves.

This book is a how-to manual for intensive no-till vegetable production on a small commercial scale. It is also a treatise on the importance of a holistic approach to agriculture and to life on a shared planet. My goal in writing it is to show that successful no-till farming not only is financially feasible and accessible to the beginning farmer, it also enables a level of care for the soil, for the farm's community, and for the planet that can guide us to a more productive, fulfilling, and prosperous way of life.

Like many farming authors, I am writing a book for my younger self. These are the pages that I would have most benefited from reading when I was taking my first steps as a farmer.

FRITH FARM LOAF

$7 SIFTED WHEAT, HAND-MILLED RYE, ORGANIC AP FLOUR, WATER, SALT

A GOOD ALL-PURPOSE SOURDOUGH

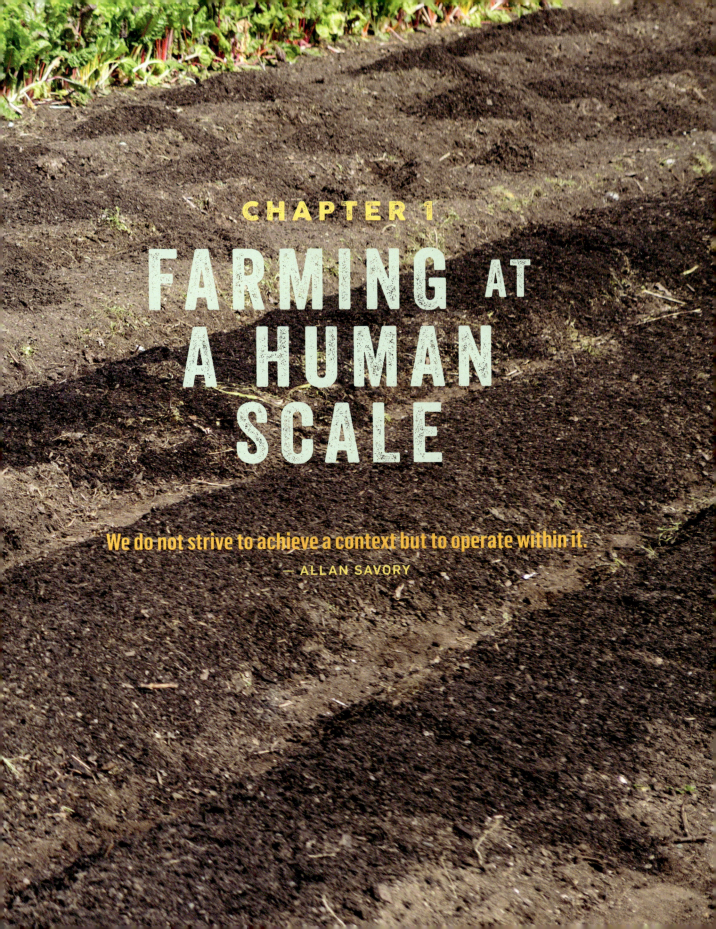

CHAPTER 1

FARMING AT A HUMAN SCALE

We do not strive to achieve a context but to operate within it.
— ALLAN SAVORY

No-till human-scale farming is about so much more than avoiding tillage. I believe the methods described in this book can lead to healthier soil, higher productivity, fewer weeds, lower costs, and a more natural way of growing food. Understanding the principles behind no-till will help clarify the practices detailed later in the book. This chapter lays out the clear benefits of this way of farming, as well as the values that guide our no-till practices at Frith Farm.

Nature as Model

Ten years ago I attended graduate school to study issues of sustainability and energy efficiency in the design and construction of buildings. The essential questions asked were, "What are the most efficient systems to install?" and "What are the greenest materials to use?" (The answers almost always involved clever new technologies and some form of bamboo.)

Years later, I realize why I left my higher educational experience feeling unsatisfied: we were asking the wrong questions. It is now clear to me that the most sustainable 3,000-square-foot single-family home is the one that is never built. The energy analysis of a glass building in Arizona should probably focus more on the sanity of the architect than on the properties of the glazing. No matter how "energy-efficient" those windows are, they're still fighting against the sun.

Not unrelated, the best approach to caring for the soil is usually to stop messing with it. If history lends any insight, the most positive step we as westernized humans can take toward sustainability is to slow down and rethink our relationship to the natural world.

In the mid-1900s, Masanobu Fukuoka developed a "do-nothing" way of farming, and his philosophy offers much insight for agriculture, and for human activity in general. Our busyness as a capitalist culture, and as an increasingly mechanized world, is tied to the root of our problems; we have trained ourselves to act, analyze, and impose control rather than observe, appreciate, and work with nature.

Tillage is symbolic of this drive to engineer everything. It would seem the only meaningful result is the one we design and manufacture with our own human ingenuity. The fact that untilled soils around the globe produce more biomass and support greater biodiversity than tilled ground is lost on many of us because we did not create those ecosystems. If we want fluffy, weed-free soil to plant into, then doggonit, we'd better make a machine that will kill weeds and fluff up the soil. Who has the time or humility to wait for biological processes to build soil structure or to suppress weeds naturally with cover crops and organic mulches? Our insistence on fighting nature is astounding, and it carries profound implications increasingly evident across the planet.

But there is hope! Ecological approaches to growing food are on the rise. Many of us are starting to listen to indigenous knowledge and to the fact that the natural world holds answers to just about all our questions. Recognizing tillage for what it is - a largely unnecessary application of mechanical power to a biological system - is a step toward a more reciprocal way of farming that honors and works *within* natural systems instead of *against* them.

Adopting an attitude of minimal soil disturbance involves not only rethinking our farming methods, but also rethinking our ways of thinking. Instead of asking "What's the best way to do this?" and "What can I do to fix that?", we might step back and consider "What's the best way *not* to do this?" and "What can I *stop* doing to fix that?"

In this view, it becomes clear that tillage is not the only practice that is antithetical to farming within natural systems. Tractors, pesticides, plasticulture, insect netting, fertilizers, and even irrigation can distract from and replace biological solutions. As Fukuoka puts it, "When you get right down to it, there are few agricultural practices that are really necessary."

Since starting Frith Farm I have been conscious of how our practices are defined by what they are not: no till, no spray, no tractor in the fields, and almost no mechanization in general. I have also come to accept that perhaps the lack of practices is its own practice, as Fukuoka suggests.

Beyond Sustainability

I believe these ideas can help guide us toward a prosperous future. As modern industry begrudgingly accepts that the world's resources are finite, the goal of sustainability takes on increasing urgency. Unfortunately, the word "sustainable" is often misused to describe a practice or product that is relatively eco-friendly, or less damaging than its counterparts. Rarely do we see the word stand for a comprehensive effort to maximize positive environmental, social, and economic impacts simultaneously.

Agriculture that is truly sustainable is about much more than reducing fertilizer runoff, or decreasing fossil fuel use; agriculture has the unique ability — and thus the responsibility — to have a net positive effect on the environment, the economy, and the social fabric of our communities. Farming is one of the few vocations that has the potential to actually achieve this triple bottom line. Unlike most other modern activities, agriculture can generate more resources than it depletes, and can create sustenance, jobs, and community connections without mining the natural capital of the planet.

Good farming can even reverse some of the unsustainable "progress" we humans have made, beginning with the "Age of Discovery" and accelerated with the industrial revolution. As farmers, we can build soil, reduce atmospheric carbon, restore ecosystem services, and repair human connections through our relationships with the land. And the need for a shift toward net-positive farming has never been more real.

We have trained ourselves to act, analyze, and impose control rather than observe, appreciate, and work with nature.

Whenever an idea or practice challenges convention, there is no shortage of naysayers. Small no-till farms are all too easy to write off, as they are antithetical to the conventional economic values of perpetual growth and large-scale mechanization. The goal of this book is to show that no-till farming on a few acres is not only possible — it can be at once economically, socially, and ecologically enriching.

Rethinking Tillage

The problems associated with tillage are severe and far-reaching. Through erosion and loss of organic matter, tillage is helping to degrade the very substance from which human life is built. An algal bloom the size of New Jersey in the Gulf of Mexico is more than an eyesore for vacationers; it represents the fertility of the continent running downhill into the ocean. The widespread eutrophication of ponds and lakes and the pollution of wells and aquifers tells the same story of soil abuse.

The effects of soil loss are not just downstream. The productivity of farms is dropping, even as inputs increase. The loss of organic matter — of life itself — in our agricultural soils is perhaps the gravest problem we now face as a terrestrial species. As author and geologist David Montgomery puts it, ". . . an agricultural civilization that degrades the soil will be transient — it cannot last if it destroys its own foundation."

Tillage is not the only culprit in our history of soil degradation, but it is a fundamental player. The act of tilling injects the soil with oxygen and kills a host of living creatures, causing a quick release of nutrients for the next crop. In other words, tillage cashes in long-term soil health for a short-term flush of fertility. It also breaks down soil structure, which leads to compaction and erosion.

So why till? Farmers have been tilling for thousands of years, and there are pragmatic reasons for doing so. Tillage is a temporary cure-all: no matter what state our fields are in, if we make enough passes with plow, disc, or rototiller, we are left with consistent, fluffy, weed-free soil — at least on the surface and for a moment. This step can be supremely gratifying, as it buries weeds, loosens the soil, and wipes the slate clean for a new planting.

But this satisfaction is usually short-lived. The flip side of tilling under all those seeds from last season is that the millions of weed seeds tilled under in previous years get turned back up toward the surface, causing an explosion of unwanted growth just after we catch a fleeting glimpse of the clean, freshly tilled field. Similarly, that nice-looking fluffed-up soil soon collapses under the forces of rain and gravity, its physical structure pulverized by the fast-moving metal of tillage implements. Pretty soon we are left with a compacted, overgrown field, and, yet again, turn to tillage to help us start over.

The Way Out

No-till farming is a way out of this vicious cycle. It allows us to prepare and plant beds without all the work and machinery that tillage requires — and without the harm it inflicts on the soil. This book presents an approach to no-till vegetable production that goes well beyond the USDA's Organic requirements and replaces short-lived solutions like tillage, cultivation, routine fertilization, and spraying of pesticides with methods that focus on the long-term health of the soil and the life it supports. The reasons to farm without tillage are numerous and overlapping and include environmental, economic, and human benefits.

Tasks, Tillage Implements, and No-Till Alternatives

Task	Tillage Implement	No-Till Alternative
Kill sod or established crop	Moldboard plow Disc harrow	Mow and smother with tarps or sheet mulch
Create plantable seedbed	Power harrow Bed shaper	Rake off debris to direct seed Transplant into stubble
Aerate & mix soil	Rototiller Reciprocating spader	Encourage natural action of plant roots and soil organisms
Manage weeds	Cultivators Rototiller	Prevent germination by leaving soil undisturbed and covered
Break up compaction	Chisel plow Subsoiler	Plant taprooted cover crops Broadfork

ENVIRONMENTAL BENEFITS OF NO-TILL

Preserves soil ecosystem. Soil organisms and their habitat are not pulverized by fast-moving metal.

Improves soil structure. Porosity and soil aggregates are left intact, and compacting forces of tractor and steel are avoided.

Reduces erosion. Undisturbed soil covered in plant material naturally resists the erosive forces of wind and rain.

Causes less pollution. No-till requires less machinery and causes less erosion, so air pollution from dust and exhaust and water pollution from agricultural runoff are minimized.

Conserves organic matter. Tillage hastens the loss of organic matter; no-till practices conserve organic matter, along with the associated benefits to microorganisms, fertility, pest and disease resistance, and water-holding capacity.

Decreases amount of carbon in the air. With more carbon sequestered in undisturbed soil, less remains in the atmosphere to affect the planet's climate.

Provides ecosystem services. A healthy and intact soil ecosystem provides numerous services to humans, from the purification of air and water to the regenerative cycling of minerals, water, and carbon.

ECONOMIC BENEFITS OF NO-TILL

Allows earlier planting dates. With no tractor work required, there is no need to wait for fields to dry out before planting.

Reduces weeds. The majority of weed seeds remain buried in the soil, so that only those at the surface are a concern.

Enables intensive spacing and higher yields. Without the need to follow tractor dimensions, closer spacing of crop plants is possible, along with higher yield potentials.

Cuts down on work. Forming planting beds and setting up irrigation systems are one-time operations within a no-till system.

Provides low-capital opportunities. Without the need for expensive tractors and implements, no-till farming is more accessible to farmers with low capital.

Requires fewer manufactured inputs. Undisturbed healthy soil leads to higher yields, fewer pests, and less disease without the need for fertilizers, pesticides, or other purchased products.

HUMAN BENEFITS OF NO-TILL

Invites engagement. Growing at a scale that can largely be managed with human labor (without tillage equipment) is appealing to customers, neighbors, and employees and invites engagement from community members.

Increases worker satisfaction. Farm tools, practices, and enterprises are sized to celebrate the satisfaction and fulfillment of human work.

Creates a healthier work environment. The reduced exhaust, dust, and noise of no-till farming makes for a healthier, more pleasant place to work.

Improves worker safety. Growing without large tractors and fast-moving implements creates a safer work environment.

Connects humans and the land. With a higher ratio of humans to acres, farming becomes social, and the line between work and play is blurred.

Promotes innovation. Humans will always be more versatile and adaptable than machines, and innovation on the farm is proportional to the number of human minds engaged in its work.

Conventional, "Organic," and No-Till Approaches to Common Agricultural Goals

ISSUE	APPROACHES		
	Conventional	"Organic"	No-Till
Soil Preparation	Heavy tillage	Low-till techniques	Plant into crop residues and undisturbed soil
Fertility	Synthetic fertilizers	Organic fertilizers	High organic matter and active soil biology
Weeds	Herbicides	Tillage, cultivation, bare fallow	Undisturbed soil covered in living plants and organic mulches
Pests	Synthetic pesticides	Organic pesticides, physical exclusion	Biodiversity, soil health, and habitat for beneficials
Disease	Synthetic biocides	Organic biocides, scouting and pruning	Soil health, crop rotation, and biodiversity

Farming Values

I started Frith Farm with little hands-on experience and only a very basic understanding of soil health. I read a number of books on the subject, and they all agreed that tillage was generally harmful to the soil. Having no other experience to dissuade me, I figured I would stop tilling once my beds were formed. This meant I did not need to invest in a tractor. I was also intimidated by the idea of pest control, so I was delighted to read Eliot Coleman's plant-positive philosophy, which gave me permission to ignore the practice of spraying pesticides.

The simple choice to farm without tillage, tractors, or pesticides had profound implications. Many questions having to do with scale, labor, markets, and soil care were immediately answered. Traveling this road of minimal soil disturbance opened my eyes to observations and ideas that would have passed right under me if I had been seated on a tractor (or otherwise following practices of other established farms). I learned much about the wholeness of a farm and

the modest role a farmer can ideally play within it. I experienced the value of work scaled to the human body. And I began to appreciate the importance of thinking beyond the present — whether this moment, this year, or this lifetime — to care for the future in the decisions of daily life.

There are a handful of core concepts that inspire and give context to our work at Frith Farm:

- Holistic thinking
- Ecological humility
- Sufficiency and simplicity
- Human scale
- Long-term vision

Holistic Thinking

Holistic thinking comprehends the world in terms of systems and patterns instead of objects and material. Within ecological systems, the concept of individuality is meaningless. There are no boundaries in nature. Even in the human body — the ultimate vessel of individuality — human cells are outnumbered by those of other organisms such as bacteria by a factor of ten to one. In plants, mycorrhizal fungi enter the cell walls of a plant's roots, becoming one with the plant on a cellular level. The health of an organism is inseparable from the health of the system of life it lives in and the system of life that lives inside it.

Ecologist and farmer Allan Savory applies holistic thinking to agriculture with eloquence and pragmatism. He presents the analogy that a collection of pixels, when studied individually, provide little insight toward the picture they create when viewed as a whole. Our increasingly specialized world excels at separating these pixels one by one, sorting them according to discipline, and studying each in meticulous detail. Experts from each field discuss the qualities of their given pixel and refrain from commenting on those outside their area of expertise. As a result, we often end up with an intricate jumble of disconnected information that confuses rather than clarifies the big picture. Like the collection of pixels, the phenomena of the natural world are most meaningful when considered as a whole.

Likewise, we would do well to recognize the farm as a single organism, containing a world of organisms within it, and positioned in a community of organisms that together form still larger systems, all the way up to the planet as a whole.

Examples of fragmented, non-holistic thinking are common in agriculture. When we till to break up compaction, we apply the very forces of weight and steel that cause compaction. When we spray to kill a pest, we kill off the food source for natural predators, preventing the very ecological balance that would remedy our problem. Our shortsighted actions have consequences that ripple outward through the seamless fabric of the natural world. The best way to prevent unintended consequences is to consider the holistic context of our decisions, and to make them in accordance with the examples set by nature.

Ecological Humility

Accepting our place in nature requires ecological humility. Western culture assumes humans are the center of the universe and that all else revolves around us, but this assumption could benefit from its own Copernican revolution. To say we are at the center of earthly life would suggest we are somehow separate from its seamless web. We cannot be at the top of the food chain when the patterns of life are cyclical and we are all worm food in the end.

By contrast, when we exist in harmony with the natural world — when our efforts align with natural processes and enhance ecosystem functioning — we start to heal our connection to the place that sustains us. No product or process of human invention has ever surpassed nature's powers of renewability. No human economy has been so resilient as the waste-free economy of nature, powered entirely by sunlight and run continually for millions of years. There is no other proven model.

If history is any guide, it is unlikely we will invent a new solution to our ecological problems. The path to the promised land is all around us; all that's required is to humbly follow rather than hold on to the vanity that requires a road of our own making.

Sufficiency and Simplicity

The prevailing attitude of the industrialized world is that unfettered growth and consumption form the basis of a "healthy" economy. The concept of sufficiency challenges this idea of growth for growth's sake. Sufficiency is the state of being adequate or enough, and until we are satisfied with what is sufficient, humans will continue to play a parasitic role on this planet instead of living in symbiosis with its natural systems. A healthy ecosystem generates no waste, and producing or consuming beyond our needs is wasteful by definition.

Satisfaction becomes possible only when we search out what is *enough* instead of continually striving for *more*. The concept of sufficiency challenges the classic economic assumption that consumption is the only path toward "utility," or happiness, and that endless production leads to endless wealth. As author Robin Wall Kimmerer puts it, "In a consumer society, contentment is a radical proposition. Recognizing abundance rather than scarcity undermines an economy that thrives by creating unmet desires." By basing our happiness on growth, we are chasing an economic goal that is by its very definition unattainable, and therefore self-defeating. As we unlearn this doctrine of growth and depletion, we enable a more natural system that values quality over quantity, fulfillment over ambition, and sufficiency over excess.

In the context of farming, seeking sufficiency starts with doing less, and doing it better. Taking on more than we can do well is not only bad for the farm's bottom line, it is also detrimental to our sense of accomplishment and well-being. By farming small and simply, we feel confident and in control of our work and are rested and excited for each new day. By limiting our undertakings and assets, we can devote more attention to — and derive more satisfaction from — those we choose to keep. Sufficiency is as much a state of mind as it is a set of skills and infrastructure.

Sufficiency and simplicity go hand in hand. The prevailing notions of the industrialized world are that bigger is better, progress and growth are equivalent, and success is achieved by adopting increasingly specialized technologies and machinery. Simple farming, on the other hand, embraces minimalism and allows us to declutter and shed those objects, practices, and enterprises that bring us neither joy nor livelihood. As humans, we have finite energy to plan, execute, and reflect on our activities — why waste it on unfulfilling busyness? As we simplify our work and our lives, we free up mental capacity to focus on what matters most, and we allow ourselves time and space to actually enjoy it.

Human Scale

Human scale refers to tools, practices, enterprises, and organizations that are sized for human use, satisfaction, and comprehension. When the farm is sized to celebrate the fulfilling nature of human work, the work itself benefits from the increased care that this scale affords. Human scale honors work as craft instead of monotony, and it implies a minimum of machinery. In his ever-relevant book, *Small Is Beautiful*, economist E. F. Schumacher writes about the difference between a tool and a machine — the former being an extension of the worker's hand and a positive influence on his creative ability, and the latter offering a mechanical replacement for the essentially human part of the work.

The no-till farming described in this book relies largely on hand tools and human power, minimizing the use of machinery and encouraging the healthy engagement of our bodies with our work. Farming is labor-intensive, but it can and should involve work that honors our creative spirit and provides daily satisfaction and long-term fulfillment. Physical work seldom becomes drudgery when it is performed with the right tools at an appropriate scale.

Human scale also relates to the value of community. We cannot work at a human scale if we do not live in close relation to other humans. Community, by definition, only exists at a human scale; it is what grounds us and what connects us to a place and to one another. Community is the web of relationships, places, and shared knowledge that influences our decisions and which, in turn, is shaped by their outcomes. The larger the scale of our undertakings, the more we stretch this web thin and distance ourselves from one another and from the consequences of our actions.

The low-tech nature of the no-till farm also makes the farm less foreign and overwhelming to neighbors and customers, enabling them to understand at a glance how their food is grown. Gardeners can take what they see and apply it at

home, without the need for expensive machinery or specialized equipment. Knowledge is shared best through direct human interaction.

Long-Term Vision

Long-term vision supports decisions that give priority to the future of the farm, its community, and the world, even if those decisions require more work or offer less financial reward in the short term. As a consumer society, we prefer what benefits us *now* over what might benefit us in myriad ways down the road. Economic development follows the formula of the parasite: extract, consume, deplete, and move on.

A vision of long-term sustainability is just the opposite. The no-till farmer can strive to create a holistic context of prosperity instead of focusing on individual benchmarks of success. Through diverse and active soil biology, rather than tillage or an injection of fertilizer, no-till farming promotes healthy soil structure and sustained fertility. Soil health and biodiversity create stable conditions that protect against outbreaks of pests and disease, avoiding short-term fixes, like pesticides and fungicides, that are counterproductive in the long run.

Long-term vision requires patience and persistence and recognizes that present prosperity is hollow if it sacrifices posterity's well-being. In pursuing our desired life we must protect and replenish the resource base that will sustain that quality of life into the future.

CHAPTER 2
ECOLOGICAL AGRICULTURE

It cannot be attained, but will happen of its own accord,
if we will only let it.

— CHRISTOPHER ALEXANDER

Following nature's model is easier when we understand the principles that drive ecosystem health. This chapter looks at the science of soil health, and how farmers can generate their own cycles of fertility, pest and disease resistance, weed prevention, and productivity by following nature's template.

Science and Soil Health

The science of soil is often divided into three main disciplines: physics, chemistry, and biology.

Physics looks at the physical properties of soil, such as structure, porosity, aggregation, and holding capacity. These properties determine the soil's ability to accept air and water and to hold moisture and nutrients and convey them to plant roots. They also allow for the movement of soil organisms.

Chemistry involves the essential chemical elements — nutrients — of soil, primarily nitrogen, phosphorus, and potassium, as well as dozens of trace minerals. Plants need a balanced spread of accessible chemical elements in order to thrive.

Biology focuses on the *life* of the soil — the vast and infinitely intricate system of plant matter, bacteria, fungi, and other organisms that form the soil food web.

Physics, chemistry, and biology illuminate fragments of the soil's holistic reality. Analyzing one without considering the whole yields an incomplete picture. The physical properties of the soil provide a setting for chemical reactions and help retain (or leach) nutrients. The soil's physical structure also affects biological habitat by allowing (or inhibiting) the movement of air, water, roots, and soil organisms. In turn, the biological activity in the soil changes and improves the soil structure over time, creating a positive feedback loop of soil health.

Plants need the correct balance of chemical nutrients, while biological interactions tie up and release these nutrients into the soil solution. All these processes form the soil ecosystem. When they are in balance, they support the diversity and abundance of underground life that defines soil health.

Where conventional agriculture gets it wrong is in its nearly myopic focus on chemistry. Chemical analysis of soil "health" typically involves testing the levels of available nitrogen, phosphorus, and potassium (and maybe a handful of other nutrients in a soil or crop sample) and then correcting the apparent deficiencies with fertilizer applications. But basing the needs of an entire underground ecosystem on a snapshot of chemicals provides an oversimplified view of soil health and ignores a whole world of biological soil interactions and long-term sources of fertility.

By contrast, biological approaches to agriculture focus on the life of the soil. The billions of organisms that form the soil food web, when properly cared for, create optimal conditions for plant growth. As the soil guru Dr. Elaine Ingham puts it, "If we want clean water, we have to get the biology back in our soils. If we want to grow and harvest crops, we have to build soil and fertility with time, not destroy it. The only way to reach these endpoints is to improve the life in the soil."

Any time science attempts to isolate an aspect of the living world there is immediate risk of oversimplification. There is something lost when infinitely complex systems of life are reduced to replicable test results. If we speak of agriculture in the language of science, we can at least use the appropriate dialect of Biology (the study of living organisms), or better yet, Ecology (the study of systems of organisms).

The word *ecology* comes from the ancient Greek word *oikos*, which encompasses the meaning of family, their belongings, and their home. Equipped with the lens of Ecology, we can ground ourselves in science without losing touch with a reverence for the holistic systems that enable health and vitality for our crops, our livestock, and ourselves.

Succession and Disturbance

Succession and disturbance are basic concepts of Ecology. Succession is the natural development, or progression, of a community of organisms. It is the combined force of every living organism's urge to multiply. A disturbance is any event that interrupts succession. Ecosystems are forever propelled by the forces of natural succession, while being steered and set back by disturbances. As farmers, we disturb a piece of land in such a way that its natural response (we hope) is to grow food. This is the song of agriculture — the call and response that must remain in harmony if we want a future with any music.

Nature seeks to clothe the earth with living plants, maximizing the biological storage of solar energy and the generation of further life. This constant push toward productivity is self-nourishing — a positive feedback loop of perpetual creation. But not all plants are food for humans, so farmers interrupt the serenity to steer succession in an edible direction.

Disturbances occur naturally in the form of animal activity, wildfires, floods, and strong winds and other weather events. Agricultural disturbances take the form of tillage, cultivation, mowing, grazing, burning, flooding, spraying, crimping, and smothering. The fundamental goal of ecological agriculture is to apply the minimum disturbance necessary to steer natural succession toward producing the crops we want.

The no-till farmer draws the line of intervention at the soil surface and strives to minimize bare ground. Exposed soil is the antithesis of ecological health: with bare soil, the diversity and net productivity of a system are at their lowest point, while the system's biomass is actively diminishing with no photosynthesis to drive the natural forces of regeneration. Through the use of cover crops, interplanting, intensive spacing, and organic mulches, the no-till farm keeps the soil covered and photosynthesizing, enabling the natural succession toward soil health. Disturbances are minimized to above-ground practices like mowing, grazing, and smothering.

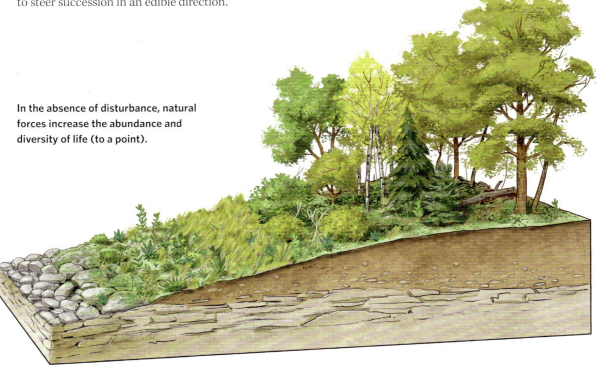

In the absence of disturbance, natural forces increase the abundance and diversity of life (to a point).

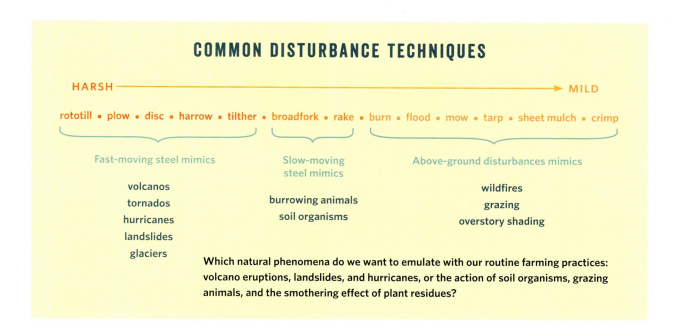

COMMON DISTURBANCE TECHNIQUES

HARSH ──► MILD

rototill • plow • disc • harrow • tilther • broadfork • rake • burn • flood • mow • tarp • sheet mulch • crimp

Fast-moving steel mimics

volcanos
tornados
hurricanes
landslides
glaciers

Slow-moving steel mimics

burrowing animals
soil organisms

Above-ground disturbances mimics

wildfires
grazing
overstory shading

Which natural phenomena do we want to emulate with our routine farming practices: volcano eruptions, landslides, and hurricanes, or the action of soil organisms, grazing animals, and the smothering effect of plant residues?

Soil Creation and the Soil-Plant Food Web

The soil-plant food web is the vast network of organisms — from microscopic bacteria, fungi, and protozoa to worms, insects, plants, and animals — that creates soil, promotes plant health, and enables our existence as land-dwelling animals.

I use the term "soil-plant food web" to highlight the inherent connection between soil health and living plants. A holistic view of the soil-plant food web draws no boundary between soil and plant. Rudolf Steiner, the founder of biodynamic agriculture, wrote that ". . . there is simply no hard and fast line between the life within the plant and the life of the surrounding soil in which it is living." As Sir Albert Howard, the first westerner to anglicize indigenous practices into what is now called organic farming, put it, "The health of soil, plant, animal and [human] is one and indivisible." In short, the plant-soil partnership, powered by photosynthesis, is the basis of healthy life above ground.

As a beginning farmer I did not adequately appreciate this partnership. In my mind, organic farming was all about the soil, so I proceeded to "feed the soil" with all sorts of imported goodies, applying thousands of pounds of compost, leaves, rock powders, biochar, and seaweed to my few acres of land. While these efforts certainly increased the depth and fertility of my soil (from which I continue to benefit years later) they overlooked the one and only mechanism for actually *creating* soil: photosynthesis. The only renewable source of stored energy is the photosynthesizer — the world's original and irreplaceable "power plant." It is just as accurate to say that vibrant plant life is the basis of soil health as vice versa. Applying organic materials to the soil can never replicate or replace the soil-generating power of living plants.

Soil ecologist Dr. Christine Jones coined the term "liquid carbon pathway" to describe how plants transform water, air, and sun into soluble carbohydrates (liquid carbon) that are exchanged for nutrients with the underground players in the soil-plant food web. This constant injection of

THE SOIL-PLANT FOOD WEB

A thriving soil food web is inseparable from healthy plants and animals.

With an effort to maintain a diversity of living roots in the ground at all times, annual agriculture can mimic the inherent health of perennial polycultures.

photosynthesized fuel, like an intravenous drip of solar energy, feeds and sustains the system of organisms in the soil and in turn stimulates the formation of humus, the portion of organic matter in the soil that is relatively stable and enables soil health. When we cut off this lifeline by removing plants from the soil, whether with herbicides, tillage, or smothering, we initiate a period of underground starvation and subsequent soil degradation. Conversely, by maintaining a thick, three-dimensional cover of living plants on the soil, we let nature do the work of feeding it — a job she has perfected over millions of years.

It is crucial to see the soil-plant food web as a whole, since the interactions among organisms are what drive the system. But there are a few key categories of players that are worth highlighting: mycorrhizae, diazotrophs, and heterotrophs.

Mycorrhizal Magic

Mycorrhizal magic happens in the rhizosphere, the underground region in contact with plant roots and the most biologically active part of the soil. This is where plant roots respire, take up nutrients, and exude proteins and sugars that feed soil life. Mycorrhizae (from the Greek words *myco*, meaning "fungus," and *rhiza*, meaning "root") are fungi that form symbiotic relationships with plant roots,

extending their reach through mycelial hyphae, a vast array of fungal filaments. This network of fungal filaments expands the rhizosphere into the mycorrhizosphere, which through its increased surface area comes into contact with up to 100 times more soil.

Besides increasing the availability of nutrients to plant roots, mycorrhizal connections have been shown to improve plants' drought tolerance, resistance to pests and disease, and timing and speed of development (producing earlier and more numerous flowers and fruits, for example).

MAINTAINING MYCORRHIZAL CONNECTIONS

Paying attention to the soil's mycorrhizal populations is an important aspect of soil care. There are several types of mycorrhizal fungi. The most important for vegetable growers are arbuscular mycorrhizae, which form connections with over 70 percent of all plants on Earth, including most vegetables.

There are a handful of notable plant families, however, that do not form these connections, and these can weaken the mycorrhizal network if grown by themselves (see Non-mycorrhizal Plants below). These plants are able to make the soil connections they need without mycorrhizae.

NON-MYCORRHIZAL PLANTS

The following plant families are not known to form relationships with mycorrhizal fungi:

Amaranthaceae (beets, chard, spinach, pigweed, lamb's quarters, etc.)

Brassicaceae (broccoli, brussels sprouts, cabbage, cauliflower, cress, horseradish, kale, kohlrabi, mustard greens, radish, rutabaga, turnip, etc.)

Polygonaceae (buckwheat, rhubarb, sorrel, dock, etc.)

Various other botanical families less common to vegetable production (see page 226 for information on finding a complete list)

Fungal communities can suffer in soils that grow only non-mycorrhizal crops without other host plants. An easy way to prevent fungal depletion is to undersow or interplant these crops with other plants that do form mycorrhizal connections.

The same care is needed for the off-season. As farmer and author Michael Phillips explains, "Farmers opting to leave ground bare over the winter months unwittingly allow the fungal system to become much weaker by the time soil temps rise enough to put in a warm-season cash crop." The aim is to support a continuous population of mycorrhizae with host plants throughout the year, since rebuilding this fungal community takes time, during which plant growth can suffer. With an effort to maintain a diversity of living roots in the ground at all times, annual agriculture can mimic the inherent health of perennial polycultures.

There are other practices besides poor crop rotation that negatively influence mycorrhizae. These include tillage, bare fallowing, and overfertilizing. Tillage chops up the physical structure of mycelia and hyphae and buries or destroys mycorrhizal spores. As a result, the partnerships formed with subsequent crops may suffer as the mycorrhizae struggle to re-establish. Leaving a field in bare fallow starves fungal populations of the living plant carbon they need to survive. And fertilizing can inhibit mycorrhizal growth. When too much nitrogen or phosphorus is present, mycorrhizal spores germinate poorly and fungal development slows.

Mycorrhizal fungi multiply the connection between root and soil. Shown here is a microscopic tree of mycelial hyphae growing from an allium root.

Diligent Diazotrophs

Diazotrophs are microorganisms, mostly bacteria, that fix atmospheric nitrogen in the soil. They take nitrogen out of the air and convert it into forms usable by soil organisms and plant roots — nature's answer to nitrogen fertilization. As demonstrated over the last 470 million years, a healthy soil-plant food web requires no imported fertilizer. In fact, adding nutrients from outside the functioning soil-plant-animal system can actually shut down natural fertility cycles and thus cause the apparent need for even more fertilizer.

There are two categories of organisms that enable atmospheric nitrogen fertilization: symbiotic and free-living. Symbiotic diazotrophs form relationships with plant roots and offer nitrogen in exchange for photosynthesized carbon from the plants. The most common of these bacteria are rhizobia, which partner with the roots of legumes, but there are also the *Frankia* genus and some Cyanobacteria, which partner with a variety of other plants.

Free-living diazotrophs provide for a lesser-known, yet more versatile, form of nitrogen fixation. Free-living diazotrophs do not require a host plant and are ubiquitous in most soils. *Azotobacters* are the most commonly studied free-living diazotroph, though there are many others. These bacteria can fix over 100 pounds of nitrogen per acre per year. Their fixation of nitrogen, however, is in balance with their appetite for organic matter, and plant root exudates are their preferred meal. While they require no direct host plant to survive, their ability to flourish, like that of nearly every soil organism, is powered by photosynthesis. Without a healthy plant population feeding the soil through its liquid carbon pathway, free-living bacteria cannot fix nitrogen at their full potential.

When we fertilize the soil with supplemental nitrogen, the nitrogen fixation of diazotrophs is slowed or shut off altogether, thus disrupting the very fertility we are trying to improve upon. Another limiting condition of nitrogen fixation is the presence of oxygen. When the soil contains excessive levels of oxygen, as is the case after tillage, diazotrophs can slow or cease their nitrogen fixation.

Hungry Heterotrophs

Heterotrophs are organisms that cannot produce their own energy (like plants do) and instead feed on other organisms or their by-products. Many bacteria and fungi are heterotrophs, as are all nematodes, insects, mollusks, earthworms, and animals. All of these creatures require the fuel that is originally supplied by photosynthesis, and each fills a niche within the soil-plant food web. They are the decomposers, the predators and prey, and the aerators and mixers. They comprise the stabilizing diversity that protects the whole system from run-away populations and imbalance. Like other soil organisms, heterotrophs rely on the energy derived from photosynthesis, and thrive in undisturbed soil that is covered in plant material.

Nature's Principles of Soil Care

Proper care of the soil can be summarized with four principles. If we uphold them, the health and resilience of our soils and crops should mirror those of the natural world:

- Maximized photosynthesis
- Extensive diversity
- Complete soil coverage
- Minimal soil disturbance

Maximizing Photosynthesis

Our fundamental job as farmers is to capture the energy of the sun. Photosynthesis converts carbon dioxide and water into oxygen and organic matter. Much of this organic matter is injected deep into the soil via plant root exudates to feed microorganisms. The remainder fans out over the ground to absorb more sunlight and carbon while protecting the soil surface from the elements.

Anytime we leave our soil without green growth we are squandering the opportunity to turn sunlight and atmospheric carbon into stored energy and soil organic matter. Yet even the best farming practices rarely maximize photosynthesis. This is partially due to the flatness of our thinking. We describe our plants in two dimensions — acres, square feet, or hectares — when in fact we live in a three-dimensional world. A plant's ability to photosynthesize is proportional to its surface area, which is affected by its height as much as by its width. A mature oak tree, for instance, may have a photosynthesizing surface area of over 10,000 square feet, while the space it actually takes up on our two-dimensional "acreage" is merely the cross section of its trunk — maybe a few square feet.

As vegetable growers, we may not grow many oak trees, but we can still utilize this third dimension of photosynthesis with multiple tiers of vertical plant growth. Taking advantage of the fact that certain crops, like lettuce, radishes, and mustard greens, prefer less intense light and heat, we can grow them

An interplanting of peppers and lettuce increases diversity and photosynthesis.

under or between taller crops, such as tomatoes, peppers, snap peas, or brussels sprouts. Like sea corals with their extended branches swaying in the currents — maximizing surface area and contact with their environment — plants seek to maximize their surface area contact with sunlight and air.

Often it is carbon dioxide, not sunlight, that is the limiting ingredient of photosynthesis, as the amount of CO_2 around the leaves can drop dramatically as the plant absorbs it. There may be plenty of CO_2 in the atmosphere above the plant (410 parts per million, and climbing), but at ground level the concentrations can drop considerably each morning as the sun kicks off photosynthesis for the day. In the tiny volume of air that is actually in contact with plant leaves, the levels may be lower still. More surface area means more access to available CO_2.

A living, breathing soil high in organic matter releases a lot of CO_2, much of which can be reabsorbed by plants and pumped back down into the soil via root exudates. With sufficient photosynthesis, soils can cycle nutrients with little to no loss.

Increasing Biodiversity

Just as soil health is the basis for health in plants and animals, the diversity of above-ground life in turn feeds the soil food web. Biological diversity is the foundation of ecosystem vitality. As soil stewards, we strive to maintain not only a diverse cover of living growth but also a prolific diversity of non-plant organisms throughout the farm. Flowering plants bring in a multitude of flying insects. Birdhouses support winged pest control. Livestock rotate through cover-cropped fields to feed the soil with their biologically rich manure. Ideally, the level of on-farm diversity goes well beyond the classic crop rotation, wherein blocks of similar crops are rotated through fields from one year to the next.

Most of our agricultural "problems" are actually symptoms of a greater underlying problem common

Fruit trees and flowering perennials planted throughout pastures add diversity and revenue.

Laying hens control insect pests and stimulate soil biology.

to modern agriculture: a lack of life, either in quantity, diversity, or both. Pests, disease, weeds, and depleted soils are all examples of such symptoms.

Many indigenous agricultural systems acknowledge the importance of diversity, not just for the health of the soil but also for the health of our human diet. The author Charles Mann writes about the *milpa* farming technologies of indigenous people of the Americas:

> A *milpa* is a field . . . in which farmers plant a dozen crops at once including maize, avocados, multiple varieties of squash and bean, melon, tomatoes, chilis, sweet potato, jicama (a tuber), amaranth (a grain-like plant), and mucuna (a tropical legume) . . . *Milpa* crops are nutritionally and environmentally complementary. Maize lacks . . . the amino acids lysine and tryptophan . . . Beans have both lysine and tryptophan, but not the amino acids cysteine and methionine, which are provided by maize . . . Squashes, for their part, provide an array of vitamins; avocados, fats. The *milpa,* in the estimation of H. Garrison Wilkes, a maize researcher at the University of Massachusetts in Boston, "is one of the most successful human inventions ever created."

The diversity of life these combinations generate, both below ground and in our gut, feed natural mechanisms of fertility and nutrition and create natural resistance to pests and pathogens. Biological diversity inspires complex synergies that indigenous agricultures have employed for millennia and that modern science is just beginning to explain. Nature's model of diversity has a proven track record.

Ensuring Soil Coverage

Soil coverage isn't just about maximizing photosynthesis; it's also critical for erosion control. Erosion goes hand in hand with bare soil. Consider this description of how erosion begins, from an article in the USDA's 1938 *Yearbook*:

"Water falling as rain on bare soil dislodges silt and clay particles by its impact. These are taken into suspension and carried into the tiny pores and channels between the soil particles as the water makes its way downward. Very shortly the filtering action of the soil causes the openings to be clogged by the particles; water can no longer move downward through the soil, so it flows over the surface carrying with it the dislodged silt and clay; and erosion is actively underway."

The article goes on to highlight the importance of keeping the soil covered:

"A protective layer of litter prevents this [erosive] chain of events by absorbing the impact of the falling drops of water. After the litter becomes soaked, excess water trickles gently into the soil surface, no soil particles are dislodged, the water remains clear, pores and channels remain open, and surface flow is eliminated except in periods of protracted heavy rains."

LAYERS OF SOIL COVERAGE

Soil coverage ranges along a spectrum, and it is never as simple as "it's covered or it isn't." In nature, soil coverage exists in a multitude of overlapping layers that help to maximize protection of the soil as well as photosynthesis, as described above. While natural layers of soil coverage are intermingled rather than neatly stratified, they can be thought of in seven different layers, from the ground up:

1. O-horizon — crop residues and organic mulches
2. Ground cover — low-growing, shade-tolerant plants, like undersown white clover
3. Short herbaceous plants — crops that prefer cooler temperatures or partial shade, like most salad greens
4. Tall herbaceous plants — crops that take up more space and prefer full sun, like tomatoes or Brussels sprouts
5. Shrubs — smaller woody perennials, like berry bushes or hazelnuts
6. Understory trees — taller woody perennials, like apples, pears, cherries, and stone fruit
7. Canopy trees — the climax species, like chestnut, oak, and hickory

As with maximizing photosynthesis, it is important to move beyond two dimensions when covering the soil. A thin layer of plant material is a huge improvement over bare soil, but soil health is maximized by maintaining as many layers of coverage as possible. Obviously all seven layers will not grow well right on top of one another, but there are many combinations that increase net productivity without competing too much for water, air, sunlight, and nutrients.

On the farm, I find it reasonable to maintain at least one of the above layers at all times on any given bed, while two or three layers are possible for most of the year. A bed with two layers might have kale (short herbaceous layer) undersown to clover (ground cover layer). A bed with three layers might have tomatoes (tall herbaceous layer) with lettuce heads (short herbaceous layer) planted underneath through mulch (O-horizon layer). There are brief periods when dropping down to a single layer of coverage may greatly facilitate a task, such as mowing or transplanting. During these times, bare soil can be avoided by maintaining a layer of mulch or compost to mimic the O-horizon of natural soil profiles.

Diverse layers of living plants are nature's model of soil care.

Multicropping infuses the farm with perennial diversity and helps keep living roots in the ground as much as possible.

Treeline of large canopy trees

Berry bushes with groundcover underneath

Paths mulched deeply with leaves or wood chips

Trellised tomatoes with salad greens on bed shoulders

Rows of lettuce heads

Brussels sprouts

Dwarf fruit trees with low-growing flowering perennials at base

A HEALTHY O-HORIZON

The O-horizon is the layer of plant residues that rests on the soil surface. This is the soil's last line of defense against the eroding effects of wind and rain and the desiccating effect of the sun.

In the context of vegetable farming, I think of the O-horizon as a sort of "minimum requirement" for maintaining soil health. Even when a cover of green growth is not possible, whether in transitioning a bed between crops or during the dormancy of winter, a protective layer of organic material is always possible.

And this layer doesn't just protect the soil from elemental forces; it sponsors an underground party for soil organisms, for which it is both venue and caterer. It is no coincidence that the most biologically active part of the soil is just below its surface.

Ecological soil care involves maintaining a cover of living plants, or at the very least keeping an O-horizon in place by leaving plant residues in the field and by spreading a layer of mulch or compost if soil starts to show through. The best possible soil cover is achieved when we couple a healthy O-horizon with multiple layers of living plants to mimic the level of soil protection that is found in nature.

Minimizing Soil Disturbance

Any soil disturbance increases the risk of erosion, compaction, nutrient leaching, and weed germination while decreasing the soil's organic matter, porosity, and water-holding capacity. Tillage is rarely performed with the goal of improving soil health; more often, soil health is sacrificed to meet other management goals, such as weeding or bed preparation. By achieving those same goals through biological processes that avoid mechanical disturbance, we allow the soil ecosystem to flourish and pass on its health to plants, animals, and people.

The tradeoff between soil health and ease of management is a common concern for farmers, mostly because we are so entrenched in our current disturbance paradigm. We have attached our farming identity to the tractor, the ultimate disturber. We marvel at the sight of freshly turned soil and take satisfaction in the mechanically denuded ground, "primed" for the next crop.

By contrast, nature does not compromise on soil health, but rather finds the win-win solution. There are ways to transition between crops that require a mere nudge of disturbance. And minimizing or avoiding disturbance is not just good soil care, it also liberates the farmer to focus on more productive tasks.

Healthy as a Prairie

These principles of soil management are clearly overlapping and are part of a cohesive whole outlined by nature. All four principles are honored by simply allowing a diversity of living plants to cover the undisturbed soil.

As a natural example, consider the prairies of the Great Plains that helped create some of the most fertile soils in history. The indigenous peoples who managed these perennial grasslands maximized photosynthesis with a diverse mix of year-round living growth. They kept the soil consistently protected with layers of plants above a thick O-horizon of decomposing residues from previous years and exposed the soil only to above-ground disturbances (until European settlers arrived with the plow). Imagine emulating the soil health of native prairies while growing vegetables!

Even as we get caught up in the practical considerations and inevitable compromises of starting a farm and earning a living, we can keep our eyes on these natural principles of ecological health. It is photosynthesis, diversity, and soil coverage that generate ecological health when the soil itself is left undisturbed. This is the standard by which we can evaluate our success as stewards of the earth.

As Edward Faulkner put it, "The fact is that untidiness to an extreme — a surface covered or filled with abundance of decaying [plant residue] — is really the proper condition."

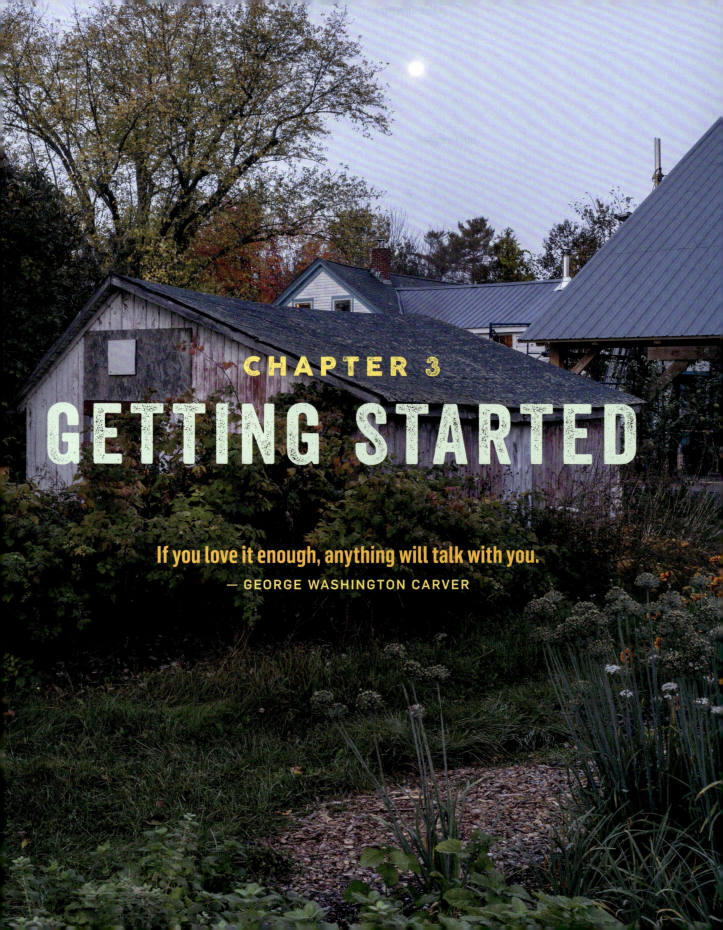

CHAPTER 3
GETTING STARTED

If you love it enough, anything will talk with you.
— GEORGE WASHINGTON CARVER

With an understanding of the principles behind no-till farming, and an appreciation for the ecological model that nature provides us, let's get down to business: how to start a farm enterprise. This chapter lays out the steps I took in creating Frith Farm, and highlights the lessons I learned along the way.

Taking the Leap

Change is afoot in the farming world. Paradigms of conventional chemical agriculture have proven destructive and unsustainable, and growers are slowly overcoming the inertia of acceptance. A decentralized system of small farms providing fresh produce to local communities is not a utopian fairy tale. We have begun the journey — with vegetables, at least — toward the Gandhian vision of production by the masses instead of mass production.

According to the USDA's Census of Agriculture, the number of young farmers in the United States is increasing for the first time in decades. In more populated areas, the trends are even stronger. The number of young farmers and the area of farmed land are growing in every state in New England. New farms are increasingly focused on community supported agriculture, farmers' markets, and other forms of direct marketing. As a part of this new wave of back-to-the-landers, I can personally say it is an exciting time to be a farmer.

If you think you want to farm, I encourage you to start growing food in some capacity immediately. There are plenty of reasons floating around for why you shouldn't farm, or why you should get more education or a "real job" first. I started out with relative privilege — a supportive middle-class family, a private education, and an agricultural system designed for people like me — so I can't speak for others, but I found that a hunger for challenge and a yearning pragmatism were the underpinnings of my success. If your heart pounds and your fingers itch at the thought of growing food, and you are eager and excited to figure out what it takes to succeed, then perhaps the best time to start farming is *now*.

Reality Check

As thrilling as the idea of farm ownership may be, a new farmer's first steps generally do not include purchasing land. There are countless ways to get your feet wet in agriculture without diving in over your head. The lessons and inevitable missteps of the learning process are challenging enough without being saddled by debt right off the bat. Traversing the steepest part of the learning curve while working on other farms is a great way to leave the mistakes behind when you eventually strike out on your own.

When ready, starting small on borrowed or rented land can be an intermediate step toward ownership that helps build experience without taking on undue risk. If land ownership or long-term land security is your goal, there is no reason why you can't start working toward it immediately without going into debt.

There is no substitute for experiential learning, especially in agriculture. Podcasts, tutorials, books, and lectures can be of great value when they are grounded in actual farm work. Educational resources are but windows into the world of farming — if you like what you see through them, open the door and go outside. Even growing a handful of plants in a backyard or community plot will teach you countless lessons and help you determine when (and if) you are ready to pursue farming for a living.

There is no need to reinvent the wheel; reap the benefits of years of trial and error by starting with models shared by experienced farmers. But keep in mind that no farmer, despite their air of confidence, has it all figured out, so take every lesson with a grain of salt and feel free to be selective about which ideas you run with. If "experts" tell you there is no way you can make a living from an acre of vegetables, feel free to prove them wrong.

The payoff of this learning process is not realized overnight. Starting a farm involves long hours and grueling work. There were many times during my first couple of years as a farm owner that, despite working 90 hours a week, I wondered if I would make it financially. I now work reasonable hours and live a comfortable life supported by the farm, but the early years were not so glossy. I share this not to discourage new farmers but to temper expectations. Expect the first two or three years to be filled with intense physical, mental, and emotional challenges. Perseverance pays off, however, as the fruits of this initial labor will potentially be reaped for the rest of your life, if not for generations to come.

Writing a Business Plan

Before jumping head over heels into starting a farm, the first step is to write a business plan. This document details your farm's philosophy and goals, and the steps to reach those goals. It is also a required part of most business loan applications. When I was looking for land, I balked at what felt like a bureaucratic task of typing up 10 pages of marketing analysis and financial predictions when all I wanted to do was start growing food. But the process helped clarify my objectives and made me think through my plans more carefully than I otherwise would have. And I still enjoy reading back over my business plan every year or two to reflect on how things are going relative to my original projections.

There are many resources that address business planning, and many websites offer free templates. There are also some helpful business planning publications specific to small-scale agriculture, such as *Building a Sustainable Business: A Guide to Developing a Business Plan for Farms and Rural Businesses*, which is available in print as well as a free download. This guide walks the beginning farmer through the business planning process and offers plenty of

Writing a business plan is the responsible first step toward realizing your dream.

examples to help you get started. Another excellent guide to developing enterprise budgets and projected revenue is Richard Wiswall's *The Organic Farmer's Business Handbook: A Complete Guide to Managing Finances, Crops, and Staff — and Making a Profit*. Developing a quantitative picture of the farm's economic potential and how it will be realized is not just an exercise to please prospective lenders; it is a prudent first step for any new business enterprise, regardless of its size.

While a business plan is a useful planning tool and a means to the end of borrowing money, don't let it bog you down. Focus on the structure and content that illuminate a path toward your goals, and don't get flustered by obscure jargon and questions from non-farming financial experts. In the end, the business plan should refine and guide your progress, not confuse and hinder it.

ON FRITH FARM
NEW BEGINNINGS

My decision to start a farm happened to fall soon after the passing of my grandfather, James Mays. The timing was meaningful in several ways. Born American, James met his wife, Mary, in England while stationed there during World War II. Mary was born and raised on the original Frith Farm in Wickham, near the southern coast of England. After the war ended and James and Mary were married, my father, Stuart, was born on Frith Farm, in the same room of the 16th-century farmhouse that his mother was born in. At that time, James was a United States diplomat, and he and Mary were stationed all over Europe until they retired back in England, close to the farm.

Throughout my life, my father has shared with me stories of summers on Frith Farm and his many adventures there with cousins and other kin. This is all to say that when my grandfather James passed away and my father was due to inherit a portion of his assets, it seemed like a natural investment opportunity to help me begin a Frith Farm in the New World. To me, this was a chance to connect with family members and an agricultural past that I had known only through my father's stories, and a way to carry on the family history with seeds of many Frith stories yet to come. I feel privileged and grateful to have had this opportunity and am glad that the interest I pay on the loan stays within the family.

Start-Up Costs

No-till market gardening focuses on human-scale methods and minimizes investment in expensive machinery. That said, there are unavoidable expenses involved in starting any commercial vegetable farm. Below is a list of the minimum set of tools and infrastructure I believe are worth acquiring at the outset of an intensive vegetable operation, along with their approximate cost. This includes suggestions for taking the next step toward efficiency in year two or three, based on the trajectory that was successful for my farm.

It is certainly possible to pinch pennies and spend less money than I suggest here, but I found that borrowing enough money to get up and running with these initial investments made sense economically. Every farm is different, and investment priorities should be tailored to your particular enterprises, scale, and available capital, but here is a simplified version of what worked for me.

The Sample Start-up Costs chart on the next page is a simplified cash flow — on an annual basis — based roughly on my first four years starting the farm. Because these numbers represent the unique location and starting time of my farm, they may vary widely with other plans and markets. I share them simply as one example of how small-scale no-till farming can be economically viable. The revenue and expenses related to livestock are separated on their own lines, even though some of these sales were made through CSA or at farmers' market.

You may note from the sample cash flow table on page 35 that profits were reinvested in the farm's infrastructure at an increasing rate. A good chunk of this money was used to pay for the much-needed renovations to the farmhouse, and the rest ($60,000) was used for the various start-up costs suggested in years two through four. As you can see, by the end of the farm's fourth year, there was plenty of cash coming in to support increased pay for workers and further investment in the land and its infrastructure.

Acquiring Capital

Acquiring the capital needed to start a small farm can be a challenging proposition. Navigating the financial bureaucracy of lending institutions and credit applications is difficult enough; add in the limited understanding that most lenders have of market gardening, and the process gets even more frustrating. The good news is that there are several alternative avenues for accessing capital that are more approachable (and often have lower interest rates) than conventional bank loans. There are also some great organizations out there that want to help you succeed.

Government Funding

The USDA's Farm Service Agency (FSA) exists to help farmers. One of its primary forms of aid is providing subsidized loans for buying or operating a farm. These loans are for farmers who do not qualify for a bank loan (in other words, almost every beginning farmer), and FSA personnel offer substantial help with the rather complicated application paperwork. More information is available on the FSA's website, www.fsa.usda.gov, or at any of its county offices throughout the country. With its low interest rates and minimal credit history requirements, an FSA loan is an invaluable resource and a good place to start when considering a farm loan.

Currently, the FSA requires three years of experience to qualify for a loan. This can be a combination of education, on-the-job training, and actual farming experience — yet another argument for spending a few years learning, working on different farms, or leasing land before trying to make a land purchase. But some beginning farmers, like me, do not want to wait to qualify for an FSA loan. I had less than one full season of farming experience when, despite all sage advice, I decided to start my own farm and was fortunate enough to have an alternative source of funding.

Sample Start-Up Costs

	Year 1	Years 2–4
PROPAGATION		
Greenhouse, 26×48	$4,000	
– automated heat	$2,500	
– automated ventilation		$2,000
Soil Blockers	$1,000	
Cement Mixer		$500
Seedling Pallets	$500	$500
Heat Mats, Trays, Watering	$500	$500
FIELD PRODUCTION		
Compost and Mulch	$5,000	$10,000
Pickup Truck (used)	$2,000	$10,000
BCS Walking Tractor	$4,000	
– flail mower	$2,000	
– rotary plow	$1,500	
Tarps	$1,000	
Hand Tools & Trellising	$1,500	$1,500
Riding Mower		$2,000
Irrigation System		$3,000
High Tunnel, 30×96		$12,000
Utility Tractor, 35 HP (used)		$12,000
HARVEST AND HANDLING		
Wash Shed	$300	$5,000
Walk-In Coolers	$2,500	$5,000
Harvest Carts	$500	$1,000
Crates & Flip-Top Totes	$500	$1,500
Wash Tubs & Tables	$500	
Salad Spinner	$200	$500
Delivery Vehicle (used)		$3,000
TOTAL	**$30,000**	**$70,000**

Family and Friends

While most young farmers have limited financial resources, some of us are privileged to have family or friends with financial means. Sometimes large sums of money sit in bank accounts or mutual funds with relatively low interest or other earnings. Convincing loved ones to shift their money to a more local and personal investment may be easier than you think, especially if you can offer a better interest rate than their current investment, and you have a business plan to back it up.

If there are resources available, a loan from friends or family can make sense for everyone involved. The lender can feel good about making an ethical investment — a phrase that can sound like an oxymoron in today's financial world — and see the immediate benefit of their money being put to use by someone they know and trust. The borrower gets access to capital that a conventional lender might not have granted, and enjoys the knowledge that loan interest stays in the community. For those of us fortunate enough to be connected to people with money, making them a proposal for investing in your farm dream can be an ideal way to help make that dream come true.

Regardless of how well you know a lender, it is a good idea to follow all the recommended steps of making a loan official, including drafting a promissory note that spells out repayment terms and what happens if the borrower is late on payments or defaults on the loan. Defining contingencies can reduce friction on the relationship and can help both parties feel more at ease with the idea of debt between friends or family members.

Crowdsourcing

As farming author Leah Penniman points out, those with limited financial resources are often rich in social capital. Crowdfunding through internet platforms like Kickstarter or Indiegogo is a modern version of an age-old practice. Before banks existed, communities pooled their resources to support causes they believed in. If someone had an idea and convinced the community it was a good one, it was natural to receive support for the initiative. Modern crowdsourcing applies the same concept in the Information Age, taking advantage of the pace and breadth of online social exchanges. I have no personal experience with this type of fundraising, but I have seen it prove effective for other farms, especially with smaller sums that form part of a larger funding effort.

Cooperatives and Nonprofit Lenders

There are a variety of borrower-owned cooperatives and nonprofit lenders that help farmers acquire working capital. Many of these institutions offer favorable interest rates or simplified loan procedures for beginning or otherwise disadvantaged farmers. Any organization that works with beginning farmers should be able to provide a list of potential lenders.

The quest for capital can be daunting — even disempowering — but hang in there! There are many great individuals and institutions out there who want to help you succeed. With a solid business plan and the right list of potential lenders, there is no good reason why the challenges of accessing capital should keep you from farming.

MONEY STARTING OUT

Prior to buying land, I had saved roughly $15,000 from two years of teaching. To start the farm, I borrowed $180,000. After paying for the land ($150,000) and the start-up expenditures listed on page 32 ($30,000), I was left with about $15,000 cash entering my first season. On the facing page is a highly simplified view of how the cash flow looked those first few years, with all numbers rounded to the nearest thousand.

Cash was tight the first two years. I spent the first winter in a condemnable old farmhouse with no plumbing and only a woodstove to keep from freezing. I slept in all my winter clothes inside a down sleeping bag on a secondhand futon mattress. I remember trying to lift the mattress one morning only to find that it had frozen to the floor in a thick layer of ice.

I survived these challenges in high spirits, partly because I was in my mid-twenties and had a safety net of family and friends, and partly because I sensed that there was light at the end of the tunnel. I felt that I was starting something bigger than myself and that the farm's trajectory would lead to the life I wanted. And maybe part of me knew that the hardships endured during those early years would later make the farm's success all the more rewarding.

Sample Cash Flow Years 1–4

	Year 1	Year 2	Year 3	Year 4	Year 5
Cash on Hand (beginning of year):	45,000	12,000	5,000	16,000	58,000
CASH RECEIVED					
CSA	15,000	33,000	42,000	48,000	
Farmers' Markets	7,000	7,000	25,000	47,000	
Grocers & Restaurants	4,000	11,000	19,000	54,000	
Farm Stand	0	0	0	3,000	
Sales of Eggs and Meat	14,000	31,000	38,000	77,000	
TOTAL CASH RECEIVED	40,000	82,000	124,000	229,000	
CASH PAID OUT					
Inputs (seeds, amendments, supplies, energy)	4,000	6,000	7,000	9,000	
Livestock Costs (animals, feed, equipment, butcher fees)	12,000	17,000	22,000	45,000	
Labor Costs (including farm manager)	10,000	23,000	32,000	52,000	
Overhead (taxes, insurance, fees, maintenance)	9,000	13,000	16,000	19,000	
Loan Payments (after 2.5 year grace period with interest accruing)			6,000	12,000	
Start-Up Costs (listed in previous table)	30,000	25,000	25,000	20,000	
Farmhouse Renovation	8,000	5,000	5,000	30,000	
TOTAL CASH PAID OUT	73,000	89,000	113,000	187,000	

The Land Search

Whether you're renting, buying, or looking for a more creative land tenure arrangement, finding the right land can make or break a small farm operation even before it gets off the ground. But don't let the land search discourage you — it is an exciting part of the process, full of opportunity and potential! With the right focus and patience, you will find a parcel that will set you up for years, if not the rest of your life.

Nevertheless, even in an age where almost every consumable item is a mere click away, finding land is surprisingly difficult. Open land is often priced for and advertised to developers, and the average real estate agent knows little about farmland beyond its development potential. So how does a new farmer start the search? Below are some resources that can help you connect with the right property.

Land trusts, easements, and FarmLink Programs. Connecting with the right local or state land trust can be a great way to initiate a land search. Land trusts are designed to preserve land for specific uses, and a trust's interpretation of the word "preservation" may or may not include agriculture. Unfortunately, some organizations see farmers as a group from whom the land needs protection. But there is growing recognition that protecting the natural landscape means finding our place as humans within it, not outside of it, and many progressive land trusts now protect farmland with agricultural conservation easements. These easements are essentially legal amendments to a property deed that stipulate what can and cannot happen on the property. Agricultural easements typically restrict development and other activities that might damage agricultural resources, while maintaining flexibility for farming the land. The land is thereby protected from development and is priced for its value as farmland rather than its potential as a strip mall or subdivision.

There are growing efforts, especially in crowded regions of New England, to protect existing farmland with agricultural easements before it is paved over. This type of land protection works only if there are farmers ready to purchase or lease conserved land, so getting in touch with organizations that oversee agricultural easements is a natural place to start a search for land. Many land trusts also organize FarmLink programs that work specifically to connect aspiring farmers with owners of agricultural lands.

Most states or regions have one or more land link programs to help farmers find land. The National Young Farmers Coalition has compiled this information here: https://www.youngfarmers.org/wp-content/uploads/2019/10/Land-Link-Directory-2019.pdf

The right real estate agent. Just because most real estate agents know nothing about farming doesn't mean they're all clueless. Ask your local land trust, extension office, or USDA service center if they can suggest an agent who is familiar with buying and selling farmland. The right agent will understand what to look for and can keep an eye out for new properties as they come online.

Word of mouth. Spread the word that you're looking for land, and you never know what connections might be made. Send group messages to local friend networks, put up fliers, post to online forums, and talk to neighbors and community members. There just may be opportunities lurking, especially if you need only a few acres.

Knocking on doors. If you're comfortable with this kind of approach, try driving around a desired area and stopping to knock on doors of houses with unused land. The odds of success may be low and the process may lead to some awkwardness, but I know of at least one farmer who found his land in precisely this manner (my introverted nature generally prevents me from pursuing this type of strategy). Often it is worth looking up property information for acreage and soil characteristics (see page 38) to make sure the prospect is worthwhile before ringing the doorbell.

Primary Land Search Criteria

When seeking land for Frith Farm, I found it helpful to organize my priorities into primary and secondary considerations. Primary criteria are the most important qualities to look for, as they are difficult to overcome or impossible to change later.

PROXIMITY TO POPULATION CENTERS

I believe this is the single most important search criteria for starting an economically successful small farm. Almost every other aspect of the farm can be improved with time and effort, but once land is acquired, this aspect of the farm is permanently set. This criterion is also one of the easiest to ignore, since expansive rural farmland can be so visually appealing and often has a very attractive price per acre. But resist the seduction of those endless rolling hills and quiet country lanes! A 3-acre parcel near a big city is far more valuable to the no-till market farmer than 300 acres in the middle of nowhere.

It makes sense to leave large parcels of rural land for farmers growing crops that need more space and store and travel well, such as grains, pulses, or tree crops, or those raising pastured livestock. Fresh vegetables, on the other hand, lose quality with travel, so ideally are grown as close as possible to the people who eat them.

Land near towns is also at the highest risk of development, so preserving it through farming is a double win. As Brian Donahue explains in his book, *Reclaiming the Commons*, "what we [need is] to protect the places we [live]." In many ways, urban and suburban spaces are the front line of the fight for local agriculture.

Since the success of the human-scale farm relies on the vibrancy of its community connections, growing near the population it sells to is critical. This proximity leads to incalculable benefits, including ease of finding employees, connecting with customers, selling food directly from the farm, hosting on-farm education and events, and minimizing time spent driving. Less driving means less money spent on fuel and vehicles, less pollution from emissions, and more time spent on the farm.

Proximity also enables a level of connection with customers not possible on more isolated farms. At Frith Farm, many of our customers are our neighbors, and they identify with the farm to the point of feeling ownership. They have raised their children on our food, picking our flowers, walking our fields, and visiting our animals. The loyalty they show us goes well beyond any concept of economics or marketing.

For the no-till market farm, I'd recommend looking for land within 10 minutes of a population

A 3-acre parcel near a big city is far more valuable to the no-till market farmer than 300 acres in the middle of nowhere.

center of at least 10,000 people. Established tourism can improve the market potential of smaller towns, but often with large seasonal fluctuations that can lead to cash flow challenges in the off-season. Land in densely populated areas is obviously harder to come by, but with intensive small-scale farming, a very small piece of land goes a long way.

SOIL CHARACTERISTICS

The quality of the native soil on a piece of land can determine what and how you grow on it. Many soil traits can be improved with soil building, but characteristics like slope, distance to bedrock, and distance to seasonal high water table are key concerns when looking for vegetable land.

You can save a lot of time in a farm search by researching the soils of a potential property before traveling to visit it in person. The USDA's Web Soil Survey is a remarkable online resource that allows you to view the soil classification of almost any agricultural land in the U.S. Soils that are classified

as "Prime" are the best agricultural soils, while those classified as "Of Statewide Importance" are reliably good for growing. Think twice before trying to grow vegetables on soils that are listed as "Not Prime Farmland," as there are likely some serious issues with bedrock, drainage, or slopes.

CLIMATE AND MICROCLIMATE

While you can get a sense of a farm's growing climate by finding its location on a regional USDA Plant Hardiness Zone Map, there are local factors beyond latitude and elevation that affect the microclimate on a farm. Two of the most important are site aspect and air drainage.

Site aspect, or the slope of a given piece of land, determines how the sun hits it and how quickly its soils warm in the spring. In the northern hemisphere, fields with a very slight slope toward the south or southeast are generally best for growing vegetables, though any relatively flat land is perfectly fine.

Air drainage is the ability of sinking cold air to settle below and away from the farm. Examining topographical maps of the farm and surrounding area can give clues about how well cold air will drain away from it. Depending on the niche you try to fill in your local markets, this can be an important consideration.

The USDA's Web Soil Survey is a free online database that describes the soil characteristics of almost any land in the country.

ON FRITH FARM
TOPOGRAPHY AND MICROCLIMATES

My farm in Maine is in a subtle geographic bowl (in this case, a swamp) that catches cold air as it sinks and settles, thus becoming a frost pocket that is consistently 5 to 10°F (3 to 5°C) colder at night than the neighboring farm up on a hill three miles away. This temperature difference puts my farm a half zone colder than other local farms, and my early outdoor vegetables tend to be a week or so behind everyone else's at market.

When farmers see land as a resource to be mined, a short-term lease may seem attractive. But when we view soil as an asset with a value that is built slowly over time, with sweat equity and reinvestment of profits, land security becomes a key component of sustainability.

SOIL CONTAMINATION

Contamination is mostly a concern in urban areas or on land where pesticides were applied for many years. Test for buildup of heavy metals in the soil from lead paint, tire dust, pressure-treated lumber, pesticides, and other industrial pollution prior to acquiring land, because remediation is often costly or unfeasible. University labs and private soil testing services can usually screen for heavy metal contamination, and performing such tests is highly recommended before acquiring land in developed areas. Airborne contamination, such as pesticide drift or exhaust fumes, is also a concern for land that abuts conventional farms, busy freeways, or industrial areas, though windbreaks in the form of hedgerows or trees can help reduce blown-in pollution.

ACCESS

The entrance to the property may seem like a trivial detail, but for a business that encourages and relies on customers visiting the farm, a safe and inviting entrance (and exit) is important. Farm entrances on busy highways or blind curves are not ideal. Landlocked parcels with no right-of-way are even worse. The extent to which the farm fields are visible from the road will also help market your farm to neighbors and passersby.

LAND SECURITY

No matter how perfect the physical attributes of a property might be, a lack of land security should be a deal breaker if you are looking to pour your heart, soul, sweat, and tears into a piece of land. A short-term lease is great for getting started and gaining experience, but the soil amendments and infrastructure needed to establish an intensive no-till farm warrant a legal agreement that protects your right to continue farming the land you improve beyond the short term.

Even a 30-year lease is not long enough, in my opinion, to justify the level of financial and emotional investment needed to establish a no-till farm. When farmers see land as a resource to be mined, a lease may seem attractive. But when they view soil as an asset with a value that is built slowly over time, with sweat equity and reinvestment of profits, land security becomes a key component of sustainability.

COST

There are limits to every budget. The maximum loan amount for a starting farm will vary depending on its goals, scale, available markets, and access to financial resources. Currently, the upper limit for an FSA direct ownership loan is $600,000 — much more than necessary for most market garden startups. A loan for $300,000 with an interest rate of 4 percent and a 30-year payback period would have payments totaling less than $18,000 per year. Once established, a well-run market farm can gross $80,000 to $100,000 per acre per year, with a profit margin of 30 percent or more.

Again, these figures depend on a variety of factors, and your budget for land should be determined carefully within a comprehensive business plan before your land search begins. Once you've determined a maximum purchase price, avoid the temptation of looking at properties that fall outside your price range.

Secondary Land-Search Criteria

Secondary criteria matter less because they can be worked around or improved with a reasonable amount of work.

SOIL TEXTURE AND FERTILITY

Clays and sandy soils can be improved with generous applications of compost and mulches combined with cover crops and minimal soil disturbance. Soils that are compacted or low in fertility can be healed in the same manner. While the ideal is to start with healthy soil, depleted or abused land can be regenerated with the no-till practices described in this book, and the state of a property's soil should not necessarily be a deal breaker. Seasonal flooding or distance to bedrock, on the other hand, are more permanent features of the landscape and should factor more heavily into the evaluation. The USDA Web Soil Survey lists the approximate distance to bedrock and to seasonal high water table for all soils.

PROXIMITY TO SERVICES

The distances to supporting businesses, such as a hardware store, a feed mill, sources of quality

Finding the right land is both challenging and exciting. This photo shows the property I visited in late 2010 that would become Frith Farm a couple months later.

compost or mulch, and a slaughterhouse for meat processing, can be major factors in the efficient operation of a farm. The importance of proximity depends on how often a trip is made and the cost of making it. In this age of online ordering and streamlined delivery, if your farm is located near a population center (a top priority), chances are you will have little problem accessing the supplies and services you need, though this is worth verifying as part of your land search.

INFRASTRUCTURE AND UTILITIES

Having roads, utilities, and a house, barn, or outbuildings to move into can accelerate establishment of a farm. That said, these improvements often add significant cost to a property, and their location, orientation, and design may not fit within your ideal farm layout. Starting with a lower-priced blank canvas might make more sense than paying for a property where major development decisions have already been made. For the bootstrap beginning farmer, living on a new property with minimal amenities can be a cost-saving way to get to know the land and plan future infrastructure.

Either way, roads and buildings can be constructed, modified, or even moved, so they are of secondary concern in a land search. The land itself is what matters most, as it will long outlive whatever infrastructure is on it.

WATER

Access to clean water is essential for any vegetable farm, and the cost and feasibility of water source development should be factored into a land purchase if no source currently exists. To the extent that water is already available from a pond or river, public utility, or private well, the land is that much more farmable and the time and money saved on developing a water source should be factored into its cost. Confirming the flow rate and quality of water available is a critical step in considering a piece of land.

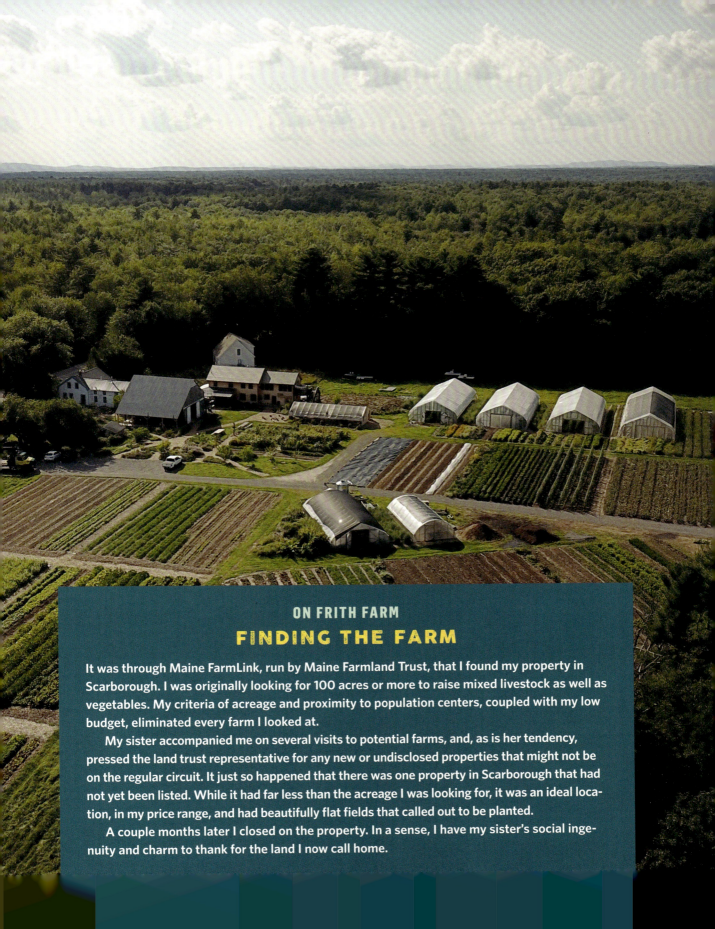

FINDING THE FARM

It was through Maine FarmLink, run by Maine Farmland Trust, that I found my property in Scarborough. I was originally looking for 100 acres or more to raise mixed livestock as well as vegetables. My criteria of acreage and proximity to population centers, coupled with my low budget, eliminated every farm I looked at.

My sister accompanied me on several visits to potential farms, and, as is her tendency, pressed the land trust representative for any new or undisclosed properties that might not be on the regular circuit. It just so happened that there was one property in Scarborough that had not yet been listed. While it had far less than the acreage I was looking for, it was an ideal location, in my price range, and had beautifully flat fields that called out to be planted.

A couple months later I closed on the property. In a sense, I have my sister's social ingenuity and charm to thank for the land I now call home.

WIND PROTECTION

Wind can be devastating to a vegetable farm. Besides blowing off row covers and tarps, wind can topple mature plants and kill tender transplants. If soil is ever left unprotected, wind can cause desiccation and erosion.

Although wind is a worthwhile concern while shopping for land, keep in mind that long-term solutions to most wind problems do exist. A variety of windbreaks can greatly reduce wind speeds, and all but the most exposed hilltop farms can be adequately protected with treelines, hedgerows, or (in the short term) constructed barriers.

CLEARED OR UNCLEARED

Clearing land of trees requires a lot of time or a lot of money, or possibly both. I have cleared about an acre of forest over the years with a small chainsaw and a rented stump grinder, and it is no small task. But farmers have been doing it for millennia with far less powerful tools than we have today. If the other criteria on a property are favorable, clearing some trees needn't turn you away, though the additional time and expense should be accounted for in your business plan and budget.

GUT FEEL

While many criteria can be quantified, there is a gut feeling when you walk onto a piece of land. How does it make you feel? Can you see customers bringing their children to play here? Can you imagine marrying yourself to this landscape for the rest of your life? Your intuitive sense of a place has a role in your search for land, but also keep in mind that these feelings can grow and evolve with time.

Building Farm Infrastructure

Once land is acquired, the real fun begins! The success of any farm starts with the health of its soil, but also depends on how well the farm is set up. Designing a farm for efficiency is important for any style of agriculture, but it is particularly important for no-till farming, which relies on human power for most of its practices. Thoughtful planning of farm layout and workflow is critical. Once permanent infrastructure is established and the overall layout designed, major changes are unlikely, so early design decisions should be made carefully.

KEYLINE DESIGN

Understanding the flow of water on a landscape allows you to use the subtle shaping of its features to make the most of water resources. P. A. Yeomans, an Australian farmer and engineer, developed a system for maximizing a landscape's water retention capability with small amounts of earthwork. The system is called "Keyline design" and is described in a number of books by Yeomans and others. Vegetables grown on a couple of acres may not benefit from Keyline design strategies, but when farming larger landscapes, it is prudent to incorporate principles of water management broader than standard irrigation and drainage.

There are six basic categories of permanent infrastructure needed for a small vegetable farm:

- Earthwork and drainage
- Buildings
- Water
- Electrical service
- Roadways
- Fencing

Proper sequencing of these installations can help prevent having to work around existing elements. For instance, digging a trench across a gravel access road to bury a water line is more work and has messier results than burying the line before the road is installed. Similarly, installing drainage tile across buried electrical lines can be stressful and time-consuming. In many cases, you can combine installations, such as by burying water and electric lines together in the same trench (when allowed by local code). But in the end, constraints of time and money, the urgency of particular needs, and the unique attributes of each property will dictate the order in which you install your infrastructure elements.

Earthwork and Drainage

Earthwork and drainage are usually the first issues to address. If it is good farmland, chances are there will be little or no such work required. But if there is uneven topography or evidence of seasonal pooling where vegetable beds will be, then leveling and adding drainage may be a good idea before proceeding with other infrastructure.

Small bumps in topography can be leveled with a tractor or bulldozer, and small dips can be filled with topsoil removed when constructing access roads or building foundations. More significant unevenness of the land may require removing the topsoil, grading the subsoil, then replacing the topsoil. This is a level of earthwork that carries significant cost and environmental impact, so proceed down this route only if alternative sites are unavailable.

Poor drainage in agricultural soils is most often caused by bedrock, a high water table, or compaction. Little can be done to change the bedrock or water table on a piece of land, but compaction can be improved in the short term (through deep tillage

CROSS SECTION OF A FRENCH DRAIN

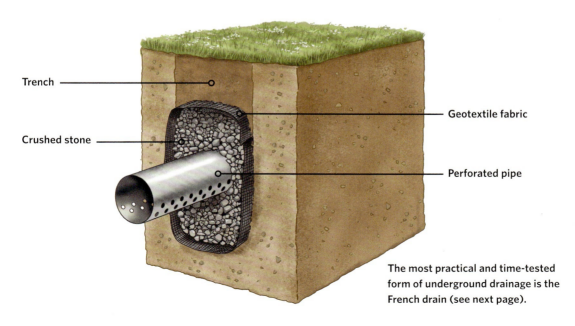

Trench

Crushed stone

Geotextile fabric

Perforated pipe

The most practical and time-tested form of underground drainage is the French drain (see next page).

with a subsoiler, chisel, or yeoman's plow) or in the long term (by growing plants with strong taproots that will reduce compaction over time).

Adding drainage tile, or an underground drainage system, is a common solution for specific areas that collect a lot of water. A French drain consists of a buried channel containing a perforated drain pipe surrounded by crushed stone. The stone is wrapped in geotextile fabric to prevent clogging from soil and roots. The trench for the drain is carefully angled at a pitch of at least ¼ inch per foot in the direction of drainage, so that the water flows by the force of gravity. Ultimately, the drain discharges onto the surface, so the area must have sufficient drop in elevation for natural drainage.

I installed about a thousand feet of French drain through portions of my farm that pooled every spring, and though laborious, this investment has proven well worth the effort.

Buildings

Once potential drainage issues are addressed and access to utilities is determined, the location of buildings becomes the principal design consideration. In my opinion, seven basic structures or spaces are needed for a small vegetable farm:

1. **Housing.** Housing is often overlooked when considering farm infrastructure, but a healthy home for the humans who operate the place is perhaps the most important space on the farm. With a lease arrangement, housing might have to be off-farm, but whenever possible, I recommend living on-site. I find countless efficiencies and joys arise from living where I work.
2. **Greenhouse.** A climate-controlled, sunny space is critical for getting plants off to a healthy and early start each season.
3. **Wash and pack area.** A central processing area is needed to efficiently chill, clean, sort, and pack vegetables coming out of the field.

4. **Walk-in cooler(s).** Well-insulated space outfitted with refrigeration keeps vegetables fresh.
5. **Customer area.** An attractive space to display produce provides a welcoming experience for customers picking up their farm goods.
6. **Dry storage.** An organized space for storage and a workshop keep tools and supplies organized and accessible.
7. **Engine storage.** A separate enclosure for engine-powered equipment and fuel keeps fumes and fire hazards away from other spaces.

CO-LOCATING UNDER ONE ROOF

As farming author Ben Hartman points out, the most efficient layout of farm buildings involves combining them all into a single multipurpose structure, except for engine storage, which should be physically distant due to the odor, mess, and fire hazard associated with liquid fuels. Co-locating the other six elements (from the list above) in the same building is often easier said than done, considering that many parcels of land come with buildings already in place (as mine did). Nevertheless, combining as many elements as possible under a single roof will save countless footsteps over the life of the farm. The cost of constructing and maintaining one large building is also much lower than the cost of numerous smaller buildings with the same total square footage.

This is a long-established strategy on New England farms like mine, with the old timber-frame houses and barns connected by a central "ell" so all living and work spaces were contiguous. A co-location layout is especially beneficial in cold climates because it saves you the time and energy of winter snow removal and outdoor travel.

MULTIPURPOSE SPACES

Another way to combine infrastructure elements is to assign multiple uses to a given space. For instance, our seedling greenhouse is full of seedlings only from

March through July. The garlic harvest falls shortly after the last seedlings go outside to harden off, so it is natural to use the greenhouse to dry garlic. Shortly after the garlic is dry, the first storage onions are ready to be cured, so the greenhouse remains in use well into the fall. Over the winter, it serves as a heatable, bright, snow-free work space for any number of projects. This stacking of infrastructure functions is a great way to reduce construction costs and make efficient use of time and space.

Another multipurpose space on Frith Farm is the 200-year-old barn that came with the property. It is a beautiful, historic timber-frame structure and thus adds value to our customers' experience as a CSA pickup area. But our CSA pickups are just two days a week, so the other days the space becomes a packing area for our wholesale orders. The barn also houses our hand tools (arranged neatly on one wall where customers can see and appreciate how much work we do by hand!), stored packaging and supplies, and a workshop. Our wash area and walk-in coolers are attached to the barn, as are the living quarters for our crew.

BUILDING LAYOUT AND DESIGN

When possible, orient new buildings so their longest facade faces south to make the most of the sunlight hitting them throughout the year. This orientation

Contiguous work spaces save countless footsteps over the life of a farm.

How does one compute the value of this commute to work?

also optimizes the output of rooftop solar panels; whether or not the panels are initially installed, it is nice to leave the option open.

When designing buildings, it is easy enough to plan for small gardens and communal gathering places, such as south-facing courtyards or porches. These little details often get overlooked in design plans, but they create the aesthetics and pleasure that lead to sustained human productivity. Considering the morale boost of living and working in beautiful, inviting spaces, these touches can add as much to overall farm efficiency as the most finely tuned workflow layout.

Water

Every farm requires a reliable source of potable water. Potential sources may include public or "city" water, private wells, and surface water such as from a river or pond. Collecting rainwater in barrels or cisterns is a great way to suppliment your water needs, but unless you have sufficient storage to maintain supply during the longest drought that

might occur, you will need a more reliable water source in addition to the captured water.

Public water is guaranteed to be "clean," or free of unwanted organisms, but this sterility is usually achieved by adding some form of chlorine. Chlorine, the active ingredient in bleach, is the most ubiquitous and accepted biocide in the United States, and most Americans are accustomed to drinking it and bathing in it on a regular basis. Generally, the concentration of chlorine in public water is low enough that it poses minimal concern for plant health, though I do wonder to what extent it affects soil organisms when public water is used heavily for irrigation.

A private well, like the one I had drilled when I started out, costs from $20 to $30 per foot of depth in my area. What depth you need depends on your location and your desired flow rate. Talking to neighbors and a local well driller is a good way to estimate the depth you will likely require, and the associated cost.

The productivity of a well is one matter; water quality is another, and many wells may have undesirable levels of minerals. In Maine, naturally occurring arsenic is common in private wells, and extra filtration is recommended before drinking the water. Mineral content is less of a concern for irrigation than for drinking water, but make sure to check with local and state recommendations before turning on your irrigation lines.

Surface water is the most renewable source of water, especially if it is replenished by local precipitation. Building a pond (or several ponds) on a piece of land is a great way to increase the resilience and sustainability of a farm. There are resources available for designing and building ponds, such as Tim Matson's classic book, *Earth Ponds*. There are also plenty of hoops to jump through with local, state, and federal regulations. Renting an excavator and digging a pond on the farm is a project I've looked forward to for a long time. In addition to conserving a precious resource, ponds provide unique ecological habitat and increase biodiversity in a farm's ecosystem.

Once a water source is established, distributing water throughout the farm is generally achieved with pipes and a pump. For year-round access, water pipes should be buried below frost line (4 feet below grade here in southern Maine), and even seasonal water lines can be buried at least 18 inches to protect them from damage and to declutter the landscape. Frost-free hydrants allow all-weather access to buried water lines, and can be installed throughout the farm. I recommend installing a frost-free hydrant in each greenhouse, and in strategic locations that will provide easy access for washing vegetables, cleaning tools, watering animals, and connecting to irrigation lines.

Electrical Service

If power is not available on a property, access to electricity is one of the first concerns in starting the farm. It might be as easy as calling the utility company and having them install a meter, or it might be as complicated and expensive as installing a large off-grid solar-electric system with a battery bank. Whatever your source, ensuring that your electrical power is sufficient and reliable will prevent many problems down the line. I paid an electrician to install 200-amp service at the farm my first year. It seemed overkill at the time, but now when multiple walk-in coolers, chest freezers, and power tools are running at once, I am grateful for every available amp.

Once the main service panel (breaker box) is installed professionally, the property owner can legally (in many areas, like mine) run circuits and install fixtures and subpanels on their own. Make sure to check with your local code authority before starting any electrical work, because permits and inspections may be required. I have saved many thousands of dollars over the years by doing my own wiring for farm infrastructure.

There are risks of shock and fire associated with any electrical project, so make sure you understand the principles and best practices before diving in, and seek professional help when warranted. I

An electrical subpanel brings power where it is needed.

A frost-free hydrant provides year-round access to water.

Building a farm road can be as simple as removing topsoil, laying geotextile fabric, and spreading gravel.

recommend picking up a copy of a simple how-to book on basic wiring. I learned from such a book that consisted mostly of pictures and found the process surprisingly straightforward.

Roadways

An efficient farm requires easy access to all buildings regardless of the time of year or the weather, as well as seasonal access to growing areas. The most practical way to provide this access is to construct gravel roads. One person on a small utility tractor can build several hundred feet of gravel road in a day or two.

In essence, installing a gravel road involves removing the topsoil, laying geotextile fabric, and spreading gravel on top. Culverts may be necessary when crossing low spots or ditches, but even so, road construction is a relatively straightforward

task that new farmers can tackle on their own and save a lot of money. Small tractors are relatively inexpensive to rent by the hour or day. Adding a driveway entrance to a public road often requires a permit, and may have to meet certain specifications. As with all infrastructure projects, check local codes and regulations before proceeding.

Fencing

Of all the crop loss I have experienced, none is more severe than that caused by deer. Depending on the level of pressure in the area, deer damage is a variable that can be removed from the list of concerns by fencing in the farm. I try to look for solutions to all pest problems within the ecosystem, which, in this case, would mean fostering habitat for the natural predators of deer. Unfortunately, one of the few remaining deer predators in populated areas is the human hunter, and relying on humans with guns or bows to protect crops is not always a reliable long-term plan.

So I turned to constructed barriers. I started with a single strand of electrified polytape nine years ago and have been adding strands ever since as the deer started to figure out what tasty treats we are growing. Last year, the pressure was high enough that the psychological barrier proved insufficient, and I estimate that we lost close to $30,000 worth of produce to our wild ruminant neighbors! Putting a few of them in the freezer helped us feel somewhat better but made little impact on the continued feeding. This year, we installed an 8-foot physical fence around the entire farm — an effort that should save us much worry and money in the long run.

You can consult with an agricultural fencing company such as Kencove, Wellscroft, or Premier 1 Supplies to determine the best options for wildlife exclusion based on your terrain, budget, and level of pressure. Once you have a plan and the right materials, installing the fence yourself requires little specialized skill and is an easy way to save money.

DIY Infrastructure

Many farmers are also do-it-yourself experts, performing their own earthwork, plumbing, electrical, welding, carpentry, masonry, mechanical repairs, and more. Starting a farm — even a small and simple one — requires significant infrastructure, and when money is scarce, deciding what to do yourself and what to hire out can be a tough call. You must estimate the potential cost savings of doing projects yourself, while also considering opportunity costs and the challenges of learning new skills, navigating local codes, and acquiring the right materials.

An 8-foot-tall woven wire fence on 11-foot T-posts reliably excludes deer from the farm.

Deciding what to tackle yourself and what to leave to the pros is a personal decision, but I find that the skills learned and the sense of empowerment that come from doing a job on your own are often worth the extra time and frustration of pushing past the steepest part of a learning curve.

When I started Frith Farm nine years ago, I didn't know much about construction, machinery, or even power tools. I was a typical suburbanite with eighteen years of expensive education and an embarrassing lack of hard skills. What I did have was an eagerness to learn and a willingness to make mistakes — two ingredients that I believe are necessary when tackling any new project.

Even with the right mindset, however, the beginning farmer faces some tasks that require skills or expensive machinery that can be impractical to acquire. The following table lists some of the common tasks you may encounter when starting a farm, along with my subjective assessment of their difficulty level and required equipment.

For those like me, starting with minimal trade skills, I suggest beginning with the "low"-difficulty tasks, and hiring contractors for other jobs until you feel confident to take them on.

Whatever you choose to attempt yourself, the important thing is that you stay safe. Some of the tools and equipment involved in these tasks can be dangerous or even lethal if not handled properly. There is no shame in hiring out any or all of these jobs. Indeed, sometimes contracting is faster and less expensive overall, especially when most contractors prefer to start a job from scratch rather than take over one that was botched or abandoned partway through by a DIYer.

The decision to farm for a living is the beginning of a journey that never ends. From writing a business plan and acquiring capital, to finding land and building the farm's infrastructure, the first steps of starting a farm are filled with new and staggering challenges. Whether or not you realize your farming dreams, the time spent trying is guaranteed to be some of the most exciting and adventure-filled of your life. Hopefully, the resources and strategies outlined here and elsewhere can give you the confidence to go for it, and the fortitude to succeed. If so, what better time to get started than now?

WHERE TO FIND THE INFORMATION YOU NEED

Living in the Age of Information, we have ready access to tutorials on almost every aspect of construction, maintenance, and repair. There are links, videos, and written information on the ins and outs of any task, and usually more than you can possibly absorb. Personally, I find reading a simple and respected book on a topic like carpentry, plumbing, or electrical wiring to be more helpful than sorting through online blogs and videos, though each certainly has its place.

The most helpful resource, however, is a seasoned friend or neighbor who can teach you the ropes far better than any book or internet resource. And when you do hire professionals for a job, you can learn a lot by hanging around, observing, and asking some questions while the pros do the work.

Technical Difficulty and Equipment Needs of DIY Infrastructure Projects

Infrastructure Project	Difficulty	Equipment Needed
Drilled well	High	Drilling rig
Pond	Moderate to high	Excavator
French drain	Moderate	Trencher
Burying water & electric lines	Low	Trencher
Irrigation setup	Low	*
Plumbing, PEX	Low	Crimper
Plumbing, copper	Moderate	Soldering tools
Plumbing, drain-waste-vent (PVC)	Moderate	*
Wiring lights, switches, outlets	Low	*
Wiring subpanels and equipment	Moderate	*
Gravel road	Low	Front-end loader
Fencing	Low	*
Greenhouse or high tunnel kit	Low	*
Concrete footings or small slab	Low	Cement mixer
Concrete foundation or large slab	Moderate to high	Formwork
Walk-in cooler	Low	Carpentry tools
Temporary or seasonal housing	Low to moderate	Carpentry tools
Year-round housing	Moderate to high	Varies
Clearing land	Moderate	Chainsaw, stump grinder

* Only inexpensive hand tools are required.

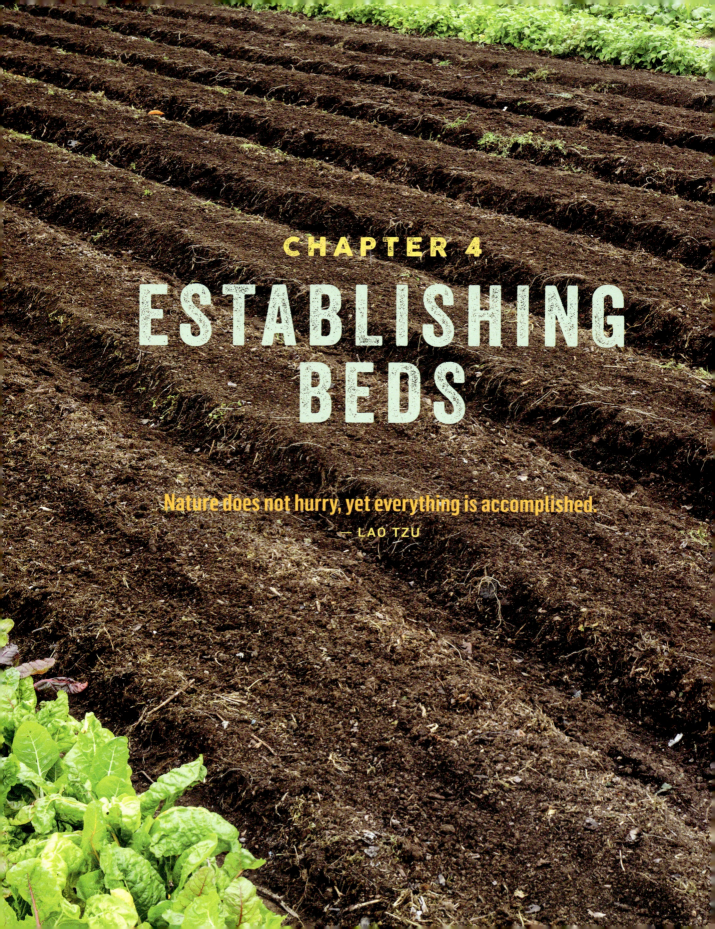

CHAPTER 4

ESTABLISHING BEDS

Nature does not hurry, yet everything is accomplished.
— LAO TZU

Building garden beds marks the essential beginning of the farm — the first step in turning soil and sun into food. This chapter describes how to go from a field of sod to a well-planned system of beds with healthy, plantable soil — all while keeping nature's principles of soil care in mind.

Permanent Raised Beds

No-till practices pair perfectly with permanent raised beds, which require no time spent on measuring, marking, or shaping for each crop. They allow application of amendments and compost right where the plants grow — on the beds — and more enduring mulches in the paths. Unlike the layout in tractor-managed fields, permanent beds facilitate intensive spacing and prevent compaction, since foot traffic is confined to the permanent paths.

Raised beds warm and dry out faster in the spring (in hot and drought-prone areas, consider permanent *non*-raised beds), and they are that much closer to us for easier planting, weeding, and harvesting. They have deeper topsoil and provide a larger root zone for all crops — think long straight carrots that exhibit no forking. And best of all, since further soil disturbance is off the table, the task of forming beds need not be repeated every year.

Optimal Dimensions

I highly recommend sticking to a single set of bed dimensions throughout the farm, even if it results in slightly less-than-optimal use of the geometry of your land. Making all of the beds the same width and length streamlines a host of subsequent tasks, including seed ordering, crop planning, reusing tarps, covering rows, trellising, and recordkeeping.

I prefer beds that are 5 feet *on-center*, meaning that the distance from the center of one path to the center of the next is 5 feet, or 60 inches. No matter how hard we try to make them otherwise, the paths seem to end up being 18 inches wide, so that leaves 42 inches of bed space. Other farmers prefer beds 4 feet on-center, with 30 inches of bed space. There are pros and cons to each width.

▲ **Newly formed beds, 5 feet on-center.**

The argument for narrower beds is mostly ergonomic: narrow beds are easier to step over, and the middle of each bed is easier to reach. Many implements for a walking tractor are also sized for a 30-inch width, which enables "single-pass" efficiency on these beds. The no-till farm requires very few such passes, however, so sizing beds for implements makes less sense. Remember, one of the benefits of no-till farming is the freedom to create your own intensive spacing without being confined by the width of tractor wheels or implements.

The main reason I prefer 42-inch beds is that a higher percentage of the field is plantable than with narrower beds, allowing for denser plantings and higher yields from the same area. With 30-inch beds that are 4 feet on-center, 62.5 percent of the field is plantable bed space; the other 37.5 percent is devoted to paths. With 42-inch beds 5 feet on-center, the split is 70 percent bed space and 30 percent paths. On an acre, that's an extra 3,267 square feet of plantable area.

I am over 6 feet tall, so the extra planting area feels worth the longer step over beds, but the right choice of bed size comes down to personal preference.

Field Layout

As with designing the farm's permanent infrastructure, the decisions around field layout will affect management and production practices for years to come. Creating an organized, intuitive, and functional layout of vegetable beds sets the stage for continuing efficiency.

I find that 100 feet is an ideal length for a human-scale vegetable bed. This length simplifies calculations for seeding, planting rates, and production data and is a standard length for trellis, tarp, and row-cover materials. It is also a suitable scale for the human body and psyche — a reasonable length to rake, weed, or harvest without feeling exhausted or demoralized.

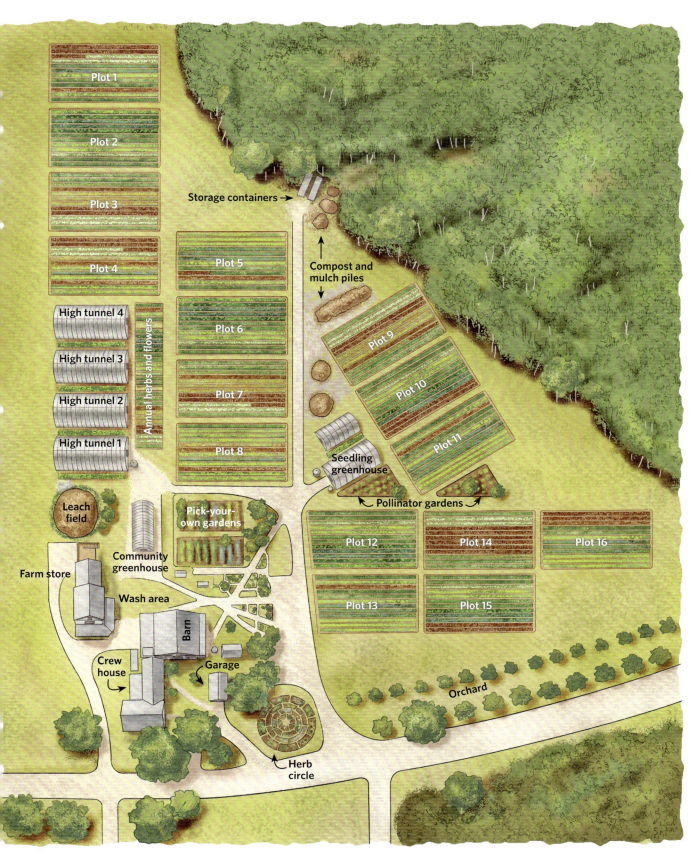

Standardizing the dimensions of beds and plots leads to many efficiencies.

Plots

To further organize the farm, I recommend grouping beds in standardized plots of roughly 10 beds each. These modular plots facilitate planning and crop rotations as well as organizing the landscape of the farm so that crew members can easily identify a given plot (and bed within it). At Frith Farm we have 16 plots of 12 beds each, with each bed measuring 5 feet on-center by 100 feet long. This organizational strategy, as rigidly rectilinear as it may feel, enables a level of clarity and efficiency that facilitates our work on a daily basis.

To help delineate one plot from the next, we planted perennial hedgerows and insectary strips between them. These not only clarify field layout, they also benefit pollination, pest control, wind abatement, soil health, and economic diversification (discussed in detail in chapter 9).

In laying out plots, it is also important to consider practical concerns, like vehicle access, water drainage, and potential shading from nearby trees or buildings. Even though we do almost all field work by hand, I find it helpful to be able to drive a vehicle to the head of every plot on the farm for larger harvests or for spreading compost and mulch. This requires a roadway or grassy swath at least 8 feet wide.

Beds of flowering perennials separate plots and make navigating the farm easy and enjoyable.

BED ORIENTATION

To facilitate drainage and spring drying, beds with clay soils in climates where rain is abundant can be oriented *with* the slope of the land instead of across it. This goes against the conventional wisdom of contour terracing and depends on how well your soils drain, how steep your slopes are, and how much precipitation you expect. With ample soil coverage and no soil disturbance, concerns around erosion are minimized in a no-till system. But what works in New England might make less sense in other climates, and bed orientation should be tailored to your local conditions.

Jump-Starting Soil Health

For me, the process of jump-starting the biological health of the soil is the most thrilling part of starting a farm. Watching the land respond to the application of compost and mulches, and taking part in the growth of living plants, is an ongoing source of wonder and satisfaction. Figuring out which materials to apply, at what rate to apply them, and how best to acquire them is an exciting (if challenging) project.

Revitalizing depleted or abused soils can be achieved naturally with no inputs, but for earning a living from vegetable production, an initial importation of organic matter and fertility from off the farm enables a faster start and a shorter lean period without cash flow.

Using Inputs

Some might question the sustainability of importing so much material to the farm. I agree that in a perfect world, farms would supply their own fertility and require few, if any, inputs. But in our imperfect world, this takes considerable time and hard work. Few of us are able to commit to this goal without some income to keep us afloat in the meantime. Importing organic matter to the farm is a way to jump-start soil health, crop production, and farm revenue without waiting years for living plants to improve the soil more gradually. And what better place to direct streams of local organic matter by-products than a productive farm?

Self-sufficiency can exist at a community level as well as on individual farms. A network of local farms and businesses that supply one another's needs with surpluses or by-products is more resilient than an isolated farm trying to do it all alone. I am happy to support a local dairy farm that sells compost made from their cow manure and am equally happy to buy every last fallen leaf from my town transfer station, which would otherwise truck the leaves an hour north to a larger facility.

These imports do not replace the need to cover-crop and care for the soil in other ways, but they accelerate the soil-building process and enable the development of a fertile, productive, profitable farm in very little time. Once biological health is kick-started, the farm can use this self-enriching productivity to develop a system that requires few inputs.

Soil Testing

Any time we bypass natural cycles and add nutrients to the land, it is prudent to start by taking a snapshot of soil chemistry with a comprehensive soil test. Most tests measure the pH and concentrations of major plant nutrients and make input recommendations based on the results. Some tests also measure organic matter content and levels of certain micronutrients. These soil tests are generally quite affordable (in Maine, the cost is $18 per test), and soil samples can be submitted through the mail. Check with your local university agricultural extension program, or search out a private testing service to get your soil tested.

A sampler with a footstep and soil ejector speeds up the collection process.

```
SOIL TEST SUMMARY & INTERPRETATION
(see Numerical Results section for more information)
                    Level          LOW          MEDIUM              OPTIMUM
                    Found
Soil pH              5.9   XXXXXXXXXXXXXXXXXXXXXXXXXXXXX
Organic Matter(%)    3.7   XXXXXXXXXXXXXXXXXXXXX
Major nutrients
Phosphorus (lb/A)    4.2   XXXXXXXXXXXXXXXXXXXXXXXX
Potassium  (% Sat)   1.3   XXXXXXXXXXXXXXX
Calcium    (% Sat)  38.2   XXXXXXXXXXXXXX
Magnesium  (% Sat)   5.1   XXXXXXXXXXXXXXXXX
Sulfur     (ppm)     10    XXXXXXXXXXXXXXXXXXXXXXX
Micronutrients
Copper     (ppm)     0.19
Iron       (ppm)     6.7
Manganese  (ppm)     2.0
Zinc       (ppm)     0.4
```

The farm's first soil test shows plenty of room for improvement.

Testing facilities also offer advice (and sometimes tools) for collecting the soil samples.

I recommend taking soil test results with a large grain of salt. Though they are useful for giving an idea of chemical excesses and deficiencies, keep in mind that life, not chemistry, is what drives soil health. There are certainly connections between nutrient levels and biological activity, but it is easy to lose sight of the broader ecological picture when examining the detailed numbers from soil tests. Remember that concentrations of a half-dozen chemical elements in a handful of soil will never summarize an entire underground ecosystem. That said, soil tests are helpful in preventing overapplication of certain nutrients and addressing glaring mineral deficiencies and pH issues in your soil, as described below.

I test my soil once each season, partly to ensure general balance and partly to record the organic matter's growth over the years. This number is a decent representation of the improved soil structure, biological activity, and water retention capability, as well as the carbon that is no longer in the atmosphere.

What Does Your Soil Need?

Once you receive your initial test results, you can start planning what you will add to the soil, and in what quantities. The following are the materials and techniques I consider to be foundational for establishing productive no-till beds quickly and effectively.

Compost

Compost is decomposed organic matter in a relatively stable form. It provides food and habitat for the soil's web of microorganisms. Finished compost is a crucial ingredient for the beginning no-till farm and is an ideal input to spread liberally before preparing beds. The best compost is dark and smells like soil; it should be screened to a fine texture and be certified for organic use. Organic standards require certified compost to meet specific temperature guidelines, which generally ensure it will be free of weed seed and pathogens.

Cost and quality can vary widely, so it's a good idea to research compost sources in the early stages of starting a farm. Most organic compost in New England costs between $25 and $50 per cubic yard, and it is typically cheapest to buy whole dump truck loads at a time. The types and uses of compost are discussed in further detail in chapter 8.

If a soil test reveals low levels of fertility and organic matter, generous applications of compost, up to several inches thick, add life and vitality to your soil very quickly and can enable a healthy first crop right out of the gate. Three cubic yards will cover 1,000 square feet to a depth of 1 inch. A layer that's 3 inches thick takes 9 cubic yards. This is a lot of compost, and how much you spread may be restricted by your budget. But any amount you can afford will pay off quickly when used on depleted soils, providing increased yields and the many other benefits of improved soil health.

Quality compost is one of the most effective amendments for jump-starting soil health.

Straw is a wonderful soil-building mulch.

For soils that are already high in phosphorus or other nutrients, selecting an organic matter input that is less nutrient-rich makes sense (more on this in chapter 8). This might include peat moss, rotted leaves, composted bark mulch, or other decomposed plant residues. Organic matter derived from plants (as opposed to animal by-products) can generally be applied to soil in large quantities with little risk of overloading nutrients. Raw materials with a high carbon-to-nitrogen ratio (sawdust, wood chips, shredded newspaper) are best used as surface mulch, since incorporating them into the soil can tie up nitrogen and inhibit plant growth.

Whatever organic matter you find and apply, take pleasure in the fact that it will feed your soil for years to come. The soil is a farmer's most valuable asset; investing in it is the same as investing in the farm's future.

Mulch

The no-till systems described in this book require copious quantities of plant residues to cover all exposed soil. These mulches can be anything that was recently a plant. The best material is almost always the one that is readily available locally (or even grown in place). Leaves, straw, and wood chips are common mulches, but there may be many other possibilities (see chapter 7). Whatever sources you find, make sure the cost and the quantity available

will fit your needs, as it takes a lot of material to mulch vegetable beds at a commercial scale. We use about 130 cubic yards of leaves per acre each season. That's a lot of spreading, but it more than pays off with decreased weed pressure and increased soil health. Ensuring a reliable source of plant material should happen long before you start forming beds because mulching is far less effective once weeds establish.

Altering pH

An initial soil test will estimate the pH of your soil and may provide recommended rates at which to apply lime (to sweeten it) or sulfur (to sour it). Wood ash is a more sustainable option for raising pH. It mimics the natural sweetening process of soil that occurs after a wildfire. When sourcing ashes, be careful to avoid those from treated lumber, plywood, and painted wood, all of which contain toxic residues.

When wood ash is unavailable or its origins are unknown, agricultural lime is an inexpensive and readily available alternative. Dolomitic limestone is best for soils low in magnesium, while calcitic limestone is better for soils low in calcium. Soil test results can indicate which type of lime is preferable. For acidifying soils, materials like peat moss or coffee grounds can lower pH somewhat, but elemental sulfur lowers pH more predictably and is an inexpensive and effective amendment.

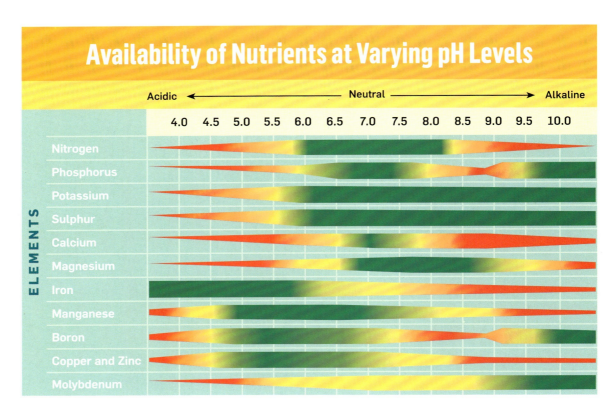

Availability of Nutrients at Varying pH Levels

The optimal pH range for growing most vegetables is between 6.5 and 7.0. While healthy produce can certainly grow outside this window, it is easy enough to adjust pH to favor vegetable production. Different minerals are more available to plants at certain pH levels and less so at others (see chart above), and homing in on the optimum range is worth the relatively small one-time task of spreading some inexpensive powder. Once amended, soil pH changes very slowly over several years, so it makes sense to start the process early.

Soil Amendments (or Not)

Beyond altering the pH, I do not recommend getting sucked too deep into the world of specialty soil amendments. Many of these inputs are mined from finite deposits far from the farm, at great environmental cost. Unless a soil test reveals extremely low levels of certain nutrients, generous applications of compost and mulches, along with the boost in soil biology from growing cover crops, will likely address minor deficiencies. For major deficiencies, or if the deficiencies persist after several years of biologically invigorated soil, then targeted applications of rock powders or other soil amendments can make sense.

Remember, natural systems are capable of growing 100-foot trees out of marginal soils with no carefully formulated inputs of trace elements or fertilizers. Following nature's model means focusing on the life of the soil, fostered through a diverse abundance of living plants growing through organic residues on undisturbed soils. Soil chemistry does not produce this health but rather falls into place as a result of it.

The soil is a farmer's most valuable asset; investing in it is investing in the farm's future.

Compost applied on beds acts as a mulch that can be planted directly into.

Layers of mulch can be used to smother sod.

Ramial wood chips feed fungal communities and keep paths weed-free.

Acquiring Local Organic Materials

Unlike fertilizers and mined rock powders, compost and bulky plant residues are both local and organic. They are biomass produced within the farm's regional ecosystem, and their bulky nature makes them difficult to ship, so they tend to remain affordable and accessible to local farms. Large quantities of organic material are required to establish productive no-till beds, but the environmental impact of putting local biomass to use in our soils is positive.

I brought in hundreds of cubic yards of compost and wood chips and closer to thousands of yards of leaves over the first few years of starting the farm. Spreading organic compost thickly can get expensive fast, and organic mulches can also be pricey. But it's worth it! I would argue there is no higher priority than creating fertile beds to grow your produce. It is better to scale down acreage rather than to scale back on soil quality.

One perk of farming small is that we can concentrate the resources we have on a fertile area of highly intensive production. Considering that the revenue from a single bed can be $500 to $2,000 per year (depending on the crops and your markets), spending a fraction of that for a yard or two of compost pays off the same year in increased yields, fewer weeds, and reduced pest and disease pressure.

If you are starting with soil low in organic matter and fertility, I recommend spreading quality compost at a rate of *at least* 3 cubic yards per 1,000 square feet (130 cubic yards per acre) as you establish your first beds. Before spreading, confirm the nutrient levels of your soil and your compost with a lab test to ensure you do not overapply certain nutrients. I recommend acquiring similar quantities of mulch — whether leaves, wood chips, straw, or whatever plant matter is locally abundant. This is a lot of material, to be sure; the ease of acquisition, the cost of purchasing, and the time spent spreading should be factored into the establishment of the farm.

SOURCING COMPOST AND MULCHES

Sourcing compost and mulches is often more complicated than calling your local garden center, especially if you want to buy in bulk at lower prices or tap into waste streams that are free. Connecting with local landscapers, homeowners, municipalities, and other farms are great ways to make relationships that can help divert flows of organic matter onto your land and into your soils. (Sourcing compost and mulch is discussed more in chapters 7 and 8).

Establishing sources for quality compost and mulch is a priority when starting a no-till market farm. It might even be a consideration in deciding where to put down roots. Getting started without organic matter inputs is certainly possible, but it will take much longer — and the need for short-term cash flow does not often afford the beginning farmer the luxury of waiting.

This is another argument for finding land as close as possible to population centers, since these sources of organic matter tend to be harder to come by in rural areas. Here in southern Maine I am able to buy leaves directly from my municipality for about $5 a cubic yard, delivered. We have also called every landscaping company within a 20-mile radius to invite them to use the farm as a dump site for leaves, stump grindings, and wood chips (but not grass clippings, which are often contaminated with applied chemicals). The result is a steady flow of organic matter onto the farm, at minimal cost.

Breaking Ground with and without Tilling

There are two methods that I have used to form raised beds at a commercial scale without tillage. One requires a longer wait time before planting, and the other requires more organic material. However, in my experience, a single till establishes beds in a shorter time and with better initial productivity than either of these no-till methods. Therefore, to get a crop growing quickly and with less work, I recommend considering one-time tillage. Let's take a look at all three methods.

Tarp and Compost

A necessary step in going from hayfield to productive vegetable beds is to kill whatever grasses, legumes, and weeds are currently established. A simple way to do this without tillage is to mow the plants and smother them with tarps.

The most common tarps used for smothering are black-on-white silage tarps that are 5 or 6 mils thick. To smother an area, simply lay the tarp flat on the ground, black side up, and secure all edges with sandbags, rocks, boards, soil, or my personal favorite: 8 × 8 × 8-inch concrete blocks. Unlike other weights, these blocks do not degrade in the sun and are easy to pick up with one hand.

Smothering established perennial sod can take anywhere from a few weeks to the better part of a year, depending on the temperature and the mix of species in the field. This is clearly a long time to wait when you are starting a farm and need revenue as quickly as possible. In such cases, smothering for *this* season may be impractical, but perhaps it makes sense for an area you might need for *next* season, while you follow a faster preparation method for the beds you need immediately (keep reading). Laying a tarp on the ground is incredibly easy relative to working the soil over with tillage implements; a little forethought can save a lot of work and prevent unnecessary soil disturbance.

After the sod is fully killed by smothering, remove the tarp, spread a thick layer of compost where you want your beds, and plant right into it. If the soil is at all compacted (see Breaking

Up Compaction on page 127), it is a good idea to broadfork it before applying the compost (or you could use a subsoiler or chisel plow before tarping). Be forewarned: it takes a lot of compost to achieve good results this way, especially if your soil is initially low in fertility or organic matter. I find a 1½-inch layer is the minimum necessary for ease of transplanting and good weed suppression.

It is important to note that this must be fully aged, finely sifted compost that smells and feels like rich soil. Using unfinished compost or raw manure can chemically burn your plants and lose nutrients through leaching into groundwater and volatilization to the air. Unsifted, bulky, or chunky compost also allows excessive air infiltration and is prone to drying out.

This method not only requires a lot of compost but also the forethought to lay down tarps up to a year in advance, which may not be feasible for the starting farmer. It also skips the opportunity to jumpstart soil health by mixing in soil amendments; so again, I prefer to till a single time to establish new beds.

Sheet Mulch and Cover Crop

An even less conventional method to establish beds is to cover the entire area you want to plant with mulch thick enough to smother the underlying vegetation. Compost is then added on top to plant into.

The effectiveness of sheet mulching relies on a layer that smothers, followed by one or more layers that can be planted into immediately. Leaves make an ideal smother layer since they tend to form an impenetrable mat when spread thickly. Alternatively, overlapped cardboard is often used at smaller scales. Regardless of the smothering material used, compost is generally the best layer to top

Sheet mulching takes us from sod to plantable garden beds in a single day — without soil disturbance.

TASK
SHEET MULCH

At Frith Farm we follow these steps to sheet-mulch at a commercial scale:

1 Mow. Cut or crimp all plant material as close as possible to the ground in the area where you want your permanent raised beds.

2 Amend to correct pH. Spread wood ash, lime, or sulfur, based on soil test results.

3 Spread leaves. Spread partially rotted leaves (leaves that have sat in a pile for a year or two) evenly to a depth of 2 to 4 inches over the entire area. You can also add a layer of cardboard under the mulch (with all edges fully overlapped) for more protection against perennial regrowth, but this is not necessary if the mulch is spread thickly enough.

4 Spread compost. Cover the leaves with a 4-inch-thick (minimum) layer of compost where beds are desired, leaving the pathways empty.

5 Mulch paths. Fill in the path areas with wood chips, straw, or more leaves. Since wood chips take several years to break down, spreading them in paths is a loose commitment to a given bed configuration (with no tillage!) for at least that long.

6 Plant beds. You can plant into the compost as soon as it is spread. Make sure to keep the newly formed beds irrigated as needed, since the compost will dry out faster than native soil. While sheet-mulched beds can be planted to cash crops immediately, I recommend planting cover crops first. The biological action of their dense network of roots and partnering microbes will mix and mellow the sheet mulch, facilitating the breakdown of the underlying sod. After a half to full season of cover crop growth, the new beds will be primed to grow amazing vegetables.

off with, since it can be planted into immediately with decent results. The idea is that the underlying vegetation is smothered and dying as the newly planted crop sends down its roots, which eventually feed on the decomposed residues below.

Despite being able to plant into the sheet mulch immediately, I find that many vegetables grow best after the mulch has had a chance to mellow. To hasten this process, it helps to seed a newly sheet-mulched area to cover crop before trying to grow a cash crop. This process ends up taking about as long to prepare the soil as tarping, with the key difference that the cover crop actively feeds the soil through photosynthesis while the underlying sod is breaking down.

Although the combination of sheet mulching and cover cropping results in amazing soil, this method requires huge amounts of organic materials and plenty of hard work to spread them.

There are various homestead-scale recipes for sheet mulching, and no single way is necessarily better than another. The formula can and should be adjusted according to the materials you have access to in large quantities.

One-Time Tillage

What if you don't have the time to smother sod with tarps, or you can't afford the vast quantities of mulch and compost needed to sheet-mulch? For many starting farmers a few thousand dollars can break the bank. I've been there.

In this case, strange as the suggestion may be for a book on no-till farming, I believe the best option is tilling a single time to transition a field from sod to plantable vegetable beds. The no-till alternatives described above require time, inputs, and effort, and with the economic and time constraints of starting a farm, sometimes corners must be cut. As Michael Phillips writes, "Incorporating sod to start a garden or restoring severely damaged soil justifies a degree of up-front compromise on biological principles."

Much of the world's farmland has experienced such prolonged abuse that a final shaping of the soil to get a new no-till system up and running is hardly the difference between paradise and damnation. Don't let purism keep you from actually breaking ground — it is better to start farming imperfectly than never to start at all!

Black tarps smother sod on a new plot of garden beds.

Initial tillage with a BCS walking tractor and rotary plow

USING A ROTARY PLOW

I formed the majority of my beds with a rotary plow made by Berta Franco, mounted on a BCS walking tractor. The Berta plow looks like a bladed corkscrew and is very effective at transitioning sod to workable soil because it recreates the effects of plowing and discing all in a single pass (yes, this is aggressive tillage!). Each pass prepares a swath 10 inches wide, so tilling large areas takes a long time. Operating the walking tractor also takes more effort than sitting on a tractor seat, so don't expect to prepare much more than a quarter acre per day.

Since this is a final tilling of the soil, it is your only chance to mechanically mix in compost and other soil-building amendments. Once established, the no-till beds will rely on the slower mixing action of plant roots and soil organisms, so one-time tillage is a one-time opportunity to inject your soil with organic matter and any desired mineral inputs (based on soil test results). This is especially relevant for pH-altering amendments like lime or sulfur because these require thorough mixing in the soil to change the pH in a reasonable amount of time. While it is possible to improve the soil without external inputs, I believe it is worth accelerating the process with generous applications of compost and any soil amendments before this final tillage event. This will help jump-start the natural cycles of soil-generated fertility that reduce the need for further inputs.

Because the rotary plow ejects soil to the side, you must follow a specific pattern when breaking new ground to avoid re-plowing soil discharged from a previous pass. You start by forming a trench with four consecutive passes down the middle of the area to be plowed, then reverse direction and refill the trench, expanding outward with each pass until you reach the outer edge of the plot. The rotary plow I bought (from Earthtools in Kentucky) includes a handy diagram that illustrates the best path to follow as you open up new ground.

The side discharge of the rotary plow also makes it an ideal tool for forming raised beds once the soil is initially plowed. Some farmers also use it for hilling crops like potatoes or ginger. Marking the center line of each bed with mason's twine tied to a stake at the head and foot helps keep beds straight and the proper width. A pass up and down each path spits soil to both sides and leaves you with impressively tall and flat raised beds. A quick touch-up with a rake smooths out any high spots.

Once your land is tilled, a human-powered alternative to rotary plowing is to dig your raised beds by hand. While labor-intensive and time-consuming, this is a viable way to go if a rotary plow is not available to you and your scale is very small.

SMOTHERING PERENNIAL WEEDS AFTER TILLING

Raised beds created from tilling new ground require steps to prevent regrowth of the sod and perennial weeds. While the bed might look perfectly weed-free and ready for planting, don't be fooled. Any perennial roots and grasses present will re-emerge and overtake your crops with ease. The traditional method to kill sod is to till repeatedly until all these roots finally give up the will to live. This certainly works, but it also kills a lot of other soil organisms, destroys soil structure, and burns up organic matter in the process.

The no-till alternative is smothering. Silage tarps or landscape fabric sheets with holes cut or burned in them at transplant spacing can be reused year after year as you open new plots. Widely spaced crops such as squash, tomatoes, or Brussels sprouts require fewer holes cut and thus enable more complete smothering. These crops also tend to thrive

when planted after turned-in sod. Some weeding around the base of each plant will still be necessary, but this technique is very manageable compared to plucking blades of grass out of entire beds.

A cheaper alternative to tarps or landscape fabric is black plastic mulch. Typically about 1 mil thick, this plastic is not reusable and generally not recyclable due to the dirt caked on it after removal, which is required at the end of the season under organic standards. It is estimated that farms worldwide use one million tons of plastic mulch every year, which then end up in landfills, oceans, and incinerators. This is clearly not a sustainable practice.

That said, I believe that using plastic mulch is an acceptable transitional practice for establishing permanent raised beds that afterward rely on natural methods of weed prevention: living plants, compost, and organic mulches. Don't be afraid to embrace this compromise in the short-term to get your first crops growing. Similar to one-time tillage, a single use of plastic mulch to get the farm up and running feels justifiable.

The environmentally conscious farmer often prefers reusable landscape fabric or tarps over disposable plastic mulch. Depending on the number of uses, however, such fabric may actually be more wasteful than disposable mulch. Heavy-duty landscape fabric weighs as much as 5 ounces per square yard, whereas 1-mil plastic mulch weighs about 0.7 ounces. This means the landscape fabric must be reused eight times before it earns its claim of waste reduction.

Covering the soil with plastic is not a long-term element of ecological farming, so a single season of disposable film may make more sense than investing in much thicker plastic that ends up sitting around after its first few uses. If we embrace the ecological principles of maximized photosynthesis, diversity, and organic soil coverage, the direction of farm practices will likely move away from plasticulture within the first few years of establishment.

A thick layer of compost is ready to be mixed in, to jump-start soil health as new beds are formed.

Laying Plastic Mulch on New Beds

When opening new plots on Frith Farm, we lay plastic mulch by hand, unrolling it as we go and burying the edges with shoveled soil from the paths. This is hard work, but it progresses quickly with two or more people. A crew of three of us can "plastic" a plot of twelve 100-foot beds in a morning. The width of the plastic should be the same as the on-center spacing of your beds to allow enough to extend into the path for adequate burial (5 feet wide for us). The trick is to place just enough soil on the plastic so that it is pulled tight across the bed and no edges are exposed, but not so much that the plastic will tear when it is pulled up and removed later in the season.

Once the beds are covered, the paths can be filled with a thick mulch of leaves, straw, wood chips, or other organic material. This completes a seamless coverage of the soil, both on beds and in paths, retaining moisture and preventing weeds. At this point the bed is ready for transplanting. Holes are poked through the plastic by hand at the desired plant spacing. Direct seeding must wait until the underlying sod has been fully smothered and the plastic removed.

Running drip tape under the plastic is a good way to keep beds irrigated, but I find that if they are watered generously before laying the plastic they retain sufficient moisture to forgo irrigation altogether. This technique has worked well on my very sandy soil, so I can only imagine irrigation under plastic would be even less necessary on heavier clay soils, but this will depend on your soil type and climate.

Once no-till beds are formed and the sod smothered, the hardest work of establishing a no-till system is complete. From this moment on, no time is wasted on working the soil, and no harm is inflicted by disturbing its web of life.

Side note: Every 3 to 5 years, we make a single pass with the Berta plow up and down each path to re-form the raised beds. This kicks up the decomposed mulch onto the beds, without disturbing the underlying soil. Without this step the beds grow less pronounced over time, and eventually become difficult to distinguish from the paths. Immediately after re-forming, we add a layer of wood chip mulch to the newly formed paths.

The BCS 853 walking tractor with rotary plow attachment

The rotary plow's side discharge forms raised beds with a pass up and down each path.

TASK

A PREFERRED METHOD FOR

FORMING NEW BEDS

Once a farm establishes its initial garden plots, the urgency of forming new beds decreases, as does the number of new beds needed each season. While I advocate one-time tillage followed by plastic mulch to enable early planting in year one, the following steps are my preferred method for forming new beds in years two and beyond, when there is more time to make use of tarps, cover crops, and livestock.

IN LATE WINTER OR EARLY SPRING

1 **Amend soil.** Spread up to 3 inches of compost, as well as amendments to correct pH and any mineral deficiencies shown by a soil test.

2 **Break up compaction.** Most agricultural land has a hardpan or plowpan about 6 to 10 inches below the surface. I recommend using a subsoiler or chisel plow on a tractor (or hiring someone to do it for you) to break up the compaction before tilling with the rotary plow.

WHEN SOIL IS SUFFICIENTLY DRY

3 **Till.** Till the entire area with a rotary plow on a BCS walking tractor. A riding tractor with tillage implements can be used instead but will re-compact the soil more than the lighter BCS will.

4 **Form beds.** Measure and mark the center of each path at the head and foot of the plot with a stake or flag. A pass up and down each path with the rotary plow forms impressively high and flat raised beds.

5 **Mulch paths.** Fill paths with wood chips, straw, leaves, or other carbon-rich organic material.

6 **Smother sod.** Cover seamlessly with black tarps until all perennial roots are dead (usually a month or more, depending on the weather and the species in the sod).

ONCE SOD IS SMOTHERED

7 **Mulch beds.** Remove tarp and spread a 1½-inch layer of compost as mulch on the beds. Rake smooth, ensuring that the compost meets the path mulch with no exposed soil.

8 **Cover crop.** Direct-seed a cover crop cocktail that will winterkill. We use a mix of barley, oats, crimson clover, fava beans, and daikon radish. Since there is seamless soil coverage from the previous steps, little to no weeding should be necessary.

ONCE COVER CROP IS ESTABLISHED, BUT BEFORE IT WINTERKILLS

9 **Graze.** Run livestock over the cover crop once established in fall, but before it starts to winterkill. Their manure will activate soil biology and help fertilize the next season's crops.

THE FOLLOWING SPRING

10 **Plant.** Transplant through the dead cover crop chaff, or rake it into paths to direct seed.

A single use of plastic film smothers the underlying sod while allowing immediate planting. Note the thickly mulched paths for complete soil coverage.

USING PLASTIC MULCH

A contentious topic among organic farmers is the use of plastic mulch. Looking at plastic film with an eye toward soil coverage, at first glance it might appear to check the desired boxes. Protection from rain, check. From wind, check. From exposure to sun, check. But let's look closer.

While a layer of plastic offers some protection, it comes at a cost. The soil directly under the plastic may be safe from erosion in the short term, but the plastic diverts the erosive powers of rain and concentrates them elsewhere, usually into the paths between beds. Also, many of the benefits of the O-horizon come from its composition of organic materials, which break down and feed the soil in addition to covering it. Unlike plastic, natural mulches of plant residues are an inherent part of the soil-plant food web. This layer of organic matter is most obvious on the forest floor, but it exists anywhere plants grow undisturbed.

Synthetic mulches are yet another example of humans trying to improve on nature's model. There are key times in establishing garden beds when I think the benefits of covering the soil with plastic outweigh the negatives, but in general, I say we leave covering agricultural soils with impervious surfaces to the land developer, not the soil husband.

CHAPTER 5

PLANTING: FROM SEED TO CROP

All life begins with a seed.
— JESSIKA GREENDEER

T here are a surprising number of steps needed to go from seeds in a packet to plants in the ground. The right plan, infrastructure, and systems help this process go smoothly, even without tillage. This chapter describes how we get seedlings off to a strong start, setting the stage for resilient plants and bountiful harvests.

Crop Planning

How do we go from a mountain of seed packets to beds of healthy, correctly spaced crops in the field? Many decisions need to be made before we actually put our first plant in the ground. How much seed do we order? When do we start the seed in the greenhouse? When and where does each crop get planted?

I am fascinated by the varying degree of planning I see on different farms, from meticulous calendars with harvest and yield projections to off-the-cuff decisions made on the fly throughout the season. I fall toward the "fully planned" end of the spectrum, and I see the following benefits in establishing a thorough crop plan before the season begins:

- Better decisions are usually made during the calm of the off-season.
- With a plan in place, valuable in-season time is spent executing, not head scratching.
- Every crew member knows what plants go where without having to find and ask the right person.
- The plan can be tweaked and reused without having to reinvent the wheel each season.

When making a crop plan for the season ahead, it is worth considering how the plan might progress over the coming years. A crop rotation takes a long-term view of the health of the land and what you are asking of it. As you establish your production routines and start to learn the subtleties of your land and climate, planning out a long-term crop rotation is a helpful way of thinking ahead. Though your plan is likely to change dramatically the first few years, as you get started, planning at least one full season ahead makes sense, for the reasons described above.

No-Till Planning Priorities

A good crop plan is custom-tailored to a farm's particular production methods, markets, soils, and climate. Crop planning decisions can be affected by a multitude of factors, but in my experience, these are the most important considerations for an intensive no-till crop plan:

- Rotations to break pest and disease cycles
- Rotations to balance nutrient uptake
- Successions to maximize the growing season
- Compatibility of successive crops

ROTATIONS TO BREAK PEST AND DISEASE CYCLES

Certain crops, most notably those in the allium family (garlic, onions, shallots, leeks), can suffer from soil-borne diseases if they are grown in the same place for too long. Some of these disease organisms can persist in the soil for years but will eventually die without a plant host. A rule of thumb is to wait at least four years before returning to the same ground with allium crops. Other crops, such as cucurbits like squash and cucumbers, are susceptible to pests that migrate easily to the next succession when it's planted alongside the infested crop. For this reason we make sure to plant our cucurbit successions at least 100 feet apart. The Colorado potato beetle is another example of a pest than can be outfoxed with strategic rotation.

ROTATIONS TO BALANCE NUTRIENT UPTAKE

Every crop removes a different proportion of nutrients from the soil when harvested. Crop rotation ensures a balanced uptake of nutrients to avoid deficiencies and surpluses that would arise from endlessly growing the same crops in the same places. The specific sequence matters less than the overall diversity of crops grown on a given patch of soil throughout the rotation. Crops are often divided into generalized categories of major nutrient uptake: leafy greens require lots of nitrogen, fruiting crops are hungry for phosphorus, and root crops love potassium. While this is a gross simplification of plant nutrition, I find it a helpful reminder to make sure a given rotation includes a balance of greens, fruits, and roots.

SUCCESSIONS TO MAXIMIZE GROWING SEASON

A key purpose of the crop plan is to ensure maximum photosynthesis and productivity *throughout* the season. By planning ahead, we can identify empty beds and make adjustments to optimize the use of time and space.

The right combination of crops makes the most of your growing season. Where we are in Maine, for example, if we seed carrots as soon as the garlic comes out, there is just enough time for them to

size up before the ground starts to freeze for winter. Similarly, a cover crop of winter rye and crimson clover starts to flower at the end of May and can be knocked down and planted through with fall-harvested crops that need to get in the ground by mid- to late June (more on this in chapter 9).

The goal is for no bed ever to sit empty for more than a few hours (unless it requires smothering). Well-planned crop successions also ensure even harvests throughout the season to avoid gaps and surpluses.

COMPATIBILITY OF SUCCESSIVE CROPS

A no-till crop plan should account for the spacing and bed prep needs of successive crops. Trying to seed carrots after a vigorous spring cover crop might drive a farmer right back to tilling. Transplanting squash gives better results. A good crop plan takes advantage of the state of the soil left by the previous crop rather than fighting against it.

The table below shows a simple four-year rotation that takes into account the primary concerns of crop rotation discussed above.

Sample Four-Year Crop Rotation

STARTING WITH SOD OR OVERWINTERED COVER CROP

Year 1	Spring	Knock down and smother
	Summer	Cucurbits or Solanaceae
	Fall	Cover crop that winterkills
Year 2	Spring	Early brassicas
	Summer	Root crops
	Fall	Mulch for winter
Year 3	Spring	Salad greens
	Summer	Salad greens (continual successions)
	Fall	Cover crop that winterkills
Year 4	Spring	Alliums
	Summer	Alliums
	Fall	Cover crop that overwinters
Year 5 = Year 1		

A good crop plan is custom-tailored to a farm's particular production methods, markets, soils, and climate.

ON FRITH FARM
CROP PLAN FORMAT

The farm's crop plan goes on an online spreadsheet (see chapter 13) so that it is easily shareable and accessible to all members of the crew. I also print out a copy and tack it to a board that lives in the barn and gets referred to throughout the season.

The most intuitive and visually informative way to lay out our crop plan is to assign a row of the spreadsheet to each bed on the farm, and assign a column to each week of the season. Within this format, "time" becomes the horizontal axis, and "space" the vertical. The contents of each bed on the farm are described for every week of the season, and the information is digestible at a glance.

With a clear plan for the season, we are assured that our work of preparing beds and starting seedlings in the greenhouse is time well spent.

The Seedling Greenhouse

Propagation is the first step in successful crop production, and the right greenhouse setup makes it fun and efficient. Each year I look forward to spending those late winter days with a small crew in the greenhouse. It could be 10°F (−12°C) outside, but with the sun shining and the music bumping inside we might as well be on a tropical beach. Mixing potting soil, compressing it into blocks, and dropping in seeds give our hands something to do while we hang out and catch up after the long quiet of winter.

What a Greenhouse Needs

We transplant, rather than direct seed, the vast majority of our crops (for reasons discussed later in the chapter), so a dialed-in seedling greenhouse is an invaluable resource. An efficient seedling greenhouse includes six key elements:

- The right structure
- Adequate space
- Proximity to operations and utilities
- Automatic heat
- Automatic ventilation
- Multipurpose benches

THE RIGHT STRUCTURE

The structure of a greenhouse should be sturdy enough to withstand the harshest winds and heaviest snows your location experiences. In our neck of the continent, this generally requires a steel frame with a gothic peak and a truss assembly on each bow. A four-year UV-stabilized polyethylene film is the common covering, and two layers, with an inflation blower to keep them separated, are recommended for heated structures. For unheated high tunnels, I find a second plastic layer does not warrant the cost, unless the house is in a particularly windy area. In high winds, the inflated layer reduces chafing between the plastic and the frame.

ADEQUATE SPACE

Choosing the right size of greenhouse can be difficult when you're just starting out. Generally, money is scarce and the seedling operation will be small for the first year or two. But the greenhouse will be around much longer than that, and the cost and inefficiency of adding a second greenhouse down the line is far greater than the up-front cost of sizing up.

So how big is big enough? A good rule of thumb is 500 square feet of greenhouse space per acre of field production. This is usually enough room to grow the necessary seedlings for transplanting, plus a reasonable quantity for nursery sales. Space needs vary, however; when in doubt, go bigger. I have never heard a farmer complain that they have too much space in their seedling greenhouse.

I started with a 26 × 48-foot Gothic structure, and during my first two seasons I sectioned off half for in-ground tomatoes to make the most of the space. By the third season, the greenhouse was pretty much filled, and today we maximize the use of every square foot, without making concessions on what we want to grow.

Rugged construction and a Gothic peak allow this greenhouse to weather strong winds and heavy snows.

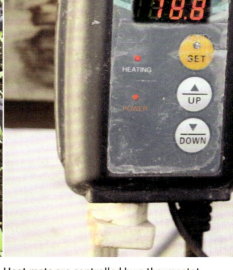

Heat mats hasten germination of warm-weather crops. Note the insulation under the mats to direct the heat upward.

Heat mats are controlled by a thermostat set to the optimal germination temperature.

PROXIMITY TO OPERATIONS AND UTILITIES

Placing the greenhouse centrally on the farm eliminates miles of needless walking over the years. Building it near — or even attaching it to — other farm structures is a great "co-location" strategy to maximize efficiency and facilitate access to utilities (see chapter 3). Pressurized water and electricity are essential features of an efficient greenhouse.

We buried our water pipe and electrical cable below the frost line (the depth to which the ground freezes in a typical winter; this is 4 feet in southern Maine) and connected to a frost-free hydrant and electrical subpanel inside the greenhouse. For most small-farm greenhouse operations, a 1-inch water line provides plenty of flow, and a 40-amp subpanel gives more than enough juice for an inflation blower, heater igniter, cement mixer, heat mats, and the all-important sound system.

AUTOMATIC HEAT

Unless you're near the tropics, a heat source is necessary to get a head start on the season and to ensure optimal growing temperatures. We use the Reznor forced hot-air propane heater that came recommended for our 26 × 48-foot greenhouse.

I am stingy with the thermostat and wait until late March to start seeding, which is a few weeks later than most farms in the area. I set the temperature at 50°F (10°C), which is plenty warm for good germination of all but the heat-loving crops. For those, I use heat mats, as described below. Unless the weather is cloudy and cold, the heater kicks on only at night, and daytime temperatures in the greenhouse are much warmer than 50°F (10°C).

For the warm-season plants in the Solanaceae and Cucurbitaceae families, we rely on electric heat mats to provide focused heat. These mats are thermostatically controlled and set to the ideal germination temperature of the crops (see chart below). I have seen various examples of DIY heat tables but prefer the flexibility of the modular 21 × 48-inch mats that can be daisy-chained together as needed. Plastic domes or row cover can be added to help hold in the heat but should be removed as soon as germination occurs to allow adequate airflow.

Ideal Germination Temperature for Common Vegetables

Vegetable	Optimal Range for Germination (°F)	Optimal Range for Germination (°C)
Bean	60–85	16–29
Beet	50–85	10–29
Broccoli/Cauliflower	45–85	7–29
Cabbage/Kale	50–95	10–35
Carrot	45–85	7–29
Celery	60–70	16–21
Chard	50–85	10–29
Cucumber/Melon/Squash	60–95	16–35
Eggplant/Pepper/Tomato	75–85	24–29
Lettuce	40–80	4–27
Onion	50–95	10–35
Pea	40–75	4–24
Radish	45–90	7–32
Spinach	45–75	7–24

Source: Adapted from *Knott's Handbook for Vegetable Growers* by Donald N. Maynard and George J. Hochmuth. John Wiley & Sons, 2007. Table 3.4 on page 108.

AUTOMATIC VENTILATION

Proper ventilation is paramount in the greenhouse. Fungal issues, especially damping off (when young seedlings rot at the base of their stem), show up when there is excessive moisture and inadequate airflow. Seedlings also tend to be spindly and fragile without the stimulation that some breeziness can provide.

Automated ventilation is well worth the up-front cost. Endwall vents and roll-up sides can be automated to operate based on the temperature and humidity in the greenhouse. I recently automated the roll-up sides on all our greenhouses, and I wish I had made this upgrade sooner. Automation eliminates the risk of catastrophe caused by forgetting to either open the greenhouse on a sunny day or to close it on a cold night. The freedom from stress alone is worth the cost for me. Automation also optimizes the conditions in the greenhouse at all times — a level of precision impossible to replicate with manual opening and closing — and plant growth benefits accordingly.

Endwall vents come with the benefit of operating regardless of the amount of snow on the ground (though I have heard of them freezing shut in winter). With automated roll-up sides, you must take care to turn off the system before the sides are buried.

In our climate, beyond opening up the greenhouse at the right times, I have never had a need for additional fans, unless overwatering occurs (see Seedling Care on page 85). If some trays get overwatered by mistake and show signs of damping off, I set up a small portable fan blowing directly onto them until the surface of the potting soil dries out, and that usually solves the problem. In warmer climates, mechanical greenhouse ventilation in the form of permanently installed fans may be worth the cost.

MULTIPURPOSE BENCHES

Tables or "benches" in the greenhouse keep seedling trays off the ground and make them easier to move, water, and monitor. We use homemade seedling pallets that rest on simple sawhorses at an optimal

Homemade greenhouse pallets make it easy to move the seedlings.

A cement mixer achieves thorough mixing of potting soil with minimal effort.

working height. These pallets are inexpensive, easy to make, and very light and maneuverable. They measure 32 × 84 inches each and are sized to fit 12 standard "1020" seedling trays. Their lightweight portability enables two people to carry a pallet full of seedlings for easy hardening off and transport to field. Handling 12 trays at a time instead of one or two saves a lot of time and prolongs the life of the trays.

When seedling production wraps up in July, we flip the pallets over and use them as curing racks for garlic, onions, and shallots. Each pallet has inexpensive plastic fencing stapled to the bottom to prevent smaller bulbs from falling through the slats. The timing works out so there is a seamless transition from seedling production to allium curing, keeping the greenhouse in full use for the whole season.

Potting Mix

Plants are as healthy as the soil they grow in, and this applies to potting mix as well. In coming up with a recipe, I started with the classic formulation for soil blocks from Eliot Coleman's book *The New Organic Grower* and adjusted it over the years. Our current concoction is shown on the next page, along with the steps we follow to prepare it. These get posted in the greenhouse for easy reference.

If you buy in your potting soil, make sure it is of the highest quality and reputation, something like Vermont Compost Company's "Fort V" mix.

Homemade mix can be of similar quality and is less expensive; every year, I do the math and the purchased ingredients to make our own mix run about one-third of the cost of finished Fort V. Even factoring in the time to prepare it, our homemade mix is just over half the cost of buying. That saves roughly $1 per tray of blocks, and we make about 1,000 trays each season.

There are certainly cheaper potting mixes available that are closer in cost to our homemade mix, but their quality is far below that of Vermont Compost (and of our mix). Cutting corners on the vigor of your seedlings costs far more in the long run than investing in quality potting soil. Given that much of the extra labor of mixing happens in the early spring when there is little other work, I am happy with our choice to make our own. For farms looking to streamline or reduce labor needs, buying a quality mix like Fort V may make more sense.

Seedling Trays

Standardized seedling trays lead to versatility and efficient use of space, which is especially important in a packed greenhouse. I considered a wide range of manufactured and homemade tray sizes when deciding on a standard for the farm. In the end, I defaulted to the standard already chosen by the nursery industry: the 1020 tray, aptly named for its 10-inch width and 20-inch length.

SOIL BLOCK POTTING MIX RECIPE

Each batch makes about 2½ cubic feet, which fits comfortably in a wheelbarrow. We mix it up in a cement mixer.

1. Add to the cement mixer in this order:

   1½ five-gallon buckets of peat moss (sifted to ½ inch)
   ½ cup of lime
   ½ cup of blood meal
   2 cups of alfalfa meal
   1 cup of rock phosphate
   1 cup of kelp meal

2. Run the cement mixer for about two minutes, then add:

   1 five-gallon bucket of perlite
   1½ five-gallon buckets of compost (sifted to ½ inch)

3. Run the cement mixer for another two minutes or so.

A strong start in the greenhouse prepares seedlings for a productive life.

As mentioned earlier, our seedling pallets are standardized to hold 12 trays, enabling easy organization and rearrangement. There are numerous options for pots and inserts that fit the 1020 tray, so any portion of the greenhouse can function as a nursery business using the same trays and configuration of greenhouse benches. We use heavy-duty solid trays with pre-cut drainage holes, inserted into a webbed "daisy tray" for added stability and longevity. The 1020 tray and insert each cost less than $1 and can last many seasons if handled properly.

There is growing interest in Winstrip trays among market gardeners. Winstrip trays mimic the air pruning of soil blocks (described below), with a vertical slit up the side of each cell that prevents plant roots from spiraling. The amount of soil in a Winstrip tray, however, is far less than that in a tray of soil blocks. Some might see this as a potential cost savings, but I see it as a potential cause of weaker seedlings, as the health of a plant is proportional to the soil contact of its roots. I also find the cost of Winstrip trays to be prohibitive.

Cutting corners on the vigor of your seedlings costs far more in the long run than investing in quality potting soil.

PAPERPOT MANIA

The use of paperpots among small-scale farmers has exploded in recent years. It is no wonder, given how quickly a bed can be planted with the paperpot transplanter. Though tempted, I have resisted using paperpots for several reasons. First, I enjoy the act of transplanting by hand, and I am wary of giving up this hands-in-the-soil experience.

Second, the paperpot transplanter performs best in smooth soil prepared by tilling, and it struggles in the stubble inherent to a no-till system. Some low-till farmers compromise with a tilther — a small battery-powered rototiller that tills only the top couple of inches of soil. While much less harmful than deeper tillage, the tilther breaks up the soil's O-horizon and drives fast-moving steel through the most biologically active part of the soil ecosystem. I am not eager to compromise soil health for transplanting ease.

Third, the complete paperpot system costs about $3,000 up front and requires continued purchases of proprietary trays with every seeding.

Lastly, there is disagreement among organic certifiers about whether the glues contained in the paperpot trays should disqualify them from use on organic farms. I appreciate the remarkable efficiency of the paperpot system and all it enables for small vegetable farms, but for now it does not fit with the values I want our farm to embody.

Soil Blocking

Soil blocking fits well with the principles of no-till production. Blocks hold much more soil than the tapered cells of plugs or other trays and so create a larger rhizosphere in the first stage of a seedling's life. This means more roots, more soil contact, and a more resilient plant. Root disturbance is minimized because the roots in soil blocks "air prune" and do not spiral and result in root-bound plants, as in plastic containers. When soil block seedlings are ready for transplant, they are simply placed in the ground, with no further disturbance or breaking apart of their roots.

Here's how the soil blocking process works. From the cement mixer, the finished potting soil gets dumped into a wheelbarrow, which is then parked alongside the soil blocking station while the next batch of mixing is started. From the wheelbarrow, the mix is added to a 15-gallon rubber livestock trough, which can stand up to the heavy abuse of soil blocking. Water is mixed in with a hoe — just enough to make the soil doughy but not soupy. The secret to soil blocking is achieving the right consistency. Mix that is too dry leads to crumbly or incompletely formed blocks. Mix that is too wet leads to blocks that slump or fall out of the blocker prematurely. When you squeeze the wetted soil in your hand, only a little water should drip out.

We use four different sizes of stand-up blockers, depending on the crop (see chart below). These are all available from Johnny's Selected Seeds (see Resources, page 223). The blocker is firmly pressed into the wetted mix so that all of the block molds are filled completely. Then the blocks are ejected into a standard 1020 tray and placed on a pallet for seeding. An experienced blocker can fill 30 to 40 trays in an hour.

I do not recommend using the ¾-inch mini blocker that is marketed for germinating seeds. The small size of the blocks leads to rapid drying, especially on a heated surface. I have lost an entire season's worth of tomatoes in a matter of hours after the last watering. Instead, we use the 1-inch stand-up blocker as the first step in our "potting on" sequence. The 1-inch blocks start on the heat mats, and once the whole tray is germinated they get transferred, or "potted on," into 3-inch soil blocks.

To make the appropriate depression, I fitted the 3-inch blocker with wooden 1-inch cubes as dibbles. The 3-inch blocks contain a remarkable amount of potting soil and produce robust transplants. This method works very well for plants that spend a long time in the greenhouse, such as tomatoes, peppers, eggplants, and greenhouse cucumbers.

Soil Block Sizes

Block Size	Blocks per 1020 Tray	Preferred Crops
1-inch	105	Lettuce, spinach, bok choy, salad turnips, herbs Germinating of tomatoes, peppers, eggplant, cucumbers
1.5-inch	78	Broccoli, cabbage, celery, chard, chicories, fennel, kale, onions
2-inch	50	Squash, melons, outdoor cucumbers
3-inch	24	Potting on of tomatoes, peppers, eggplant, cucumbers

above **Cucumbers in one-inch blocks get "potted on" to three-inch blocks made with homemade one-inch dibbles.**

left **Soil blocking requires more labor and produces a stronger seedling than other seed-starting methods.**

bottom **One-inch blocks are an ideal size for germination of warm-weather crops, like these tomato plants.**

Seedling Care

Once soil is mixed, blocks are made, and seeds are germinated, seedling care boils down to these factors: sunlight, temperature, airflow, moisture, and hardening off. Note that nutrients are not included in this list, since the quantity and quality of potting mix in soil blocks is sufficient to carry seedlings from germination to transplant without supplemental fertilization.

SUNLIGHT

Sunlight is a key ingredient of plant health. While this seems obvious, I have seen growers starting seedlings in overly shaded areas, like windowsills or sunporches or under inadequate grow lights. Most vegetables thrive in full daylight, especially during a northern spring when the sun is relatively low in the sky. Low or inconsistent light leads to weak, spindly seedlings. There is no substitute for a greenhouse

in full sun. To this end, the plastic on a greenhouse should ideally be replaced every four to six years as it yellows and becomes more opaque.

TEMPERATURE AND AIRFLOW

Under normal conditions, a greenhouse equipped with automated heat and ventilation will take care of the temperature and airflow needs of its plants. That said, shade cloth can be helpful when daytime temperatures are consistently above 80°F (27°C), especially when starting summer favorites like lettuce, which germinates poorly in the heat. The shade cloth is used less for reducing light levels than it is for reducing solar heat gain, as ventilation can only provide so much temperature regulation on hot days.

MOISTURE

Efficient watering requires pressurized water and a wand or spray nozzle. I am partial to the Wonder

The Wonder Waterer applies water quickly but gently.

Seedlings spend about a week outside to harden off before getting planted.

Waterer wand, as it creates both an alluring alliteration and a soft, uniform spray pattern with an adjustable flow rate. An overhead sprinkler or mister system can greatly reduce watering time, but hand-watering will still be necessary in spots to ensure each tray gets enough water without some trays getting too much.

It's best to give seedlings a good soak when watering, rather than applying water more often but only getting the surface wet each time. Frequent light waterings increase the risk of damping off and can cause algal buildup on the soil, which reduces water penetration. After a thorough watering, we wait for the surface of the soil blocks to dry out before reapplying water. This may mean no watering for several days during cool, cloudy weather, or it can mean watering every few hours on a hot, sunny day.

HARDENING OFF

Hardening off can be an important middle step before transplanting. Greenhouse seedlings are pampered: they have all their needs met while experiencing minimal exposure to wind, direct sun, strong rain, or harsh temperatures. The transition from a sheltered environment to an open field can stress a plant and even kill it. To ease this transition, we set our seedlings outside for about a week before transplanting. If severe weather is expected, we might throw some row cover over the seedlings or move them back into the greenhouse, but we aim to move them just once and leave them to acclimate to the harsher conditions of the outdoors.

Without their roots being jostled and exposed, plants generally make this partial transition smoothly, and they are transplanted a week (or so) later with few signs of shock. This hardening-off treatment, combined with the benefits of soil blocks, creates robust seedlings that can handle the stubbly terrain of no-till beds.

Hardening off is less important when the transplanted crops will be under row cover, since the cover replicates the condition of the greenhouse. For this reason I often reduce or skip hardening of these crops. A seedling can usually adjust well to the following changes one at a time, but not both at once: (1) any kind of root disturbance, and (2) exposure to unbuffered rain, wind, sun, and temperature swings.

Transplanting by hand is a social affair.

Transplanting

We opt to transplant, rather than direct-seed, the majority of our crops for three reasons:

1. Photosynthesis is maximized with transplants, since there is no time when a bed is completely empty waiting for seeds to germinate. In other words, bed space is available for other crops while the seeds germinate and grow in the greenhouse.
2. Transplants fit well within a no-till system, as they can be planted through mulch or other residues, and beds require minimal preparation.
3. Transplants allow fully planted beds. Problems with germination are minimized in the greenhouse and can be solved by starting extra seedlings. The result is no empty bed space and maximized productivity, with minimized seed cost.

We do all our transplanting by hand. Mechanized transplanting can increase efficiency in larger operations, but I believe there is no substitute for the sublime act of kneeling and pressing a plant into the earth with two hands. This work becomes drudgery only when the area to plant is out of proportion to the number of hands.

If there is one way to increase the success rate of transplanting, it can be summed up in a single word: water. Even with soil blocks, roots are jostled slightly as the seedling goes in the ground. If the disturbed roots dry out for even a moment, they die and the plant's foundation is weakened. Keeping roots moist during every step of the transplant process helps tremendously, and saving transplanting for rainy or overcast days is a natural way to keep seedlings happy.

I have tested a number of rolling multi-dibbles and am most satisfied with the rugged and adjustable Infinite Dibbler (see Resources, page 223). If you want to save some money, I recommend building your own dibbler by drilling holes in a 55-gallon steel drum and attaching wooden pegs to the drum with carriage bolts. Drill a hole in each end of the barrel, and insert a metal rod through holes to create an axle. Bend some metal tubing and bolt it together (no welding required) and attach it to the axle to create a handle. We still use our homemade dibbler for 3-row spacing (so we don't have to adjust the Infinite Dibbler, which is set at 4-row spacing). Both dibblers are set to mark every 12 inches in-row, since all other spacing is easily based off these marks (see table on page 90).

Garlic gets special planting treatment. We use homemade step-in multi-dibbles that ensure correct spacing and create deep enough dibble holes that no further digging is required. We just pop in each clove and cover it with soil. When the bed is done, we cover it with leaves. We use the rolling dibble to first mark the rows so that the step-in dibble follows a straight line down the bed.

One benefit of well managed no-till beds is their natural tilth, which makes for easy transplanting with bare hands. Harder soils that must be loosened with a trowel signal the need for increased soil care. Beds covered in plant residues and living growth naturally heal compaction and create biological tilth that welcomes new seedlings.

Whether purchased or homemade, a rolling bed marker saves time and keeps plant spacing consistent.

A homemade garlic dibbler ensures proper spacing and prepares holes for cloves in a single step.

Correctly planted, this seedling is buried up to its first true leaf.

This seedling is planted too shallow. Its roots are at risk of drying out and its stem will lack support on windy days.

TASK
TRANSPLANTING

These are the steps we follow when transplanting a crop into a prepared bed (See Flipping Beds on page 116.)

1 **Pre-irrigate.** Wait until after a rain, or irrigate the bed prior to transplanting.

2 **Transport.** Cart a greenhouse pallet of seedlings to the head of the bed. When transporting many trays or planting distant plots, we use a pickup truck.

3 **Soak.** Submerge the seedling trays in a wheelbarrow of water until the soil blocks are fully saturated (usually a few minutes). Mycorrhizal inoculants or compost tea can be added to the water to give transplants a biological boost.

4 **Mark.** Push a rolling multi-dibble over the bed to mark the transplant spacing.

5 **Transplant.** One person lays out seedlings while one or two others tuck them in the ground at the designated spacing (see table on page 90), ensuring they are buried up to their first true leaf and are pressed firmly into the soil.

6 **Irrigate.** Irrigate immediately, or as needed based on the weather.

7 **Cover (optional).** If warranted, protect transplants with floating row cover (see box on page 91).

Transplant Spacing at Frith Farm

CROP	ROWS PER BED*	IN-ROW SPACING	SEEDLINGS PER HOLE
Basil	2	6"	1
Beets	3	12"	3-4
Bok Choy	4	6"	1
Broccoli/Brussels Sprouts	2	18"	1
Cabbage, Mini	3	12"	1
Cabbage, Storage	2	18"	1
Celery/Celeriac	4	8"	1
Chard	3	6"	1
Cucumbers	1	12"	1
Eggplant	2	18"	1
Endive/Escarole	3	12"	1
Fennel, Bulbing	3	6"	1
Garlic	4	8"	1
Ginger/Turmeric	2	6"	1
Kale/Collards	3	12"	1
Kohlrabi	3	12"	2
Lettuce Heads	4	12"	1
Onions	4	12"	3-4
Parsley	4	6"	1
Peppers	2	12"	1
Potatoes	2	6"	—
Radicchio	4	12"	1
Rutabagas	3	12"	1
Shallots	4	12"	3-4
Squash/Zucchini	1	24"	2
Tomatoes (Field)	1	18"	1
Tomatoes (High Tunnel)	1	14"	1
Turnips, Salad	4	6"	3-4

*42" beds (60" on-center)

FLOATING ROW COVER

Floating row cover, or garden fabric, is a spunbound material that allows the passage of light, air, and water. This translucent blanket is used to cover crops for any of the following reasons:

- Increase crop growth or protect from frost by retaining heat
- Reduce transplant shock
- Protect crops from insect damage

I try to avoid the use of row cover and typically cover beds only when there is a clear need, and when doing so fulfills at least two of the above purposes simultaneously. We cover the first summer squash planting, for example, not only to speed its growth and protect against late frost but also to exclude the first generation of squash bugs and cucumber beetles.

Other crops we cover include certain brassicas (to reduce transplant shock and keep off flea beetles and cabbage moths) and potatoes and eggplant (to speed growth and exclude Colorado potato beetles). For crops that require pollination, it is important to remove row covers once flowering begins.

Since insect damage is only significant when farm diversity is out of balance (more on this later), using row cover or insect netting — a more durable and expensive material that excludes pests without retaining heat — as pest control should be recognized as the treatment of a symptom. Ideally, pest exclusion is a transitional practice that is used while the underlying lack of diversity and plant health is addressed. That said, when the row cover accomplishes other goals at the same time, I see it as a worthwhile tool.

Direct Seeding

Relative to transplanting, direct-seeded beds require more seed, a higher level of bed preparation, and closer attention to weed control. While I prefer to transplant whenever possible, closely spaced crops often lend themselves better to direct seeding, since transplanting so many seedlings would be laborious. Salad greens like lettuce mix and arugula germinate quickly and reliably when direct seeded. So do radishes. Carrot seedlings like to send down a long taproot that is often constricted and deformed if started in seedling trays. Cilantro is especially susceptible to transplant shock.

All of these seeds tend to be relatively inexpensive, so the extra seed required by direct seeding is a negligible cost. For all these crops, we take extra care to prepare a smooth, weed-free seed bed, since direct seeded plants do not have the head start on weeds that transplants have.

For putting seed in the ground, I am a loyal fan of the Earthway Seeder. This simple and inexpensive tool creates a furrow, drops in seed at a rate determined by the selected seed plate, covers the furrow, and tamps it in — all in a single pass. It works wonderfully for small to very large seeds, but it can struggle with very fine round seeds, such as arugula and other mustards, which can get behind the seed plate, resulting in uneven seeding rates and seed that has been ground. Regardless, I have used the Earthway Seeder for almost all our direct seeding since starting the farm, with very good results.

The Jang JP-1 Seeder performs the same function as the Earthway but with higher-quality construction and more precise seed singulation. The Jang is a worthy investment (at roughly four times the cost) for farmers who want such precision, but I have found the Earthway to be more than adequate. When it comes to pushing through the debris typical of no-till beds, I find the more compact geometry of the Earthway actually outperforms the Jang. The latter tends to pop a wheelie when a lot of downward pressure is applied, whereas the Earthway can muscle through just about anything.

That said, the Jang is available with an optional double disc opener instead of the standard furrower, and this upgrade allows the seeder to perform well in beds with moderate amounts of plant residues. Both the Jang and the Earthway can be purchased in multi-row ganged assemblies that seed a bed in a fraction of the time of a single seeder, though the up-front cost of this efficiency may not pencil out for the very small farm.

I have experimented briefly with the four-row pinpoint and six-row seeders from Johnny's Selected Seeds, and I've found they both require a level of seedbed preparation that is not always realistic within a no-till system.

Direct-Seeded Crops at Frith Farm

CROP	EARTHWAY SEED PLATE	ROWS PER BED*	THIN TO
Arugula/Mustard Greens	Fine seed — light	10	—
Carrots	Fine seed	4	—
Cilantro	Radish	8	—
Cover Crop Grasses (Barley/Oats/Rye)	Beet	12	—
Green Beans	Jumbo pea	2	—
Lettuce Mix	Fine seed	10	—
Parsnips	Beet	3	2"
Radishes, Fresh	Radish	6	1"
Radishes, Storage	Radish	4	2"
Sugar Snap Peas	Sprout, then plant by hand	2	1"
Turnips, Storage	Fine seed	3	2"

*42" bed (60" on-center)

TASK
DIRECT SEEDING

These are the steps we follow to direct seed a prepared bed (see Flipping Beds on page 116).

1 **Rake** the bed so that it is flat and smooth, with only fine plant residues on its surface. Rake any larger residues into the paths.

2 **Adjust** the Earthway Seeder: install the appropriate seed plate, and set the furrower depth to roughly 3 times the diameter of the seed you're planting.

3 **Inoculate** the seed (optional). Coat the seed with an organic microbial inoculant such as Myco Seed Treat. It helps to add a drop or two of water to the seeds first so the powder sticks and coats them thoroughly, though keep in mind this will reduce the germination rate of any leftover seed.

4 **Seed** the bed with the Earthway Seeder, starting with outer rows, followed by the middle row(s), then filling in the remaining rows (see planting chart on facing page). This pattern facilitates even row spacing with no measuring or marking necessary.

5 **Irrigate** immediately, then daily or as needed based on the weather, until germination. Once seeded, the soil should never dry out until the seedlings emerge. Sprinklers achieve more uniform coverage on a bed with no row cover, but irrigating through a row cover works in a pinch.

The Earthway seeder pushes through remaining stubble from a previous crop after the loose debris has been raked into paths.

CHAPTER 6

IRRIGATION

No artist or artisan ever has such broad
control of the medium through which [they]
express [their] own character and personality
as does the farmer or grazier in the control
[they] can exercise over [their] land.

— P. A. YEOMAN

Getting water when and where you need it on the farm is no trivial matter. This chapter describes how to set up a permanent, low-maintenance irrigation system, so that any bed can be watered with the turning of a single valve. But prudent use of water is about more than pumps and pipes, so first we'll delve into how following the principles of natural soil care will reduce the need for irrigation and increase our farms' resilience in the face of unpredictable weather patterns.

Water Resilience

Water is the source of life, and throughout history agriculture has focused on designing and engineering systems of moving water. But the most sustainable and efficient irrigation system is the one that is not needed. Undisturbed, biologically rich soil covered with layers of mulch and living plants is naturally resilient in the face of drought. Layers of plants harvest humidity from the air as dew. Mycorrhizal fungi extend the rhizosphere, connecting plant roots with as much as a hundred times more soil moisture than they would otherwise access. The natural capillary action of undisturbed soils pulls water up from reserves deep underground. A thick O-horizon of residues on the soil surface protects from the desiccating effects of wind and sun. The organic matter content of the soil multiplies its water-holding capacity. Nature provides a model of water management worth following, even if we supplement with irrigation.

Irrigation design begins with proper soil care, as pumping water is not always a sustainable solution to our irrigation needs. Much of the world's vegetable production takes place where precipitation is less than the water needed by crops. Water is often supplied by diminishing aquifers, receding glaciers, or weather patterns that are shifting with climate change.

Every 1 percent increase in organic matter soaks up an additional 20,000 gallons of water per acre. If a 10-acre farm went from 3 percent to 8 percent organic matter, 1,000,000 gallons of extra rainwater would be held right where it counts, every time it rains.

If we could make these kinds of increases at scale, we would reduce the atmospheric carbon that may be responsible for the water shortages to begin with. It seems foolish to run ever bigger pumps and pipes without focusing on the role of soil health in natural water cycles. Irrigation is the icing on the cake, but the cake itself is the spongy soil that catches and holds the water that we're given for free.

While proper care of land should be the primary focus of water management, a reliable water source and well-designed irrigation system are invaluable for the commercial vegetable farm, as they essentially eliminate the variable of drought from our farming concerns. This is huge. Even in regions like New England that get over 40 inches of precipitation a year, there is no guaranteeing when the rain will come, and in many summers there are periods of several weeks without rain. While established crops in undisturbed, covered soil weather these dry spells with little harm, direct seeding and transplanting achieve better results with some supplemental water.

A commonly quoted rule of thumb is that vegetables need about 1 inch of water per week throughout the season. I find this suggestion misleading. In reality, plants do not care how much water is applied from above; what they care about is the moisture content of the soil, which is affected by far more than irrigation or rainfall. Keeping track of applied water is a helpful reference, but plants in healthy, undisturbed soil require much less irrigation than crops in tilled or bare ground.

There is no substitute for watching plants for signs of their water needs and probing down into the soil to check moisture levels. Keep in mind that the smaller the root system of a plant, the more susceptible it is to drying out, so err on the side of extra water when direct seeding or transplanting. Once established, however, crops in a healthy soil ecosystem need far less water than most farms are used to applying.

As with watering in the greenhouse, I prefer to irrigate generously and infrequently. The idea behind this is that plant roots reach deeper into the soil if their water needs are not met near the surface. Deep roots not only build resilience for the plant, they mine nutrients and open up channels for other organisms and future plant roots. Keeping the leaves and stems of plants dry also helps prevent rot and foliar disease — another reason to use sprinklers less frequently. Whenever possible, I try to irrigate overnight to minimize evaporative losses and to allow plants to remain dry during the day. In our climate, plants often soak with dew overnight anyway, so it is a natural time to apply more water if needed.

Irrigation Design

A typical irrigation system for the small vegetable farm has four basic components:

1. Water source
2. Pump
3. Distribution pipes
4. Driplines or sprinklers

In a nutshell, irrigation design is about sizing these components to meet the needs of the farm and of one another. There are also other less fundamental components that can facilitate the operation and maintenance of the system:

- **Pressure tank** provides ballast and extends the life of the pump

- **Filters** remove unwanted impurities and keep sediment from clogging the system
- **Check valve** or **backflow preventer** protects against water source contamination
- **Flowmeter** facilitates monitoring and troubleshooting
- **Valves** control flow to different zones
- **Pressure regulators** ensure proper function of sprinklers and drip emitters

Water Source

The water source is the first component of an irrigation system. The amount of water it can provide helps determine the size of the rest of the system. There are a few common types of water sources that can supply an irrigation system.

Municipal water, where available, is quick and easy but may contain chlorine or other undesired additives and might cost a few dollars for every thousand gallons. Still, this is likely the easiest option for small farms in urban areas.

Surface water is arguably the best option for a farm's water source. Water from a farm pond, for example, is readily accessible and at an ideal temperature for crops. It often contains beneficial microorganisms and usually relies on the renewable cycles of local rainfall for recharging. A farm pond also adds valuable habitat for biodiversity and is a great place to cool off in hot weather.

If access to fresh water does not exist on a piece of land, building a pond can provide multiple benefits. There is more to it than simply renting an excavator, however, so make sure to consult with the local code authority, relevant government agencies, and nearby pond owners before getting started. Food safety issues tend to originate with contaminated water, so ensuring the ecological health of your pond is a must.

On properties that don't have access to public or surface water, and where a pond is unrealistic, tapping into underground aquifers via a drilled well is

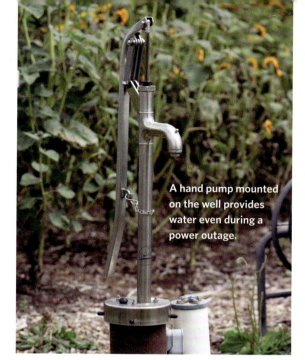

A hand pump mounted on the well provides water even during a power outage.

a common and relatively inexpensive way to access water. The necessary well depth and associated costs vary widely with location. In some areas, a productive well might be less than 100 feet deep; in other locations, it might be 10 times that depth and still not achieve the desired flow. In my area, the cost of drilling a well ranges from about $20 to $30 per foot of well depth. In the grand scheme of starting a farm, paying $5,000 or $10,000 for a reliable water source is well worth it, but be aware that well water can vary in quality, and excessive minerals can be an issue. Conducting a comprehensive water test and adding any recommended filters is a good idea before turning on the tap.

When drilling a well, I recommend shooting for a recharge rate (the rate at which well water replenishes) of at least 5 gallons per minute (gpm) for each acre you expect to irrigate, though more flow allows more irrigating flexibility. An additional 5 gallons per minute is recommended if the well is connected to a house for domestic use. The more flow your well supports, the more beds you can irrigate at once.

As a reference, supplying 1 inch of water per week to an acre would require a minimum constant (24-hour) flow rate of 2.7 gallons per minute. To apply the same amount of water only at night over the span of 8 hours would require three times that flow rate. This assumes no rain, and it doesn't account for evaporative losses or other water needs of people or livestock, but it gives you an idea of how much flow a farm can use.

Be clear with your well installer about your desired recharge rate before they start drilling, and be aware that there is no way to know a well's capacity until it is drilled. Unfortunately, many wells come up short. I got lucky; my drilled well has a recharge rate of 25 gpm from a depth of about 200 feet — more water than I need or use, which gives me peace of mind.

Pump

A pump provides the pressure that drives the flow of water. The more powerful the pump, the more water it can push.

Municipal water is delivered under pressure, so no pump is necessary. Check with your water provider to determine the maximum flow rate, cost, and any regulations restricting irrigation use. For surface water, like that from a pond or river, there are a variety of electric, gas, diesel, or PTO (power takeoff)-driven pumps available. Consult with an irrigation supply company or your local extension service to help find the best fit for your situation.

I irrigate from a well and am most familiar with this scenario. Your well installer can tell you the recharge rate of the well as they are drilling, and will typically install a well pump sized to match. It pays to build in a buffer of at least a few gallons per minute between the capacity of the well and that of the pump, as overdrawing (trying to pump more water than there is) can burn out a pump. Though my well recharges at a rate of 25 gallons per minute, my pump can move water only at a rate of 12 gallons per minute. The flow rate of the installed pump, assuming it does not exceed the well's recharge rate, then becomes the limiting factor for how many driplines or sprinklers you can run at a time.

Distribution Pipes

Irrigation pipes distribute the water pushed by the pump to sprinklers or driplines in the field. The diameter of the pipe affects the flow rate; the narrower the pipe, the more friction there is between the walls of the pipe and the water passing through it. The table at right shows recommended maximum flow rates for different diameters of polyethylene pipe (polypipe), based on a maximum safe water velocity of 5 feet per second.

The length and slope of pipes also impact pipe sizing. If any pipes carry water more than a few hundred feet, going up a pipe size is recommended to reduce pressure loss over longer distances. Significant changes in elevation can also complicate an irrigation system, so hillside farmers may want to consult with an engineer.

I recommend sizing the main distribution pipes to exceed the maximum flow rate of your well, regardless of the pump size. In general, it makes sense to oversize pipes rather than save a few dollars in the short term. As unlikely as it may seem right now, you may upgrade your pump down the line, and having larger pipes already in place will save the time and money of replacing smaller pipes. Even though my well is rated at 25 gallons per minute, I buried 2-inch main line to all my fields. There is no downside to upsizing, aside from a nominally higher cost of the larger pipe.

Lateral or secondary lines are those that branch off the main line to reach specific areas of the farm. These lines should be sized either to match the main line or to provide the maximum flow of water that may ever be needed by the area they supply, whichever is less. Header lines branch off of the lateral lines or main line to supply a given irrigation zone (in our case, a plot of twelve 100-foot beds, or 6,000 square feet) and are sized for the maximum flow needed by that zone.

A map of Frith Farm's irrigation pipe layout is shown on the next page. Whenever water, drainage, or electrical lines are buried, it is good practice to make a map of them to facilitate future repairs and improvements.

Maximum Flow Rates for Common Pipe Diameters

Pipe Diameter (inches)	Maximum Recommended Flow (gallons per minute)
½	3
¾	7
1	12
1¼	19
1½	27
2	49

Based on a maximum water velocity of 5 feet per second

An underground box keeps the header valve and regulator out of harm's way.

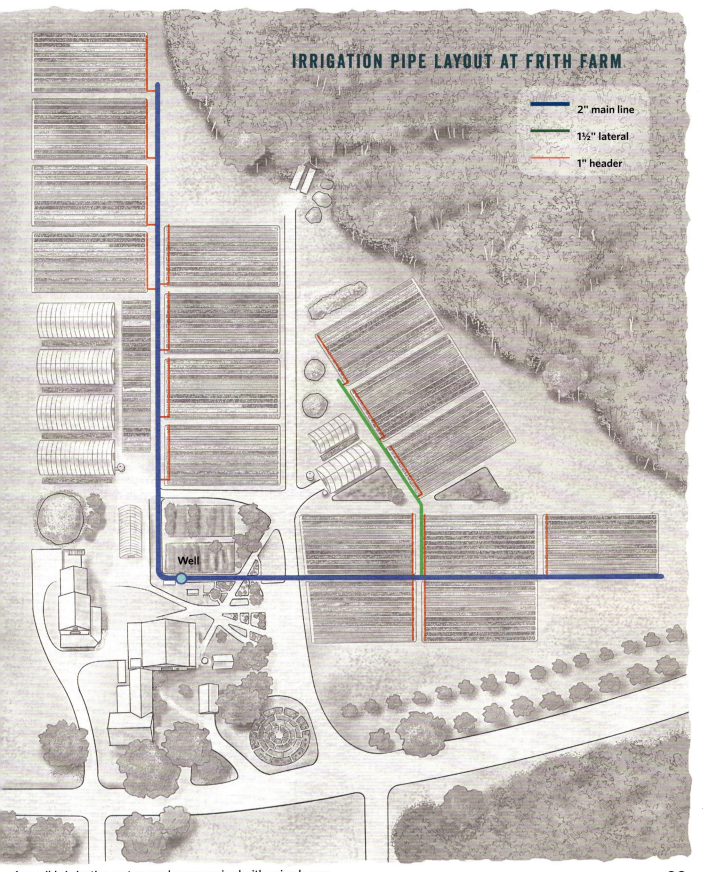

IRRIGATION PIPE LAYOUT AT FRITH FARM

2" main line

1½" lateral

1" header

Well

A sensible irrigation system can be summarized with a simple map.

In our setup at Frith Farm, each header line is fitted with a pressure regulator and is controlled by a single ball valve housed in an underground valve box at the corner of each plot. Keeping the valve underground prevents damage from both foot traffic and frost, and it enables us to keep the entire system pressurized in the shoulder seasons without fear of fittings bursting due to freezing. To prepare for winter, we disconnect the main line and open all valves in the whole system. A closed ball valve reliably cracks when it freezes; an open valve rarely does.

For header lines and sprinkler lines, we use a low-density polyethylene pipe (called "oval" or "blue stripe" pipe) that tolerates freezing and foot traffic. The softness of the plastic allows easy connection of drip tape connectors with a simple punch tool, and the pipe can be used with the same barbed fittings used in the rest of the system. Keep in mind that the low-density pipe is not designed to hold pressure for extended periods of time, as it will stretch and eventually burst, especially if it's exposed to sun or heat.

Driplines and Sprinklers

Every sprinkler and dripline (also called drip tape, or T-tape) has specifications for how much water it applies at different pressures. This information can be obtained from the manufacturer or the irrigation supply company selling the product. A pressure regulator reduces the system pressure and maintains it at a specified level for the line it serves, so the regulator you choose for the header line determines the flow to each dripline or sprinkler it supplies.

I opt for regulators that limit the water pressure at 15 pounds per square inch (psi) at all of my header lines. This pressure works well with both drip tape and low-pressure sprinklers. Dripline flow rates are usually given in gallons per minute (gpm) per 100 feet, while sprinklers are gpm per sprinkler head. Adding up the total length of dripline and total number of sprinklers in a plot gives you the total flow required for that plot.

At Frith Farm, 8 sprinklers cover all 12 beds in each of our 60 × 100-foot plots. Each sprinkler uses about 1 gpm, so the whole plot requires a flow of 8 gpm. Hypothetically, if each bed had two lines of drip tape with a flow rate of 0.5 gpm per 100 feet, the required flow would be 24 lines × 0.5 gpm per line, or 12 gpm. The higher the flow rate to an area, the less time is needed to irrigate it adequately.

CHOOSING BETWEEN DRIPLINES AND SPRINKLERS

The decision between driplines and sprinklers can be a difficult one for the small farm, as each has its benefits. Sometimes, a combination of the two is best, depending on the mix of crops.

Benefits of Dripline
- Targeted application → fewer weeds
- Keeps plant leaves dry → less foliar disease
- Low flow → good fit for low-capacity wells or pumps
- Efficient use of water → minimized evaporative losses

Benefits of Sprinklers
- Uniform coverage → better germination
- Fewer pipes and connections → less work to set up, and fewer leaks
- Uses less plastic → less wasteful
- More visible when running → easier troubleshooting and more peace of mind

In our climate, I find the benefits of drip tape outweigh those of sprinklers only for long-season crops that suffer readily from foliar diseases, or whose fruits can be damaged by excess moisture. These include the Solanaceae and Cucurbitaceae families, which are the only crops we irrigate with drip. Otherwise, the simplicity of sprinklers wins me over.

Choosing the right drip tape can be more involved than you might think. The wall thickness of drip tape determines its longevity as well as how easily it will develop leaks. The cheapest tape can be endlessly frustrating and can easily cost more in the long run than investing in a higher-quality product if you aim to reuse it for more than one season.

The emitter spacing on drip tape is another variable. I recommend emitter spacing of 12 inches or less. This way, the drip tape can be used as a continuously irrigated line so you don't have to worry about lining up emitters with plants in the row. Attaching each dripline to the header pipe via a shutoff valve gives you the flexibility to control individual lines within a plot.

For sprinklers, I am a fan of the popular Xcel Wobbler made by Senninger. These accommodate various interchangeable nozzles with different watering diameters and flow rates, so you can select the best nozzle to suit the size of your fields and your system's total flow. I use wobblers that each apply about 1 gpm over a diameter of about 40 feet — enough to cover six of our beds (5 feet on-center) with a single line of four sprinklers. This fits well with the shape of our plots and the capacity of our well and pump, and we can water one and a half plots (12 sprinklers) at a time.

Each sprinkler is mounted on a 4-foot steel stake with a riser assembly (see photo on next page). The tool-free compression connections make installing and moving sprinklers (for mowing, tarping, or winter storage) nearly effortless.

Since a line of sprinklers covers six of our beds, sometimes we water a bed by hand after planting, if the adjacent beds have crops that do not need extra water. Hand-watering is made easier by installing a valve with quick-connect fitting at the end of each header line. This allows you to connect a garden hose at the head of any plot. The hose is stored in a portable hose reel that can be wheeled to the end of any bed. The reel lets you pull out the hose neatly down the path next to the bed. When you're done watering, the hose rolls up quickly without kinking, tangling, or damaging seedlings.

This wobbler sprinkler, mounted on a 4-foot steel rod, is our preferred way to water most crops.

IRRIGATION OPTIONS

A permanent irrigation setup allows you to water any part of the farm by opening a single valve.

A riser assembly with tool-free push-in connections makes installing and moving sprinklers a breeze.

A rain gauge next to our irrigation manifold helps determine when and how much to irrigate.

Installation and Maintenance

No-till methods enable a permanent irrigation that is not possible when tillage or other tractor work is part of the production system. An irrigation system can be set up once and left in place indefinitely, so watering any part of the farm is as simple as opening a single valve. No moving of pipes, untangling of hoses, or fumbling with fittings is required. Any further setup or movement increases the likelihood that plants will not get the water they need. This one-and-done approach to irrigation setup works only within a permanent bed no-till system, where tractors and equipment do not interfere with the pipes and sprinklers — another reason for farming at a human scale!

While drilling a well and installing a pressure tank are best left to a professional, the rest of the system is suitable for DIY installation, especially if you accept that mistakes are a part of the learning process. Unlike electrical wiring or indoor plumbing, the stakes are low for outdoor irrigation connections.

I recommend burying all main and lateral pipe lines. Keeping pipes out of sight and out of the way prolongs their life and reduces clutter on the farm. The depth of burial is important. I made the mistake of initially burying ours 6 inches deep, and within days we stuck a broadfork right through the main line. We then proceeded to dig up all 1,200 feet of pipe and re-bury it below the depth of errant fork tines. Learn from my mistake and bury all pipes at least 18 inches below grade! It is better not to bury at all than to bury too shallow. Renting a trencher is an inexpensive and efficient way to get lots of pipe buried quickly.

Once a permanent irrigation system is in place, it requires no moving or assembling, and it needs only minimal maintenance. The system

A hose reel facilitates hand-watering of individual beds.

Burying water (and electric) lines keeps them protected from damage and freezing. This trench was made in a couple of hours with a rented trencher.

at Frith Farm has been in operation for six years now with only minor repairs, mostly from accidents involving poorly aimed pitchforks. Preparing the system for winter is as simple as disconnecting the main line and opening all the valves. Come spring, we close the valves and connect to our well and, voila, we have pressurized water throughout the entire farm. Because our main lines are buried and our header valves are housed in underground boxes, we can turn on the system well before the danger of frost has passed.

The level of permanence inspired by no-till farming allows us to spend more time on soil care and less on nonessential busyness.

Tips for Installing Irrigation

- Use a propane torch for polypipe connections. The stiffness of polypipe can make sliding in a barbed fitting difficult, especially with large-diameter pipes. Heating the inside of the pipe end until it glistens (but not so much that it melts) makes this job easier.
- Use two stainless steel hose clamps on each barbed connection. Pay the extra pennies for the hose clamps that are 100 percent stainless steel (including the screw), and place two of them on each pipe end (e.g., six clamps per T-fitting). For more even clamping pressure, offset the clamp positions slightly so the screws are not in line with each other.

- Buy irrigation components from a reputable supply company. Don't be tempted by the incredibly cheap (in all senses of the word) generic fittings available online.

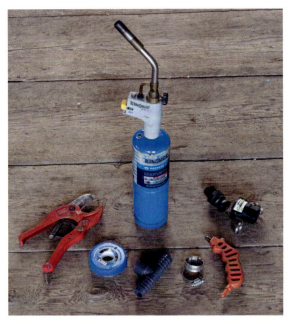

Installing and repairing irrigation requires simple fittings, inexpensive tools, and a very basic skillset.

ON FRITH FARM
QUICK FIX KIT

Repairs are inevitable with humans and harvest knives passing over beds throughout the season, but adding a splice or replacing a fitting is quick and easy. To facilitate irrigation repair, we keep a small bucket stocked with an assortment of the most common fittings and the tools needed to install them. This repair kit sits waiting in the workshop and makes fixing a leak a painless chore. Any parts used in a repair get replaced when the bucket is returned to its home.

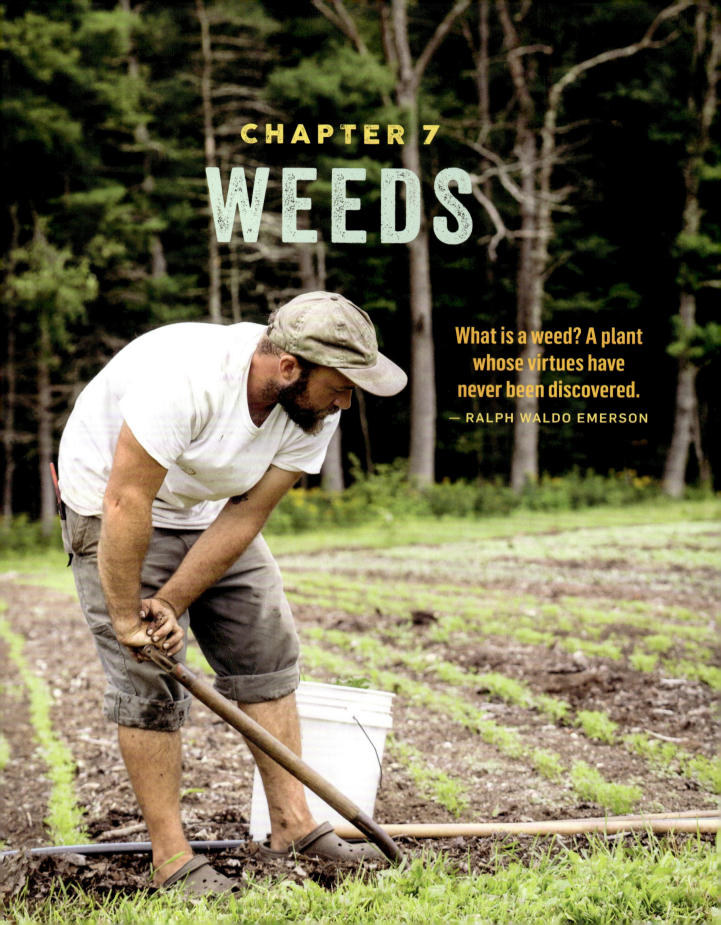

CHAPTER 7
WEEDS

What is a weed? A plant
whose virtues have
never been discovered.

— RALPH WALDO EMERSON

One of the first issues people take with the idea of no-till farming is the alleged difficulty of managing weeds. The reality is that tillage tends to contribute more to weed problems than it does to their solutions. The saying, "We till because we have weeds because we till . . ." all too often becomes a never-ending refrain. This chapter outlines a weed management strategy that leaves the earth undisturbed and covered, replacing the perennial battle against weeds with a resilient approach based on prevention rather than damage control. This follows the example set by nature; the best approach to weeding is eliminating the need for it.

Treating Symptoms vs. Causes
(Killing vs. Preventing)

Annual weeds are nature's bandages and are adapted to grow in disturbed or bare soil. Their ecological role is to cover the soil as quickly as possible, so they typically go from germination to setting seed in a very short time, dropping thousands of seeds so the next generation will cover exponentially more ground. Weeds are an ecological mechanism of healing the land, and fighting this curative natural force is not only bad for the soil, it also requires a huge amount of time, effort, and equipment. To the no-till farmer, weeds are merely a symptom of inadequate soil coverage.

Nature will do her darndest to maximize photosynthesis and soil coverage, and why should we try to stop her? These are the very forces that lead to healthy, productive soils. Instead of working endlessly to strip the ground naked, ecological weed management keeps the soil covered with plant material, both living and dead, so that weed bandages are unnecessary. Instead of weeds that would compete with vegetable crops, low-growing ground covers and organic mulches protect the soil and enhance crop growth. Intensive spacing and multi-crop combinations cover bare ground. Honoring natural tendencies of soil coverage is easier and ultimately more productive than the task of perpetual cultivation. The foundation of our weed management at Frith Farm is keeping the soil covered with organic mulches and closely spaced plants.

Zero Seed Rain

The black-and-white approach of never letting weeds go to seed is less work in the long run than fighting generation after generation of weeds in an endless Sisyphean struggle. A successful "zero seed rain" approach prevents weed seed from ever forming and dropping in the fields. Achieving this goal relies on smallness of scale and sufficiency of labor. Put another way, it requires a minimum number of hands per acre.

Whatever your approach to weed management, when weeds start overrunning your crops it is a sign that this ratio of humans to land is out of balance. I find that achieving zero seed rain within an intensive market garden requires a minimum of two people per acre. With the right number of people, weeding is not only manageable, it is even enjoyable.

Many traditional approaches to weed management aim to reduce the weed seed bank in the soil — the viable seeds that have been dropped and buried over the years. The ability of weed seed to lie dormant in the soil varies, but some seeds happily hang out for decades. When the soil is tilled, a whole history of seed is stirred up. Some catch the right flash of light and bit of moisture needed to germinate, while others continue to patiently await their turn.

To the no-till farmer, weeds are merely a symptom of inadequate soil coverage.

Every time the soil is disturbed, a fraction of the seed bank germinates, and the resulting weeds must be managed. Leaving the soil undisturbed, on the other hand, renders the majority of the weed seed bank irrelevant. Only the seeds in the soil's top fraction of an inch are within range of the light they need to germinate and grow. Practically speaking, we can "eliminate" more than 90 percent of our soil's weed seed bank with the simple decision to stop tilling.

With the ability to ignore most of the weed seed bank comes the increased consequences of letting new weeds go to seed. Without getting buried with tillage, dropped seeds remain on the soil's surface, where they can readily germinate and lead to further weed problems. A zero-disturbance approach to the soil ideally goes hand in hand with a zero seed rain approach to weed management.

Besides weeds reproducing in the fields, there are several ways in which they make deposits to the weed seed bank. To prevent weeds efficiently, each of these aspects should be addressed:

Weeds in paths, roadways, and field borders. Eliminate weed seed rain throughout the farm by mulching, planting perennial ground covers, and killing weeds in gravel roads by flame weeding (see page 113) or acidifying with elemental sulfur (most common garden weeds will not thrive at very low pH levels). Even if these weeds seem small and out-of-the-way, they can be industrious spreaders of seed; wind, water, animals, and human feet can carry these into fields.

Wind-blown seed. Plant hedgerows as natural windbreaks to reduce blown-in seed. However, some especially aeronautical seeds, like dandelions, will always find a way. I have found that dandelions compete minimally with crops, and embracing them with an annual root harvest for spring tonics turns foe into friend.

Imported seed from other farms. Importing manure or hay is an easy way to introduce new weed species to the farm. I do not advocate avoiding these valuable local resources, but additional attention to weeds is warranted when applying them. Composting manure before spreading it can create enough heat to kill some or all of the seeds in the compost. Shared equipment can also bring in seed, so hosing off implements and tractor wheels before taking them back into the fields may be a worthwhile step.

While a zero-tolerance approach to weed seed rain can feel austere at first, a few seasons of patience and perseverance pay off with greatly reduced weed pressure. The task of finding the few remaining weeds can even become fun! A serene satisfaction comes from walking around a farm that is free of weeds and fully covered in desired plants and organic mulches.

FRIEND OR FOE?

Preventing weed seed rain is not necessarily the same as zero tolerance toward weeds. As long as they are killed before they set seed, weeds can increase photosynthesis, diversity, and soil coverage like any other cover crop. We stop weeding beds the last week or two before they are scheduled to be mowed or tarped so the soil can benefit from the additional understory growth. With the right level of care, weeds can even be our friends.

Mulching

Mulching is a fundamental practice of no-till farming. As microbiologist Dr. Elaine Ingham points out, "Mother nature abhors bare soil." Keeping the soil covered not only prevents weed germination, it also encourages biological activity by maintaining moisture levels and providing habitat for soil organisms. While soil life thrives most when this cover is in the form of living plants, there are times when planting constraints favor a nonliving mulch.

There are a number of organic mulch materials, each with their own attributes, some of which are described in this section. The best mulch is almost always that which is available locally; connecting with sources of biomass can be instrumental in establishing the farm. (See Acquiring Local Organic Materials on page 62). Even if you can't find affordable mulches, you can always grow your own. Here are the mulches that are commonly available to the market gardener.

In-situ mulches. Grown-in-place plant residues are the most local mulch there is. Planting through a cover crop at the end of its life cycle is perhaps as close as vegetable farming will ever come to replicating nature's model.

Leaves. Trees are amazing producers of biomass. Deciduous leaves contain a well-balanced spread of minerals and drop in abundance every fall. In many populated areas there is an entire industry built around the removal of leaves, with little value attached to where they end up. Tapping into a reliable supply of leaves was a rewarding step I took as I started the farm. Every year, I buy all the leaves collected by my municipality, which can be as many as 1,000 cubic yards.

Straw. In areas of grain production, the straw byproduct makes an excellent locally sourced mulch. Finding a source that is free of chemical residues and weed seed can be challenging; finding the right grower and establishing a good relationship is well worth the effort. Round bales are usually less expensive than square bales and can be rolled out right onto a bed.

Hay. Hay makes a great mulch, but its seed content can vary widely. If other mulch sources are readily available, I find it safer to keep hay out of the vegetable fields. Hay is perfect, however, for covering exposed soils in pasture (i.e. reseeding the dust bathtubs left by chickens).

Compost. Seeing compost as mulch rather than a soil amendment opens up a world of possibilities for the no-till farmer (see chapter 8). In addition to performing the basic mulch functions of other materials, compost has the profound ability to be planted *into* instead of *through*. Good root contact is almost guaranteed with compost, while planting through leaves, straw, or other mulches is more difficult and time-consuming. Transplanting into compost is pure pleasure — like pressing a birthday candle into a moist chocolate cake.

Wood chips. Wood chips are another amazing resource bestowed by trees. Where trees and people live in close proximity, there are always woody residues to dispose of from the clearing of yards, roadways, and power lines. Connecting with local landscapers and utility crews is a great way to divert these "waste" streams onto the farm. There are key attributes of wood chips that depend on the type of tree (deciduous vs. coniferous) and the diameter of the branches being chipped. Small-diameter (less than 3 inches, or so) twigs and branches from deciduous trees yield what are referred to as "ramial" wood chips (*rami* means "branch" in Latin). With higher concentrations of nutrients and a lower carbon-to-nitrogen ratio than thicker logs, ramial wood is the ideal source of chips for the garden and orchard. Wood chips from coniferous, or softwood, trees do not favor the same mycorrhizal and saprophytic fungi (fungi that feed on decomposing organic matter) that enhance the growing conditions for vegetables and fruit trees, and can have an allelopathic effect on garden soils.

The perfect wood chips rarely arrive at your door, however, and making the most of mixed loads of varying quality is often necessary. I find that letting a pile sit and mellow for a season or more turns it into a good mulch, no matter its origins. Wood chips take a long time to break down, which makes them an ideal mulch for paths. They are less ideal for spreading directly on beds, where they can get in the way of seeders and tie up nitrogen if the chips are buried with transplants.

Any plant residues. Search out whatever sources of organic material are available in your area. Coconut fibers, peat moss, peanut shells, corn husks, shredded newspaper, seaweed — the possibilities abound. Get creative and tap into streams of underappreciated local biomass, but check with your certifier before applying new materials to organic fields.

Tapping into "waste" streams of underappreciated biomass can divert valuable local resources to the farm.

We never turn down an opportunity to stockpile free carbon.

THICKER ISN'T ALWAYS BETTER

One concern with thick mulches is the insulating effect they have on the soil. This can be a boon in hot weather, keeping the soil at the cooler temperatures optimal for root growth. But in colder climates (like ours in Maine), farmers go to great lengths to extend their short growing season, and mulches can get in the way. By blocking radiation from the sun and heat transfer from the air, mulches can slow spring soil warming by a week or more.

We get around this delay by raking our leaf mulch into the paths in early spring and spreading a layer of compost as mulch on the beds. The rich, dark compost soaks up the sun's energy and warms the soil beneath it. The raised height also hastens warming of the bed and creates troughed pathways that holds the leaf mulch in place. The result is fully protected soil that is ready for early planting, while the paths are mulched thickly enough to remain weed-free for the rest of the season.

Our approach to weed management focuses on complete soil coverage at all times.

PLASTIC "MULCH"

I do not consider plastic film a true "mulch." As discussed in chapter 4, plastic is inherently wasteful and does not feed soil organisms or increase water infiltration the way organic mulches do. I believe the use of plastic is justifiable when a farm is starting out, as it enables effective smothering of perennial sod while producing a marketable crop out of the gate. But covering living soil with impervious synthetic material is not an ecological practice in the long run.

GROWING A MULCH IN PLACE

LEAF MULCHING

We prepare beds in the fall, starting with a layer of compost. Also note the wood chip mulch in the paths.

Beds that are harvested too late to allow for a fall cover crop get mulched with leaves (after a layer of compost).

Cover crop seeded directly into compost comes up weed-free.

Leaves are raked into paths in the spring to expose composted beds for planting.

A thick stand of cover crop feeds the soil and provides a grown-in-place mulch. This mix will winterkill and be planted through in the spring.

Crops direct-seeded into compost need minimal weeding. Weeds are rarely a problem when the soil is kept covered.

Methods of Manual Weeding

While we should accept that weeds are not the enemy but rather nature's messengers telling us to cover the soil, sometimes we need efficient ways to knock back weeds while we establish soil coverage. There are several weed management practices common in small-scale vegetable production.

Hoeing

The hoe is the iconic tool of the vegetable farmer. Hoes come in all shapes and sizes, with two defining features: a handle and a piece of metal designed to cut or pull out weeds when pushed or pulled over the ground. The colinear hoe and wire weeder are my go-to tools for hoeing small weeds that come up between crop rows in a bed. The wire weeder is less likely to damage crops as it moves by them, but the colinear hoe is better at weeding underneath the leaves of squat crops like lettuce heads or cabbage. The upright posture and minimal effort required to use both these tools make weeding easy, as long as the weeds are small. For larger weeds (and less precision), the stirrup hoe is my tool of choice.

Whatever the implement, the key to successful hoeing lies in hitting the weed with the hoe blade at just the right height. When aimed just below the crown of a plant, it will uproot the weed cleanly, allowing its roots to dry out and die. If aimed too high, a hoe will merely damage the leaves of a weed, which will then regrow from its intact root system. If aimed too low, a hoe will dig up the weed with enough soil attached that it will re-root where it lands.

The problem with any hoe in a no-till context is that it necessarily disturbs the soil surface. Even a skilled hoer will mix the O-horizon with the underlying soil to some extent, disturbing the roots of nearby crops and stirring up new weed seed. If we embrace the message of annual weeds — that the soil is inadequately covered — then we see that

The colinear hoe allows a comfortable upright posture and kills small weeds with little effort.

Preferred weeding tools, from left to right: hand hoe, wire hoe, stirrup hoe, colinear hoe, and digging fork.

ON FRITH FARM

WORKING WITH THE WEATHER

Whenever possible, we let the weather determine when we weed, as hoeing on a dry sunny day is vastly more productive than trying to weed wet ground. This leaves the cooler rainy days for transplanting, for which hot dry weather is not ideal.

hoeing actually aggravates the problem. Certainly treating the symptom may be necessary at times, but repeated agitation of the soil surface does not fit with the long-term goals of ecological soil care.

Flame Weeding

Fighting weeds with fire is (with apologies) hot right now among organic vegetable growers. I have experienced the joy of scorching weeds in a blaze of propane-fueled glory. Most flame weeders consist of one or more propane jets shrouded in metal to focus the heat at ground level. Whether carried, pushed, or pulled with a tractor, these implements work by applying focused flame directly to the soil surface.

Flame weeders are most useful for tillage-based operations with very weedy soils. After a bed has been tilled, it can be "stale-bedded," or left empty to allow weeds to germinate. The flame weeder can burn off this flush of weeds without further soil disturbance, and then a crop can be seeded with reduced weed pressure. The flame weeder can even be used after the crop has been seeded, but before it germinates, so that any weeds are knocked back right before the crop emerges. This is a common method for crops like carrots that take a long time to germinate (careful timing of the flaming with this method is obviously critical).

For a no-till farmer, flame weeding is less useful. While weeding by fire leaves the soil undisturbed, it presents a couple of significant drawbacks. First, it kills only very young weeds. In undisturbed soil, weeds do not germinate in flushes as they do after tillage, and they trend toward perennials over time. Flaming kills only the minority of weeds that

happened to germinate recently, leaving more established weeds and root systems unperturbed.

Second, flame weeding pairs poorly with the more enduring method of weed control that is mulching. If weather is dry, applying flame to beds covered in plant residues is an ideal way to start a wildfire. I learned this the hard way one summer. I fired up my newly purchased flame weeder and blasted my way down the first bed in a plot seeded to carrots five days earlier. The weeds were few and far between, but the pleasure of torching them was immense. As I turned to start back on the second bed, however, I was met with a startling sight. Both paths of the bed I had just traversed were on fire. My heavy mulch of leaves had, quite literally, backfired. The bed looked like an emergency runway, lined with flaming paths. I dropped the flamer and started dancing my way back up the bed, stomping out the flames frantically with my sandaled feet. I imagine the scene might have looked like a fast-forwarded video of someone practicing the Cajun two-step. Despite my commendable tempo, the flames were spreading, and it wasn't until I had the obvious-in-hindsight idea to flick on the irrigation that the fire was controlled. I sold the flame weeder later that season.

Mowing and Smothering

Mowing and smothering is discussed in detail in chapter 8 but deserves mention here as well. While I advocate an approach to weeding that focuses on prevention rather than killing, at some point weeds will get out of hand. The mower and the tarp are the most efficient tools for weeding large areas without soil disturbance.

For those beds that inevitably get away from us and are lost to weeds, a quick pass with the flail mower and a week or so under a black tarp will restore them to a weed-free, plantable state with no hoeing, flaming, or soil work. In this way, mowing and tarping act as a valuable "reset" button, replacing the role usually filled by tillage. We can wipe the slate clean for the next crop without the negative impacts on soil health.

If you use this method, it is important to accept the fate of an overgrown bed and take action before the weeds go to seed. Mowing a bed too late results in a deposit of seed on the soil surface that will plague future seasons. When a limited number of weeds have just started to set seed, I find it worthwhile to go through the bed and remove these by hand before flail mowing. We place weeds with viable seed in buckets or wheelbarrows and remove them to a compost pile rather than drop them in paths or field borders. Timing is critical in preventing seed rain, and when soil coverage and scouting are adequate, no weed should ever set viable seed.

Mowing is a useful method of weed control in other areas of the farm as well. If weed seed is generated on the farm, it will likely find a way into your fields. To achieve zero seed rain, every nook and cranny near crop fields must be managed to prevent weeds from setting seed. For grassy areas, mowing is the easiest way to favor perennials over unwanted annuals. Keeping nearby pastures mowed or intensively grazed will also promote grass growth and prevent seed from migrating into crop fields.

Hand Weeding

After just a couple of years of successful zero seed rain management, the weeds should be sparse enough that hand weeding will actually make more sense than hoeing. Hands have a key advantage over other forms of weeding in that they are highly selective. Unlike flaming, tarping, or even hoeing, pulling weeds with our fingers enables us to choose exactly which plants come out and which remain.

In contrast to the traditional kill-all approach, the targeted nature of hand weeding is especially useful in the context of multicropping, cover cropping, and undersowing. Hand pulling also pairs well with mulching, which renders hoeing and flame weeding impractical. The core of a zero-seed-rain strategy is tightly spaced crops planted through organic mulches. Then a team of humans provide the final quality assurance by searching out the few scattered weeds that still come up. By focusing on prevention rather than damage control, weed management becomes synonymous with soil coverage, and hand pulling is but the cherry on top.

Pulling by hand provides the finishing touch on a weed-free farm.

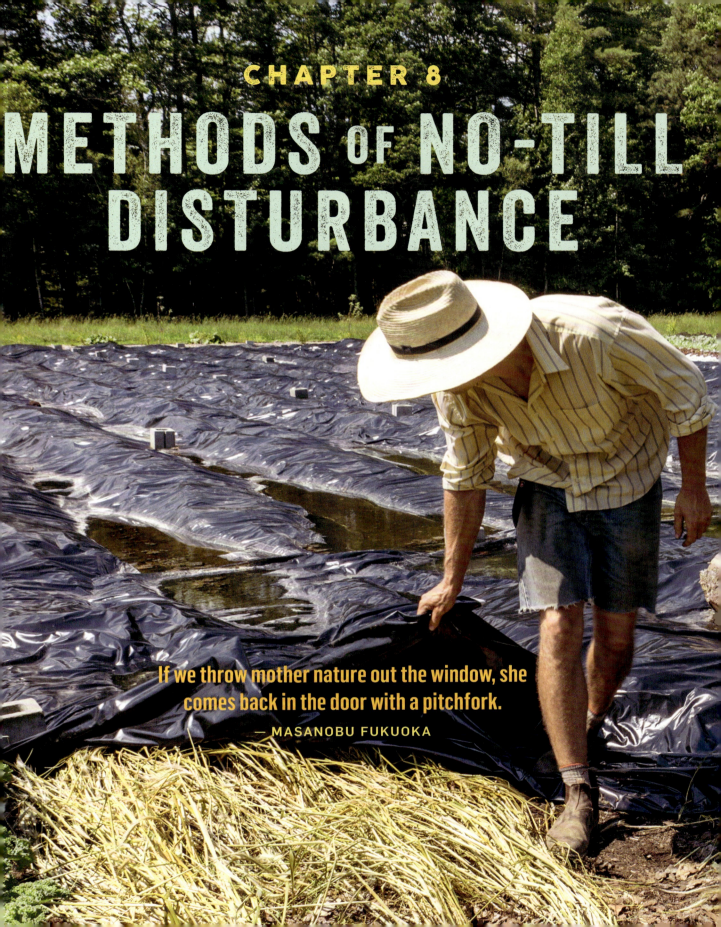

CHAPTER 8

METHODS OF NO-TILL DISTURBANCE

If we throw mother nature out the window, she comes back in the door with a pitchfork.
— MASANOBU FUKUOKA

arming requires a degree of disturbance to nature's ecological progression, but our efforts to steer natural succession in an edible direction need not resort to tillage. This chapter lays out our toolbox of no-till methods for transitioning beds between crops: mulching, mowing, smothering, breaking up compaction, and preparing for planting.

Flipping Beds

Transitioning a bed from one crop to the next can be one of the scarier parts of adopting a system of no-till vegetable production. The current farming paradigm focuses so heavily on working the soil that skipping tillage and cultivation altogether can sound ludicrous. But the steps of preparing no-till beds and flipping them to new crops are actually quite simple and one day may make us wonder why we spent so much time driving heavy, expensive equipment back and forth over our fields.

The challenge is getting a bed back to a plantable state after the first crop is harvested. Seeds and transplant roots need good contact with the soil, which can be difficult to achieve while also maximizing soil coverage and photosynthesis. In some cases, preparing a bed can be as simple as walking through and pulling a few weeds that were missed while the previous crop was growing. But what if there are lots of well-established weeds, or the previous crop was something like squash or broccoli that leaves a lot of plant matter behind after its harvest period is over? Or, what if the previous crop was a 6-foot-tall cover crop that is still growing vigorously?

Transitioning from an overgrown bed with large, fibrous plant residues and active growth to smooth, plantable soil can certainly tempt a farmer toward tillage. However, there are easy no-till steps that allow for a smooth succession, no matter the level of preparation needed.

SPRING BED PREP

Avoiding bare soil is a year-round concern. Maintaining living growth through the winter, however, is not always possible. We are in zone 4b, where the ground freezes sometime in November and doesn't usually thaw until the end of March. After late fall harvests there is little time to establish a dense cover crop, so we protect these beds with a layer of leaf mulch. In the spring, we rake the leaves into the paths to expose the bed for planting. This results in weed-free paths all season long, and soil of excellent tilth — biologically aerated by worms and other soil organisms under the leaf mulch — to plant into without soil disturbance.

Beds mulched for winter get raked off for spring planting. The thick mulch in the paths keeps them weed-free all season.

TASK
FLIPPING
A BED

Here are the steps we follow at Frith Farm to prepare an established bed for planting.

1 **Scout.** Hand pull and remove all weeds that have seed heads or are close to producing seed (see Zero Seed Rain on page 106).

2 **Mow or knock down (if needed).** Mow or knock down established plants that have not produced seed. (see Mowing and Rolling on page 122). This step is not necessary after well-weeded crops that leave minimal residues, such as root crops.

3 **Tarp (if needed).** Cover the bed with a black tarp to kill the root systems of remaining plants. Since mowing does not disturb the roots of plants, some may grow back if not smothered. Leave the bed covered for up to 10 days, depending on weather (see Occultation and Solarization on page 125). If there are no vigorous root systems to smother, this step is skipped.

4 **Clean.** If direct seeding, rake the bed clear of mulch and crop debris. Dig up and remove perennial weed roots. (Unlike annual weeds, these generally do not die after brief tarping.) If transplanting, you can clean the bed to a lesser degree, depending on the spacing and vigor of the transplants. Winter squash, for example, can be transplanted with good results into a bed with heavy mulch or other plant debris.

5 **Amend (if needed).** Spread soil amendments, if needed, based on soil test results. If soil is visible, spread compost at a rate of seven wheelbarrows per 100-foot bed (2.5 cubic yards per 1,000 square feet), and rake it smooth, ensuring the top of the bed is the correct width for the entire length of the bed (see Compost as Mulch on page 119).

6 **Plant.** See chapter 5.

OVERLAPPED PLANTING

To maximize photosynthesis, we aim to flip beds and replant them the same day. This also makes the most of every degree-day in our short growing season. Another way to maintain a continuity of living plants is to plant the next crop before the first crop is even out. Like multicropping (see chapter 9), this strategy adds diversity and minimizes unproductive planting areas.

Overlapped planting can reduce or eliminate the period of relative bareness that normally occurs after seeding or transplanting. When planted into the understory of an established crop, seeds can be germinating, or transplants can be adjusting to outdoor conditions while the first crop is still being harvested. When the older crop is eventually removed, the new plants are ready to take advantage of the extra space and sunlight. The logistics of this overlap are critical to avoid crowding and competition, but the method's potential for sustaining an uninterrupted biological party below ground is worth the effort of figuring out the details of ideal timing and spacing.

Replacing Tillage with Strategic Successions

Transitioning between crops is facilitated by careful crop planning. Direct seeding through the thick chaff of a previous crop is difficult and usually results in poor germination. Planting an overwintered cover crop before early spring crops, for example, makes no-till bed prep close to impossible. The arrangement of crops both in time and space can make or break the success of a no-till sequence.

There are two main considerations when planning a transition between crops (in addition to the traditional array of crop plan decisions; see Crop Planning on page 74).

The amount of crop residue and the level of seedbed preparation needed. In what state does a crop leave a bed after it is harvested, and what level of bed preparation does the next crop require?

Following crops that leave minimal residues with ones that need a clean seedbed is a simple way to eliminate the need for tillage or other bed prep work. Crops that are transplanted with wide spacing, on the other hand, can more easily follow those that leave significant residues. These residues can then be left undisturbed as food for the soil and mulch for weed suppression and moisture retention.

Spacing of consecutive crops. Does the direct seeding or transplant spacing of a crop work well with the spacing of the stubble left by the previous crop?

A crop plan that considers the spacing of the second planting eliminates the need to disturb the root mass left behind by the first. Here are a few examples:

- Follow arugula, seeded ten rows to a bed, with nine rows of spinach, so that the seeder with spinach passes cleanly between the stubble left by the arugula.
- Direct seed carrots in four rows around and between kale stumps that were planted three rows to a bed.
- Do a late planting of squash that is transplanted in one row down the middle of a bed containing two rows of summer cabbage.

In some cases, the beds are tarped after the first crop is harvested to ensure the plants have died completely so their roots can decompose and feed the next plants rather than compete with them for nutrients and water.

This level of spatial planning avoids soil disturbance entirely and leaves exposed the absolute minimum of bare soil necessary for good soil-seed contact and germination. It also saves the time of running soil-working implements over the beds, as well as the expense of buying such implements in the first place.

Compost acts as a slow-release fertilizer while providing soil coverage, weed prevention, and water retention.

Compost as Mulch

Compost is a slow-release fertilizer and an excellent source of organic matter, but to a no-till system it is perhaps most valuable as a mulch (see chapter 7). All organic mulches hold in moisture, prevent weeds, and improve fertility slowly over time. Compost, however, is unique — compared to leaves, straw, wood chips, or other mulches — in that you can plant directly into it, both with transplants and direct seeding.

Other forms of mulch inhibit transplanting, clog push seeders, and prevent good soil contact with seeds and plant roots. Not so with compost. Finely screened compost is an ideal medium for transplants and direct seeding and can substitute for tillage in creating a plantable seedbed. The stubble and unevenness left by a previous crop can be covered and smoothed over with a thick layer of compost, thereby avoiding soil disturbance of any kind.

In addition, all the other attributes of mulch hold true for compost. This layer of organic matter, like the O-horizon of the soil, retains moisture, protects against erosion, prevents weed germination, and feeds soil biology.

The quality and nutrient content of compost varies widely. For the purpose of simplicity, I distinguish here between two categories of compost: compost derived partially from animal products and compost derived purely from plant material.

Manure-Based Compost

Most commercial compost is made from animal manure. Any farm that imports feed in large quantities, like most dairy, poultry, or horse operations, generates excess nutrients that accumulate and eventually need to be moved off the farm to avoid polluting land and water. We can debate the sustainability of these operations, but the fact is that they exist and represent a steady source of local manure that is often composted and sold as a value-added product. Manure-based compost tends to be relatively high in the three major plant nutrients — nitrogen, phosphorus, and potassium — and can function as a slow-release fertilizer when applied to the soil. Too much of it, however, can lead to nutrient buildup and potential leaching.

Phosphorus is often the first nutrient to accumulate this way, and farms that apply lots of animal-based compost are notorious for having very high phosphorus concentrations in their soils. Phosphorus leaches minimally (which is why it builds up in the first place) but is a prime cause of water pollution through erosion. High levels of phosphorus are not only bad for water resources, but they can also cause an imbalance in the soil that affects biological activity and nutrient cycling. Thus, it's best to switch to a plant-based compost once the nutrient levels, especially that of phosphorus, approach the recommended range on your soil test.

Some of the best compost I've used is made from nothing but crop residues.

Plant-Based Compost

Plant-based (or "vegan") compost is much lower in nutrients (see chart below) and generally harder to source than manure-based compost. Locating a reliable supplier of screened plant-based compost can be difficult but well worth the effort.

Any pile of plant material will eventually break down into a compost-like mulch, so start your search with industries that collect or produce plants in various forms. Municipalities often store yard wastes and cleared brush in enormous quantities. Call your local transfer station or town hall to start the inquiry. Local landscapers are another valuable resource. Even if they don't have their own piles of plant matter, they probably know where some are. Plant nurseries usually sell expensive bark mulches but might have old decomposed piles they wouldn't mind seeing cleaned up — just avoid any with inorganic dye additives (ask the staff, to be sure). Lumber mills produce huge amounts of bark that eventually breaks down into wonderful low-nutrient compost. Think like mycorrhizal fungus: get creative and tap into whatever plant-based resources are available nearby.

Even if you can't find finished plant-based compost, it might be practical to acquire the raw ingredients (wood chips, bark mulch, hay, leaves, etc.) and let them break down into compost on the farm. Since they contain no animal products, there are no organic certification rules for how plant-based compost is made or how long to wait between application and harvest, as long as the plant material inputs are free of prohibited substances. Farm safety regulations also tend to focus on issues involving manure and largely ignore the use of plant-based mulches and compost. Stockpiling and composting static piles of plant residues on the farm is one way to make your own low-nutrient, high-value compost, if local sources do not exist.

Sample Nutrient Contents of Manure-Based Compost vs. Plant-Based Compost

	Manured-Based Compost	Plant-Based Compost
Total Nitrogen (%)	1–4	1–2.5
Phosphorus (%)	0.5–3	0.2–0.5
Potassium (%)	1–3	0.5–2

Dry weight basis. Source: https://vric.ucdavis.edu

Spreading Compost

Spreading large amounts of compost can be a laborious and time-consuming task. In the farm's first season, we spread about 300 cubic yards of compost — close to 200 tons! This might seem worthy of a manure spreader, but the no-till market farm is generally of a scale that investing in a manure spreader and extra tractor to pull it does not make sense, especially since the benefit of heavy compost applications tapers off as soil health increases. I also prefer to keep the compacting forces of large machinery off of crop fields, and a manure spreader covers paths in compost when ideally just the beds would receive it.

A drop spreader can apply compost with greater precision than a manure spreader, but it still requires heavy equipment to drive it through the fields. The old-fashioned way of shoveling compost into a wheelbarrow and pushing it across the farm, while enjoyable at a small scale, can easily fatigue a crew if spreading much more than a few cubic yards per person at a time.

A HUMAN-SCALE SOLUTION

I stumbled on a hybrid tractor-human approach to solve the problem of spreading larger volumes while maintaining a human scale. The majority of the work of spreading compost by hand is in the loading: lifting heavy compost into a wheelbarrow with a shovel. The next most tiring part of the process is pushing the wheelbarrow across the farm to the bed. The easiest and most rewarding step is dumping the compost onto the bed.

Our approach takes all of this into consideration by using a tractor for the loading and transporting of the compost (or leaf mulch or wood chips, which we spread in the same manner) and wheelbarrows for the final spreading within the field. We have a small utility tractor with a bucket that is 6 feet wide and holds about half a cubic yard — the perfect width and volume to fill three wheelbarrows, lined up side-by-side, with a single dump.

When spreading compost, a tractor does the heavy lifting but stays off the vegetable plots.

Wheelbarrows allow for precise application directly on beds.

A quick rake leaves the beds ready for planting.

The wheelbarrows are filled at the head of each bed, then are pushed a maximum of 100 feet (our bed length) and dumped precisely where the compost is needed. The timing generally works out for the wheelbarrows to be dumped and returned to the head of the bed by the time the tractor has made the round trip to the compost pile and returned with another load. Once the compost is roughly spread, we smooth it out with rakes.

With this system, the tractor does the heavy lifting, the humans work with gravity, and the fields are not subject to the compacting forces of tractors and machinery. Four people can spread 25 cubic yards of compost in a couple of hours in this manner — and still feel their arms the next day.

Mowing and Rolling

Mowing a crop is a primary form of no-till disturbance, enabling weed management, the use of cover crops, and the preparation of beds, all without tillage. The best implement for this job is a flail mower, an indispensable no-till tool. It has a horizontal axle with Y-shaped blades that are free to rotate or "flail" around the axle as it spins. The flailing action helps the mower tackle established crops, cover crops, and even shrubs and small saplings, reducing the above-ground portion of these plants to shreds. The mower is essentially a chipper-shredder on wheels that can cut right down to the soil surface. Since the residues left behind are so thoroughly chopped up, they take very little time to break down and are easy to plant through. Used in tandem with tarps for smothering, the flail mower allows for cover cropping and rapid succession planting, even with established crops and overgrown beds.

There are several flail mower models available for walk-behind tractors. I am partial to the 30- or 34-inch model made by the Italian company Berta Franco. The Berta mower features a floating deck to allow the mower to follow ground contours independent of tractor wheels as well as a removable discharge baffle to adjust how finely the plant material is chopped.

Since the finely chopped debris left after flail mowing breaks down so quickly, the flail mower is not the implement of choice when intact residues are desired as an *in situ,* or "grown-in-place," mulch. Some farmers use a sickle-bar mower for this, as it severs a cover crop with a single cut. A rotary mower can also be used, although its rotating blades result in partially chopped residues, somewhere between those left by a flail mower and a sickle-bar mower.

When possible, I prefer to avoid mowing altogether. At a cover crop's peak flowering stage, it often requires very little effort to "roll" it, or knock it down enough to secure a tarp over it. When the tarp is removed, the dead plant material remains intact and endures as a mulch far longer than its flail-mowed counterpart. (This process is covered in detail in chapter 9.)

A flail mower reduces plants to finely chopped mulch that breaks down quickly.

THE ROLLER-CRIMPER

The roller-crimper is an innovative no-till tool that allows you to terminate a cover crop without severing the plant material. It was developed at the Rodale Institute in Pennsylvania and consists of a cylinder with curved radial blades that fold down the cover crop and "crimp" or crush its stems. When timed correctly at peak flowering, crimping can achieve a complete knockdown.

The roller-crimper is a pivotal innovation for mid- and large-scale no-till operations where the use of tarps and imported organic mulches is unfeasible. For the human-scale farm, however, the implement is less useful because it is heavy (to crimp effectively) and therefore difficult to maneuver and transport. Even the smaller version designed for a walk-behind tractor is cumbersome — yet its weight is not always enough to adequately crimp the cover crop, especially on no-till beds that have soft soil of good tilth.

While not ideal for the human-scale farm, the roller-crimper has profound implications for grain growers and other larger operations, as it provides the benefits of organic mulching in tandem with those of a living cover crop, without any soil disturbance. At much smaller scales, however, simply knocking down a cover crop and dragging a tarp over it (see chapter 9) performs the same task without the need for tractors or expensive implements.

A T-post stomper provides a human-scale alternative to the roller-crimper.

Twine attaches the T-post to your foot. The bottom edge of the T-post acts as a crimping blade.

Occultation and Solarization

The ability to manipulate when and how the sun hits the ground is a powerful tool for the no-till farmer.

Occultation is the practice of blocking all light from reaching the soil surface. Every living plant needs air, water, nutrients, favorable temperatures, and light to grow, so removing one or more of these elements will eventually kill the plant. Covering a piece of earth with an opaque material occults the sun and starves any plants of the light they need to survive.

Most of us have witnessed the effects of occultation when we pick up an old board or piece of wood in a field or lawn. Underneath we find a patch of soil bereft of plants but teeming with life: spiders, beetles, and centipedes scrambling for cover between miniature mountains of worm castings and lacy fields of fungal webbing. The soil is soft and crumbly, beautifully tilthed by the activity of countless soil organisms. No-till occultation practices seek to mimic this natural phenomenon of soil preparation.

Solarization is the practice of trapping the sun's radiation in order to heat the soil above ambient temperatures. Greenhouses and row covers are examples of mild solarization, but generally the term refers to the method of laying clear plastic directly on the ground during warm weather. If the edges are buried or otherwise sealed and the weather is hot and sunny, temperatures can reach upwards of 140°F (60°C) in the top several inches of soil, killing not only weeds but also weed seeds, pathogens, and just about everything else.

This type of solarization is essentially a broad-spectrum biocidal treatment of the soil, killing almost all life in the top couple of inches. Since our goal in no-till farming is to nurture diverse and prolific life both above and below ground, reproducing

the effects of chemical soil fumigation may not jibe with our principles. But not all solarization is so extreme.

For the purposes of killing weeds or crop remains to prepare a bed for the next planting, I find that black tarps provide an ideal combination of occultation and mild solarization. Their black color enables the tarps to completely block light from the soil while absorbing the sun's rays and concentrating heat at the soil's surface. Since these tarps transfer heat to the soil primarily through conduction rather than solar radiation, the soil temperature does not increase as drastically as with clear plastic solarization; the black tarps heat the soil surface enough to hasten the death of plants without overheating the soil at lower depths.

To clean a field of weeds without pulling, hoeing, or cultivating is a revolutionary concept for the organic farmer. The practice of tarping allows us to wipe the slate clean for a new crop without spraying poison or disturbing the soil. Unlike traditional organic weeding practices, smothering with black tarps can kill every last annual weed, not just the ones that get caught by a hand, hoe, or cultivator. Another benefit of "passive" weeding with black tarps is that, once in place, the tarps are more effective the longer you wait — the precise opposite of other "active" weed control methods that almost always fall behind the progression of weeds as the season gets busy.

The success of smothering with black tarps is determined by how long they are left in place. This timing depends on the weather, as black tarps are much more effective during the heat of summer than during the cooler shoulder seasons, and in many places tarping to kill weeds may be completely ineffective during the winter.

The significance of temperature is related to both the occultation and solarization effects of tarping. Since occultation works by removing a necessary

Black tarps create a weed-free surface without disturbing the soil.

"Tarp kits" facilitate the handling of tarps and weights. Each pallet holds a 24×100 tarp along with enough 8×8×8 concrete blocks to weigh it down. The layer of blocks under the tarp keeps it from catching on the tractor forks, which we use to move the pallets where needed.

ingredient of plant growth (light), this "diet" is most effective when the plant is hungriest — when soil temperatures are warm enough for optimal growth. At lower temperatures the plant's metabolism naturally slows and a lack of light has much less effect on its survival.

Similarly, solarization relies on the sun's ability to heat the soil surface to sufficient temperatures to kill the plant, so it is less effective when the soil is cool or when the sun is lower in the sky during spring and fall. In areas where soil freezes or plants go dormant, laying a tarp on the ground over winter will do little to kill the plants.

Many perennial weeds can survive tarping for extended periods, and hand-digging is often preferable when these weeds are present at manageable levels. Otherwise, effective tarping of deep-rooted or rhizomatous perennials can take half a season or more. Most common weeds are annuals, however, and smothering for shorter periods is consistently effective at killing most of them, although certain heat-loving species like purslane and yellow nutsedge can be troublesome.

Some farmers choose to leave tarps on their beds through the winter as a placeholder for spring crops. The tarp is removed just before planting, so new plants go into completely weed-free soil. This is a great way to eliminate spring weeding, but for climates that get heavy snows, tarping through the winter has a downside. Since water cannot drain through the tarp, the full weight of snow, ice, slush, and water bears down on the soil, causing more compaction than on an untarped bed.

I witnessed this phenomenon firsthand in some of our beds, and I decided to stick to organic mulches for winter coverage from then on. Impervious material on top of soil does not exist in nature, and we should always be mindful of unintended consequences of unnatural practices.

There are various materials suitable for use as smothering tarps, but most farmers go with inexpensive 5- or 6-mil black-on-white polyethylene silage tarps, available through farm suppliers. We use 8 × 8 × 8-inch concrete blocks to weigh down the edges, and we err on the side of too many rather

APPROXIMATE TIME REQUIRED TO SMOTHER MOST ANNUAL PLANTS

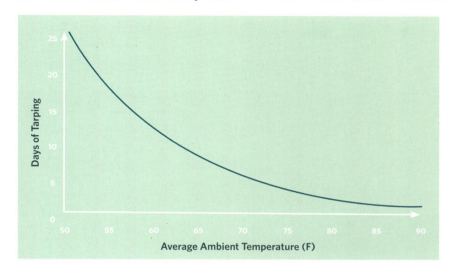

The hotter the weather, the less time tarps take to smother plants. Every day that a bed is tarped is that much less time for photosynthesis and crop growth, so we try to home in on the minimum duration needed for thorough smothering. Knowing this time helps us make the most of our short growing season.

than too few. The extra effort of placing blocks is worth the savings in time (and dignity) spent chasing tarps around the farm on windy days. The advantage of concrete blocks over sandbags is that they require no filling and do not degrade in the sun (spreading plastic residues across the farm).

Breaking Up Compaction

Compaction is a symptom of inadequate soil care. Driving heavy machinery on fields, tilling, leaving soil exposed to the elements, a lack of living plant growth — all will lead to compaction. As with any ailment, it is preferable to treat the underlying cause rather than the symptom. No-till practices avoid compacting forces by keeping the tractor off the fields and keeping the soil undisturbed and covered. Cover crops and organic mulches break up existing compaction through the biological activity that thrives in these nourished and protected conditions. In a perfect no-till world, there is no further need to break up compaction.

But the world is far from perfect, and compaction happens. Deep tillage with a subsoiler or chisel plow is the conventional response and is very effective in the short term. It is important, however, to address the underlying causes of the compaction — one of which, most likely, is the weight of tractors driving over the fields.

No-till farming favors a biological approach to soil care. Plants with deep taproots are natural subsoilers and can open up vertical channels well into the soil's B horizon, or subsoil layer. As the roots die they become a delicious highway for soil organisms, whose steady traffic continues the loosening work. In colder climates, these new openings absorb water, and the freeze-thaw cycle of winter enlarges them further. The conditions for this biological activity are achieved when the soil remains covered with plants and mulches.

In cases of severe compaction, or to jump-start the natural healing process, a broadfork is a helpful tool. With its long, slightly curved tines and two handles, a broadfork requires only moderate effort to loosen the soil to a depth of 10 inches, while causing minimal disruption to the soil's structure. I prefer the 727 model from Johnny's Selected Seeds.

We step in the broadfork every foot or so, walking backwards along the top of the bed so that any compaction from our feet is ameliorated by the broadforking. (This is the only time we step on the beds.)

I find we need to broadfork only after we have slacked on the first principle of soil care — maximizing photosynthesis with perpetual living growth. With no tillage or tractors and with adequate fostering of soil biology through mulching and plant growth, broadforking should be necessary only as an occasional practice and not a perennial task.

A broadfork alleviates compaction in the short term.

A Plantable Surface

Creating a fluffy, fine-textured planting surface is perhaps the most common reason for tilling. Since one of our goals as no-till farmers is to disturb the soil as little as possible, we aim for the minimum level of bed preparation needed to plant a crop. And the fact is, for most transplants, a smooth planting surface is simply unnecessary, and a churned, fluffed-up bed is overkill even for direct seeding.

A big part of going no-till is redefining "plantable." When we recalibrate our expectations, a bed preparation rake is often the only tool needed to prepare the surface for direct seeding, and raking can often be skipped altogether for beds receiving transplants. As farmer and researcher Edward Faulkner figured out over 75 years ago, "Planting can be done in a trashy surface."

There is a tendency among market gardeners to impose a degree of control on our vegetable beds that borders on vanity. We revel in the image of freshly exposed dark soil mounded in meticulously measured and marked beds, and we photograph the perfectly straight rows of precision-seeded crops as they emerge from the leveled soil.

In reality, however, a bed can be prepared for correct plant spacing and good contact between soil and seed with little more than a rake. Nature shows no preferential treatment for picture-perfect soil preparation. As Edward Faulkner puts it, "The fact is that untidiness to an extreme — a surface covered or filled with abundance of decaying trash [plant residues] — is really the proper condition."

While there are low-till tools, like the power harrow and tilther, that enable a higher level of bed preparation, I find such a finely worked seedbed to be unnecessary. Nature guides us to strive for the minimum of machinery and of work to fulfill a given need. For preparing a suitable no-till planting surface — if any work is even needed — the humble rake answers the call.

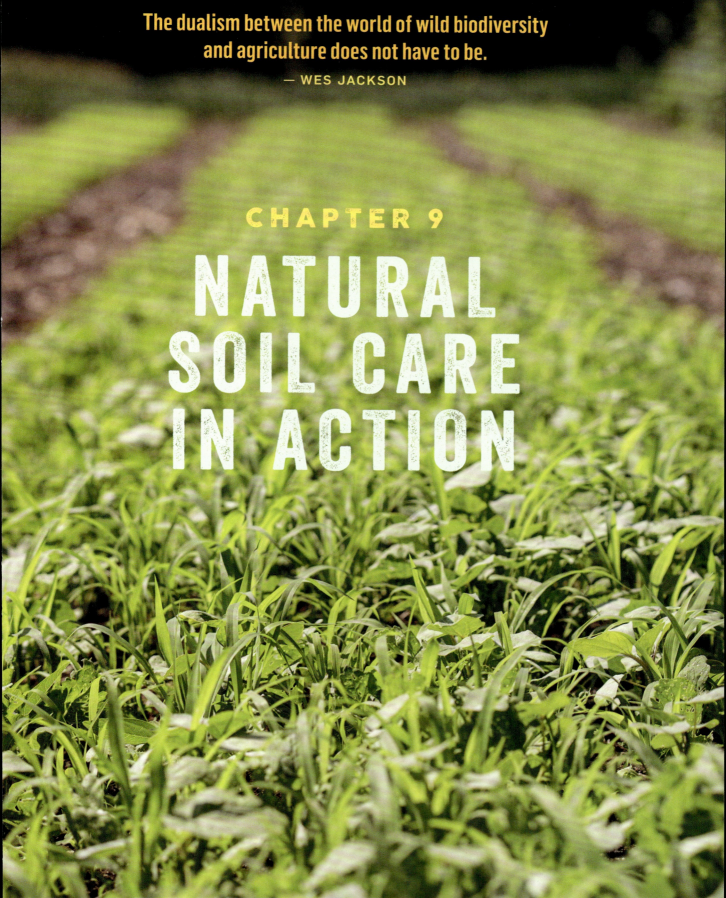

> The dualism between the world of wild biodiversity
> and agriculture does not have to be.
> — WES JACKSON

CHAPTER 9

NATURAL SOIL CARE IN ACTION

All the evidence shows we cannot improve on nature's model. So how do we put into action ecological principles of soil care that are based on non-disturbance? This chapter describes some of the techniques we employ to enhance the natural phenomena that protect and regenerate the soil.

Principles of Soil Care

As discussed in chapter 2, the health of terrestrial ecosystems can be achieved by following the four basic principles of maximizing photosynthesis, biodiversity, and soil coverage while minimizing disturbance. These overlapping ideals guide our soil husbandry efforts at Frith Farm. Some of the practices discussed here have been employed since I started the farm nine years ago, and others are relatively new additions to our system.

There are no prescriptions for how best to nurture the soil, as true care comes from a personal relationship to the land and keen observation of the particular model nature has tailored for it. In any case, by following these natural principles I believe we are at least moving in the right direction.

Cover Cropping

Living plants are the most natural way to nourish soil biology and generate soil health. Unlike soil amendments and imported organic matter, plants are living solar collectors customized to the conditions and needs of the soil. They pump the sun's energy and the air's carbon deep underground, feeding soil life in exchange for nutrients in a self-enriching cycle of symbiosis — all with minimal human intervention. This model of self-generating fertility is *the* renewable source of terrestrial wealth, and we all become poorer when we fail to maximize photosynthesis on the farm.

My definition of a cover crop is both broad and literal: a crop grown to cover and feed the soil. In this context, the distinction between a cash crop and a cover crop (or green manure) is irrelevant, as

any crop can be grown for either or both of these purposes. Keeping a garden bed covered in a variety of living plants is more important than worrying about which plant is or is not classified as a "cover crop." That said, there are particular plants that are especially effective at covering the soil, catching nutrients, and fixing carbon and nitrogen from the atmosphere. These species, many of which are grasses and legumes, are useful biological tools to help build soil and are what farmers generally refer to when talking about cover crops.

Integrating cover crops into a no-till system can be daunting. Most vegetables do not perform well when planted in a densely populated neighborhood of established plants. Without the plow, disc, and harrow to incorporate bulky residues, how are we to kill established cover and prepare beds for the following crop? Unsurprisingly, nature provides the answers to these questions. In undisturbed natural settings, plants routinely die in one of three ways:

1. They fulfill their life cycle.
2. They winterkill.
3. They are starved of light or other resources.

By embracing these natural methods, no-till cover crop management not only becomes possible, it also ends up being less work than any soil-disturbing alternative. With the right planning, we can wait for cover crops to fulfill their life cycle, stepping in at the end to mow, crimp, or knock them down prior to seed set; we can wait for the temperatures of winter to kill cold-sensitive species; or we can smother plants with tarps or with larger, faster-growing plants that outcompete them. We can use any combination of these techniques to transition beds from thick stands of maximized photosynthesis to an environment hospitable to new plants.

Note that time is a crucial element for all these techniques, and there is a waiting period involved with each. This is another way no-till practices differ from conventional methods: efficient no-till cover cropping requires greater patience and planning than tillage-based systems, as natural cycles generally progress slower than tractors.

Planning how a cover crop will be terminated and the bed transitioned to a new crop is important when tillage is off the table. In beds that will be planted early the following spring, we plant cover crop species that winterkill, allowing us to rake their remains into the paths and expose the beds for direct-seeding come April. For beds that will be planted the following summer, we seed cold-hardy annuals in the fall that survive the winter and grow vigorously in the spring, flowering in time for us to mow or knock them down, tarp, and then transplant the summer crop through the stubble (see Winter Cover Crops on page 134).

When mowing or rolling (knocking down) a cover crop, timing is important in determining how quickly the crop will die. Grasses co-evolved with grazing animals and are well adapted to grow back repeatedly if mowed when young. Mowing or rolling is most effective at terminating a cover crop when it is timed with the peak of its flowering stage. This is important, as knocking down too early will result in regrowth that extends the tarping period required or competes with the subsequent crop, while knocking down too late results in unwanted seed production. Just because it was once a desired cover crop doesn't mean it won't become a weed. Tarping afterwards ensures the cover crop is thoroughly killed.

With a plan for the termination of the cover crops, we can proceed with confidence and integrate the crops into our production rotation. There are many goals we might have when deciding to cover-crop, and any decent cover will meet many of these at once:

- Feed and sustain soil life
- Break up compaction
- Suppress weeds
- Suppress pests or disease
- Fix nitrogen
- Fix carbon (generate biomass)
- Catch nutrients to prevent leaching
- Scavenge minerals
- Feed beneficial insects
- Produce forage
- Produce a marketable harvest
- Create an *in situ* mulch

THE NO-MAN'S-LAND OF MULCHING

Placing too much confidence in an *in situ* (grown in place) mulch has a potential downside: if the cover crop has inadequate biomass it will provide insufficient soil coverage to effectively suppress weeds. While a thin mulch is far better than nothing for soil health and moisture retention, it can complicate weed management by preventing the use of hoes or other tools. I call this the "no-man's-land" of mulching: not enough to suppress weeds but too much to allow easy weeding.

The problem is easily solved by adding some additional mulch to the *in situ* cover crop after it is terminated. We often spot-apply leaf mulch to beds where the cover crop did not germinate well or grow as thickly as we hoped.

Other considerations that affect cover crop management include:

- Cover crop height (especially if undersowing)
- Winterkill temperature, or cold-hardiness
- Life cycle and flowering time
- Ease of termination
- Compatibility with other crops in mix
- Plantability of the bed after termination (ready for direct seeding, or only for transplants)

With these goals and management concerns in mind, we can start to make sense of the numerous species of cover crops available. Remember, these seeds are sparks that ignite the fire of natural fertility and soil health!

For the sake of simplicity, I group cover crops into four seasonal categories: winter, spring, summer, and fall. Their ideal uses and management are highly dependent on climate, so these categories should be adjusted to match your particular goals and setting.

Before you fixate on one or another cover crop to plant, keep in mind that there is tremendous value in expanding the diversity of cover crop mixes beyond the usual one or two ingredients. Rarely in nature do we see a field covered in just a couple of plant species; the natural soil care principle of maximizing diversity inspires us to do better. At Frith, we aim for at least three species in each mix, but some mixes may contain six or more. The way I see it, even if some varieties get outcompeted, all that's lost is a small amount of seed. Spreading a diverse mix of seed is like casting a wide net — the odds of maximizing photosynthesis and the infiltration of roots throughout the soil profile are increased with every new species. Playing with different ratios and seeding rates is an ongoing process, but I try to err on the side of more seed rather than less.

SEEDING COVER CROP

To plant our cover crop seed, we use an Earthway push seeder after preparing the bed as we would for any other direct-seeded crop. While this requires a lot more walking back and forth than a broadcast seeder, it ensures proper spacing and good germination. For grass seed (oats, barley, rye, etc.), we use the Earthway's beet plate; for peas, the small pea plate; and for small clover seed, the "lettuce, carrots, and other fine seed" plate. For most crop combinations we seed twelve rows total per bed, and we irrigate and weed the emerging cover crop as we would a cash crop.

Growing Information for Common Cover Crops

Crop	Life Cycle	Approx. Winterkill Temp. (F°)	Approx. Max. Ht. (feet)	Comments
Legumes				
Cowpea	Annual	30	2	Thrives in hot weather; vining varieties are more vigorous than bush types
Sunn Hemp	Annual	30	8	Huge warm-weather biomass producer
Berseem Clover	Annual	20	2	Heavy producer of nitrogen and biomass in warm weather
Field Pea	Annual	15	4	Most popular spring and fall cover crop; easily killed; tendrils are delicious and sell well
Subterranean Clover	Annual	15	<1	Good undersown crop; doesn't thrive in shade so is easily managed
Bell (Fava) Beans	Annual	10	6	Vigorous-cool weather growth; great in fall mixes
Austrian Winter Pea	Annual	0	4	Cold-hardy cousin of field pea
Crimson Clover	Annual	0	2	Rapid growth in spring and fall; flowers same time as winter rye when overwintered
Yellow Sweet Clover	Biennial	–20	8 (second year)	Vigorous growth breaks up compaction; most of growth in second year
White Clover	Perennial	–30	<1	Tolerates foot traffic and shade; slow creeping habit
Medium Red Clover	Perennial	–30	2	Faster to establish than mammoth red clover; tolerates mowing
Hairy Vetch	Perennial	–40	6 (with grass)	Slow to establish, then vigorous; spreading rhizomes make it difficult to kill
Grasses and Forbs				
Sorghum-Sudan Grass	Annual	30	10+	Huge warm-weather biomass producer
Japanese Millet	Annual	30	4	Heat-loving biomass producer; drought-tolerant
Buckwheat	Annual	30	2	Establishes quickly to outcompete weeds; low biomass producer; easy to kill; insects love its flowers
Forage Radish	Annual	15	3	Rapid cool-weather growth; thick taproot loosens soil
Oats	Annual	15	4	Most popular winterkill mulch and nurse crop for field peas
Barley	Annual	0	4	Fast biomass producer in cool weather
Annual Ryegrass	Annual	–10	4	Outcompetes weeds; can become a weed if allowed to set seed
Winter Wheat	Annual	–25	4	Easier to kill and slower to set seed than winter rye
Winter Rye	Annual	–40	6	Powerhouse overwinter cover crop; huge biomass producer

WINTER COVER CROPS

1. We direct-seed the beds in September.

2. The plants are well-established by mid-October.

5. We cover the beds with tarps.

6. Tarps are removed two weeks later.

Seeded by mid-fall, these crops survive winter and can be knocked down and killed in time for next season's summer-transplanted crops. The extensive residues form an *in situ* mulch through which the summer crop is planted.

BASIC MIX: Winter rye and crimson clover

The rye builds biomass, catches nutrients, and insulates the crimson clover to survive winter, and both species flower early the next season (end of May for us in zone 4b). Adding winter wheat, hairy vetch, Austrian winter peas, and red clover multiplies the diversity benefits and ensures superlative photosynthesis.

3. Rapid growth occurs the next spring.

4. We knock down by hand (or by foot), around June 1.

7. We transplant through the *in-situ* mulch.

8. Yields are strong with no machines or exposed soil. We pull only a handful of weeds from this 6,000-square-foot plot.

SPRING COVER CROPS

1. We seed peas and oats in April.

2. Crop is flowering and ready to be knocked down by mid-June.

5. We rake the pea and oat mulch into the paths.

6. We direct-seed the beds (here to storage radishes).

Planted as soon as the ground thaws, these crops establish quickly in cool weather and flower in late spring or early summer, when they can be easily killed and raked aside for direct seeding.

BASIC MIX: Peas and oats

Oats build biomass and act as a nurse crop for the nitrogen-fixing peas, supporting them as they grow. We also harvest and sell the pea tendrils. Both species flower at the same time (early June for us) and are easily knocked down, smothered, and raked into the paths to expose the beds for direct seeding. Since the crop will be killed early in the summer, allowing weeds to grow in this mix can add valuable diversity! Nature does not recognize the concept of a "weed" and benefits from all plant diversity. Just make sure to mow or tarp before viable seeds are set.

3. We knock down the peas and oats to facilitate tarping.

4. We tarp the beds.

7. Radish crop is looking good.

SUMMER COVER CROPS

Planted once the soil warms in late spring, these crops grow vigorously in warm weather, outcompeting weeds and generating large amounts of biomass before dying back with frost.

BASIC MIX: Sorghum-Sudan grass and sunn hemp

These heat-loving powerhouses produce incredible amounts of biomass and can grow to over eight feet tall. They will increase root depth and total production if they are cut or grazed periodically, and they die with the first hard frost, allowing for easy planting the following spring. To spice things up, try adding other heat-loving crops, like cowpeas, millet, buckwheat, and subterranean clover to the mix, but be ready to graze or mow before any of these set seed. Cover crops like buckwheat or millet can readily reseed themselves, and potentially become a weed for subsequent crops.

A diverse summer cover-crop cocktail pumps carbon into the soil and hosts a party for all manner of organisms.

FALL COVER CROPS

Planted in early fall, these crops establish quickly in cool weather and die back in the cold of winter, allowing for early spring planting and direct seeding.

BASIC MIX: Peas, oats, and forage radish

This mix is the same as our spring cover crop but with the addition of radishes. Sometimes called "tillage radish," these daikon relatives open up deep channels with their vigorous taproots, breaking up compaction and improving drainage and tilth. All three crops establish well if planted by early September (here in zone 4b), and they winterkill when lows hit about 10°F (–12°C). With the cold of winter as a reliable way to kill them, we can add any array of cold-sensitive crops to the mix, including tender barley varieties, fava beans, berseem clover, subterranean clover, or any other plants that don't survive a winter in our climate.

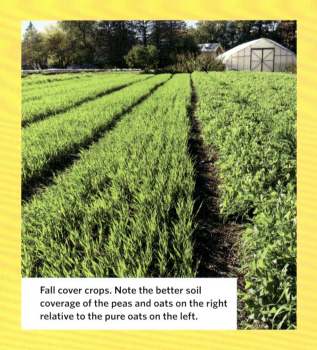

Fall cover crops. Note the better soil coverage of the peas and oats on the right relative to the pure oats on the left.

Seasonal Observations

I try to arrange the crop plan such that any beds that will be cover-cropped in the spring can be planted the preceding fall so that there is living growth through winter. Though largely dormant, these plants hold their relationships with soil organisms through the cold months and hit the ground running as soon as the thaw begins. Spring-planted crops, on the other hand, require the bed to be plantable, and thus relatively free of living growth as winter ends. If we are going to devote valuable spring bed space to cover crops, we may as well get the added benefit of living winter cover beforehand as well as eliminate the bed prep and planting required during the busy months of spring. The only exception is when a summer crop needs to be direct seeded, which is far easier after a spring crop of peas and oats than after an overwintered cover crop like winter rye.

An allelopathic effect follows the termination of certain crops, reducing seed germination for a period of up to several weeks. This effect can either be a blessing or a curse, depending on what's next in your crop plan. The allelopathy of winter rye is well-known, and transplanting through a thick *in situ* mulch of overwintered rye can lead to near-weedless beds for the rest of the season. Attempting to direct seed a crop immediately after winter rye, on the other hand, can give poor results.

The benefits of overwintered cover crops like rye are often worth the additional crop plan constraints. Maintaining living roots through the winter holds soil structure and supports a vast array of soil organisms. Of special note are the mycorrhizal relationships that are preserved into the next season, as described in chapter 2. Without this fungal bridge, the roots of the next year's crop start out naked and lonely while the mycorrhizal network recovers from a period of famine.

For climates with mild winters, cash crops can provide year-round photosynthesis and living fungal connections. In colder climates, however, not many vegetable species survive the winter. Notable exceptions are garlic and hardy biennial crops, like parsnips, carrots, beets, chard, and onions. Though typically grown as annuals, these crops can assist in the preservation of soil life when overwintered for seed production. Even for avid seed savers, however, it is unlikely that vegetable species will fully cover the soil with living growth through northern winters. Cover crop species, especially varied mixes of grasses and legumes, enable a level of photosynthesis, diversity, and soil coverage that is not possible with vegetables alone.

Multicropping

A simple way to increase photosynthesis, diversity, and soil coverage all at once is to grow more than one type of crop in one place. This stacking of functions to increase net productivity can take various names and forms: interplanting, undersowing, companion planting, interseeding, or multicropping. In a broader sense, alley cropping, silvopasture, livestock integration, and perennial polycultures are all forms of multicropping as well, though they are less commonly associated with vegetable production. One of the multicropping combinations with the longest track record is the "Three Sisters" mix of corn, squash, and beans — a version of the *milpa* agricultural system developed by indigenous peoples of the Americas, mentioned in chapter 2.

Many commercial farmers dismiss the idea of multicropping because it complicates field management, especially if mechanization is involved. Concerns around plant spacing, harvest windows, and crop rotation are multiplied when there is more than one crop per bed. While some may find this daunting, I see it as an opportunity to increase soil health with nothing but some extra planning! The no-till farmer is used to replacing mechanical simplicity with biological complexity, so why not carry this forward with multicropping?

With careful timing and spacing, a multicropped bed can achieve higher productivity than either of its monocropped counterparts.

Community Thinking

An important reality to keep in mind — and one that is often used to discredit the idea of multicropping — is that while more than one crop increases *net* productivity for a bed, it generally does not increase the yield of each crop relative to a bed with only that crop. For instance, a bed interplanted with carrots and lettuce heads may yield 300 pounds of carrots (sold for $600) and 200 lettuce heads (sold for $400), while a single-cropped bed would yield either 400 lettuce heads or 400 pounds of carrots (sold for $800 in either case). Together there is greater production value ($600 + $400 = $1,000) than either of the mono-cropped beds alone ($800). As with ecosystem health, thinking in terms of communities yields better results than focusing on individual species.

Care must be taken to ensure multicropped plants are not overcrowded. While productivity may increase by packing in a diversity of plants, lack of airflow and competition for light, water, and nutrients can lead to disease and stunted growth. Intensive spacing is great for soil health, but there are limits to what will yield a marketable crop.

When spacing two different crops in a bed, start with the average spacing for the two crops. For example, if lettuce heads are planted 12 inches between rows, and kale is spaced 18 inches between rows, interplanting lettuce and kale rows at 15 inches is a good place to start. In my limited experience, spacing can actually be slightly closer with no adverse effects, since dissimilar plants access resources in different ways. With careful observation over a couple of seasons, distance between plants can be adjusted to fill every last bit of bed space without reducing the quality of the harvests.

Multicropped bed of tomatoes, beets, and sweet alyssum. Diversity increases net productivity and resistance to pests.

Multicrop Combinations

I am relatively new to multicropping and am still experimenting with different combinations and sequences of crops. I am convinced, however, that the benefits of increased diversity and productivity can outweigh the additional management required. To keep the planning, management, and harvesting from getting too complicated, I find it useful to divide crops into two categories when planning a multicrop combination:

Widely Spaced, Large, or Slow-Growing Plants

- Tomatoes
- Peppers
- Eggplant
- Ginger
- Turmeric
- Brussels sprouts
- Kale
- Squash
- Cucumbers

Closely Spaced, Small, or Fast-Growing Plants

- Lettuce heads
- Chicories
- Bok choy
- Salad turnips
- Radishes
- Scallions
- Salad greens
- Cilantro
- Parsley
- Sweet alyssum
- Clover

Bok choy and salad turnips planted on the shoulders of cucumber beds provide photosynthesizing soil coverage (and extra revenue).

Escarole provides spring soil coverage while peppers establish.

Plants that are small and fast-growing pair well with slow-growing crops that eventually need more space. Growing herbs or greens on the shoulders of trellised tomato or cucumber beds is an easy companion planting.

The trick is to find the combinations that make the most of time and space. For example, there is not enough time for us to grow a full bed of escarole before our first planting of peppers, so we plant early escarole down the middle of the bed and leave the shoulders unplanted. The pepper seedlings can then be transplanted and take root while the escarole sizes up. By the time we harvest the escarole, the pepper plants are established and ready to utilize the extra bed space.

Not all the plants in a multicropped bed have to be cash crops. It often makes sense to undersow to a non-cash crop so that the undersown plants' needs for sun, water, or nutrients are not primary concerns. Low-growing clover is a natural choice for this application, and there are other low-growing plants that offer different benefits. Sweet alyssum is a short member of the Brassicaceae family that flowers continually over a long period. Its nectar is especially attractive to parasitic braconid wasps, so we interplant it in-row with tomatoes (see photo on previous page), which can suffer from hornworms that the wasps parasitize.

A healthy ecosystem provides its own pest control. Here a tomato hornworm has been parasitized by a braconid wasp.

Kale is nonmycorrhizal, so it is undersown to parsley, which serves as a fungal host plant.

Working with Mycorrhizal Fungi

Multicropping is a great way to increase and support populations of mycorrhizal fungi. As discussed in chapter 2, there are certain species of vegetables that do not partner with mycorrhizae, and fungal populations suffer when no host plants are present. Pairing these nonhosts (primarily plants in the cabbage and beet families; see list on page 19) with fungi-friendly partners sustains the mycorrhizal web for the plants that follow. Undersowing kale, cabbage, and Brussels sprouts to clover or other fungal host plants has benefits beyond soil coverage and weed suppression.

The value of plant diversity multiplies underground. The soil organisms that thrive with one species of plant may not thrive with another. Other organisms may depend on the intermingling of differing rhizospheres. Like the center of a Venn diagram, there are sweet spots of overlapping communities that rely on the diversity of plant life. We have seen that the whole is greater than the sum of the parts, and as we add diversity to a system, its overall health increases accordingly.

Beds of perennial flowers make the farm attractive to people as well as to beneficial insects.

Hedgerows and Other Beneficial Plantings

Growing annuals will never achieve the photosynthetic potential of perennial polycultures — so why not integrate both? Hedgerows and other beneficial plantings add numerous benefits to a farm, including:

Sanctuary for underground diversity. Perennial habitat for soil organisms bolsters underground diversity that spills over into adjacent vegetable beds.

Habitat for beneficial insects. Hedgerows provide food sources and habitat for pollinators and natural predators.

Economic diversity. Beneficial plants can also be cash crops, including berries, tree fruit, cut flowers, herbs, and medicinals.

Wind protection. A hedgerow provides significant wind protection for a distance at least five times its height. This reduces drying out and buffeting of nearby crops and lowers the risk of dust and erosion.

Shade for workers. Easy access to shade from trees and shrubs throughout the farm reduces sun fatigue and increases human productivity.

Visual markers. Hedgerows or perennial strips divide the farm visually into sections or plots. This definition facilitates planning and workers' understanding of farm layout.

Privacy. The visual privacy of hedgerows creates a more intimate work environment and a "secret garden" appeal for both customers and workers. Most animals also feel more at ease in a landscape with objects taller than they are. There is instinctual comfort in working close to a hedgerow or tree line rather than a wide-open field.

Beauty. A farm full of flowering plants is pleasant to the senses and attracts customers and workers. The business of farming makes little sense to me if it does not increase the beauty of the land.

Choosing Beneficials

Beneficial planting comes in many different forms, although I prefer to think of them all as one practice. Hedgerows separate fields with lines of woody perennials. Insectary strips focus on herbaceous flowering plants that feed pollinators and natural predators. Beetle banks create overwintering habitat for these particular friends. Field borders outline the farm with native diversity. Flowering cover crops bring insect food and habitat into the fields as part of the crop rotation. A given planting can incorporate any or all of these elements, depending on the goals of the farmer and the space allotted.

When choosing plants for a beneficial installation, consider the following characteristics:

Native region. It stands to reason that the plants that coevolved with the organisms of a region are best suited to support and enhance their populations. Native plants do well without fertilizer, irrigation, or pampering, as they have for millions of years. Flowering plants native to your region can be found through the Xerces Society for Invertebrate Conservation (see Bibliography, page 226).

Cold-hardiness. Perennials are not perennial everywhere. Make sure your plants are hardy enough to survive the winter in your climate.

Size at maturity. The types of plants in your hedgerow will determine its eventual dimensions. Most shrubs are about as wide as they are tall, so don't plant a 10-foot-tall shrub where you want a 5-foot-wide hedgerow unless you plan to prune regularly. It is also easy to space plants too closely when they are small. Plan the spacing based on the mature sizes of the plants, and use a measuring tape to ensure accuracy when planting.

Bloom period. For an insect-friendly mix, choose flowering plants with overlapping bloom periods that span as much of the year as possible. Ensuring a constant food supply is the best way to build insect populations naturally.

Below are some recommended plants for perennial hedgerows. All of these selections grow well in the northeastern United States, but many of them are native to much larger regions of North America or the world. Some genera contain a number of recommendable species (denoted by *spp.* after the genus name). Choose your own mix based on what's native to your region, or based on the criteria that you want to prioritize. Just remember: diversity and abundance!

All of the plants listed here (in order of bloom) are excellent magnets for beneficial insects, but also note that many yield marketable harvests of fruit, flowers, or medicinals. While I believe hedgerows make sense even without direct resale value, why not earn some revenue from them as well?

Tall Shrubs (8 to 15 feet tall)

Black haw (*Viburnum prunifolium*)

Buttonbush (*Cephalanthus occidentalis*)

Dwarf and semidwarf fruit trees
(*Prunus* spp., *Malus* spp., *Pyrus* spp.)

Elderberry (*Sambucus canadensis*)

Hazelnut (*Corylus americana*)

Nanking cherry (*Prunus tormentosa*)

Ninebark (*Physocarpus opulifolius*)

Short Shrubs (3 to 6 feet tall)

Chokeberry (*Aronia melanocarpa*)

Haskap (*Lonicera caerulea*)

Highbush blueberry (*Vaccinium corymbosum*)

New Jersey tea (*Ceanothus americanus*)

Shrubby cinquefoil (*Potentilla fruticosa*)

Meadowseet, Steeplebush (*Spiraea* spp.)

Summersweet (*Clethra alnifolia*)

Wild raisin (*Viburnum nudum* var. *cassinoides*)

Herbaceous Perennials (1 to 6 feet tall) — listed in approximate order of bloom

Crocus (*Crocus* spp.)

Daffodil (*Narcissus* spp.)

Golden alexanders (*Zizia aurea*)

Coreopsis (*Coreopsis* spp.)

Yarrow (*Achillea millefolium*)

Culver's root (*Veronicastrum virginicum*)

Milkweed (*Asclepias* spp.)

Mountain mint (*Pycnanthemum* spp.)

Nodding onion (*Allium cernuum*)

Blazing star (*Liatris* spp.)

Bergamot (*Monarda* spp.)

Giant hyssop (*Agastache* spp.)

Echinacea (*Echinacea purpurea*)

Rudbeckia (*Rudbeckia* spp.)

Joe Pye weed (*Eutrochium* spp.)

Boneset (*Eupatorium perfoliatum*)

Goldenrod (*Solidago* spp.)

Aster (*Symphyotrichum* spp.)

Native Grasses

Big bluestem (*Andropogon gerardii*)

Little bluestem (*Schizachyrium scoparium*)

Spreading tendencies. When in close proximity to vegetable fields, it's best to avoid plants with aggressive spreading tendencies. All plants reproduce, so don't get too hung up on this, but a quick search through online forums can reveal the level of wariness other farmers and home gardeners have toward certain plant species.

Shade tolerance. Incorporating shade-tolerant plants will increase the total productivity and diversity of the mix. This doesn't have to be complicated: if you include a wide variety of plants, they will sort out their hierarchy of shade-tolerance on their own, and new understory species can always be added later.

A multiyear study in central California showed that pest populations in fields with native plant hedgerows were significantly lower than those with weedy field borders. While these lower pest populations were observed over 500 feet into the fields, the measured impact of beneficial plantings was much higher closer to the hedgerow. At the scale of intensive market farming, it is easy to design for frequent hedgerows throughout the landscape to maximize their benefits.

At Frith Farm, our vegetable plots are 60 by a 100 feet (consisting of 12 beds, as described in chapter 4), and we have planted a strip of beneficial perennials between each plot. This means that no part of any field is more than 60 feet from a diverse perennial polyculture of beneficial insect habitat!

Beneficial insects thrive when offered ample habitat and a steady supply of nectar.

Integrating Livestock

Adding livestock to a crop plan is a great way to increase the diversity and net productivity of the farm. This type of enterprise stacking is a triple-win: soil life flourishes with the microbial contributions of animals, livestock benefit from the health and diversity of plants in fertile vegetable fields, and land use is maximized with multiple revenue streams from a single area. In addition, livestock happily perform a variety of tasks that would otherwise be left to human labor and mechanical equipment.

A pasture managed with intensive grazing builds soil faster and yields more than a pasture managed with mowing. This fact flies in the face of a chemical understanding of the soil, since the nutrients removed by the animals (and sold as meat) would seem to be a net loss for the system. But the biological interactions among soil, plant, and animal create a sort of symbiotic magic that feeds all parties at once. The minerals in the plant are biologically activated as they pass through an animal's gut, and grazing stimulates many plants to thrust their roots deeper, feeding microorganisms and improving structure.

Converting green living plants into protein-rich meat can be one of the most sustainable ways of producing food. Something is lost when we replace biological relationships with mechanical tools, like mowers. Indeed, when it comes to soil health, the mower is a poor substitute for the grazing animal.

Grazing animals do the work of mower blades and activate fertility cycles in the process. Livestock are movers of fertility and can be choreographed to rejuvenate thin soils or infertile ground. Poultry remove pests and rake out compost. Hoofed livestock agitate the soil surface and step in seed for good soil contact. Pigs help convert brushy areas to pasture and manage unwanted plants like poison ivy. Ducks can weed perennial gardens and control slugs. And as a bonus, livestock produce eggs, milk, meat, and fiber as they work!

Sheep require less acreage than cows and are easier to fence in than goats. This one is enjoying a cover crop of peas and oats.

Due to our small land base at Frith Farm, we primarily integrate poultry into our farm system. Laying hens are industrious scratchers and dust bathers and will readily compact and flatten beds without thick plant cover. For this reason, we rotate the layers around the perimeter of the farm, where they all but eliminate our tick populations.

Turkeys, on the other hand, focus their attention almost exclusively on the above-ground buffet and are ideal grazers, fertilizers, and pest controllers for vegetable fields. Since we raise our turkeys for Thanksgiving, their foraging season fits well with the organic standard that requires a waiting period of no harvests for up to 120 days after manure applications on a given plot of ground. Our turkeys glean leftover crops and graze and fertilize fall cover crops so the waiting period is fulfilled while the fields are dormant for winter.

Laying hens circle the farm and provide a nearly tick-free environment.

EMPLOYING PIGS

Pigs are happy to till up a field, but they can do more damage than a rototiller if they're left in one place too long. Following the principle of minimum soil disturbance, pigs are best kept to shrubby treelines and field borders, where they do an excellent job at managing invasive or unwanted species and exposing overgrown rock walls.

Another caution about pigs is that they can pass internal parasites to humans. Since round-worm eggs can persist in the soil for years, I prefer to keep pigs well separated from vegetable fields. Pigs evolved as woodland creatures and can easily do more harm than good if integrated with vegetable production. Following nature's models bodes well for all involved.

Turkey on rye: grazing and fertilizing a cover crop of rye and clover

Multiplying Benefits

I have mixed feelings about importing commodity livestock feed onto the farm, even if it is organic. This feed represents the fertility of another region being shipped across the continent (or world). What is replacing the grain farms' fertility? What are the impacts of this large-scale transportation of feed?

But I believe in locally raised poultry and pork, and omnivores generally need to eat more than pasture can provide. And vegetable farms are used to bringing in fertility to replace the nutrients exported off the farm with the sale of crops. If we are going to import distant fertility to the farm, it may as well be in the form of animal feed that nourishes livestock on its way to the soil. Like dollars in a local economy, the more pit stops nutrients make in their travels around an ecosystem, the more the community benefits.

Fertilizers and Fertility

Diverse and abundant biological activity is the basis for health in all living communities. The optimal conditions for growing healthy plants are therefore tied directly to soil biology, which thrives when the soil is undisturbed and covered with diverse living growth and organic mulches. With the right temperature and moisture levels, the underground world becomes a teeming web of organisms eating, breathing, transacting, reproducing, and dying, all while pulling solar energy through the conduit of plants and nourishing their roots in return. This is a perpetual process of self-generating abundance.

One spoonful of healthy soil contains more organisms than there are humans on the planet. This incomprehensibly intricate community of living relationships, when in balance, leads to a regenerative ecosystem capable of supporting more productive and nutritious plant growth than any fertilizer-based system.

So why do almost all farms rely on regular fertilizer applications? Most vegetable production replaces the biological complexity that generates natural fertility with imported fertilizer mechanically mixed into the soil. The yields of this linear system are high at first, as the leftover soil biology remains active. But after years of soil disturbance, inadequate coverage, and meager photosynthesis, crops become less productive; less resilient to pests, disease, and drought; and less nutritious, no matter how much fertilizer is applied.

Degraded soil not only fails to generate its own fertility, it also lacks the life to make the most of applied organic fertilizers, which rely on intermediate biological processes to convert nutrients into forms that are available to plants. The rational response to these observations is not to keep applying more fertilizer but to focus on the self-generating fertility of undisturbed soils covered in a diversity of living plants.

There is no way around the fact that harvested crops remove nutrients from the soil, and these nutrients must be replaced if harvests are to be sustainable long-term. Luckily for us, healthy soil is designed to create carbon and nitrogen out of thin air. Even without legumes, plants and soil organisms working together can funnel carbon into the soil and fix all the nitrogen necessary for plant growth, as described in chapter 2.

This leaves the other plant minerals to worry about, such as phosphorus, potassium, calcium, magnesium, sulfur, and others, that plants do not access as readily via the atmosphere. Harvesting some crops, like tomatoes and peppers, can remove 50 or more pounds of phosphorus from an acre of soil. Celery can remove as much as 400 pounds of potassium.

One shortcoming of chemical agriculture is its failure to consider the immense nutrient resources already present in most agricultural soils. These

COMPOST TEAS AND IMOs

I usually focus on creating the optimal *conditions* for healthy soil biology, and trust that microbial life will find its way into the soil on its own. Build it and they will come. Adding soil organisms directly, however, can hasten the process of soil rejuvenation.

Dr. Elaine Ingham is an authority on brewing compost teas and assessing biological soil health with a microscope. She founded Soil Food Web Inc., which teaches and promotes the most effective ways to get the biology back into our soils. I would encourage any farmer concerned with the lack of life in their soil to look into Dr. Ingham's work.

Another approach to adding soil biology is the use of indigenous microorganisms (IMOs), foundational to Korean Natural Farming (KNF). KNF is a system of farming, founded by Cho Han Kyu in the 1960s, that focuses on plant health through fostering soil biology. IMOs are harvested from different parts of the landscape and cultivated for application on cropland. I have no direct experience with these methods, but the success stories I've read and heard from other farmers are convincing.

Whatever name it goes by, a practice that increases the life of the soil is a move in the right direction.

reserves are usually considered "unavailable" and are dismissed without further thought. By fostering a vibrant living soil ecosystem, however, these pools become more accessible to plants. Consider, as an example, the fact that most agricultural soils contain between 25,000 and 150,000 pounds of potassium per acre. The average removal rate of potassium in harvested crops is anywhere from 50 to 400 pounds per acre. There is a lot of extra potassium just hanging out that can be made more available given the right biological conditions.

That said, we do not want to deplete the soil, even at a very slow rate, so adding back the minerals that we remove with crop harvests makes sense. In a perfect world, we would cycle all nutrients on the farm and add back what was removed with crops by applying the manure of the animals who ate them. I joke about CSA customers trading in a bucket of humanure when they pick up their vegetables each week. While this may sound ridiculous, soils of China were kept productive for thousands of years partly because the farmers built attractive outhouses along the road to entice travelers to leave behind some valuable fertility. But alas, the world is far from perfect — and humanure is prohibited in organic production — so we must find less cyclic alternatives to replace the nutrients exported off the farm with crop sales.

There are various organic fertilizers and soil amendments on the market, and they generally fall into three categories:

1. Mined resources, such as greensand, rock phosphate, or langbeinite
2. Byproducts of industrial processes, such as fish meal, blood meal, or feather meal
3. Farmed or foraged products, such as alfalfa meal, soybean meal, or seaweed

There are issues of sustainability associated with each of these categories, but their function is necessary: as long as we export nutrients off the farm in the form of food, we eventually need to import minerals back in some form. From an environmental perspective, the best inputs are almost always the ones that are the most local and the least processed, such as manure, compost, leaves, or straw. In addition to providing minerals, these materials add organic matter and can protect the soil and suppress weeds in the form of mulch. Given the multiple benefits of local biomass, it makes sense to use these materials to meet mineral needs before turning to those that are mined, processed, and shipped to address any remaining deficiencies.

In most cases, compost is the first such local resource to turn to. It is usually easy to purchase, has relatively high levels of nutrients, and — if

CHEMICAL BALANCING

When thinking about minerals in the soil, it is easy to go down a chemical-balancing rabbit hole and lose sight of the biological picture. Whatever your soil test results, remember that long-term fertility comes from diverse and abundant life, not from a perfectly proportioned spread of chemicals dissolved in the soil solution at any given moment. Addressing mineral deficiencies can bolster biological health but should not seek to replace it.

certified organic — is likely to be free of contaminants and weed seed. Most commercial composters can give an analysis of their product upon request, so application rates can be matched to nutrient needs shown by a soil test.

Other bulky organic materials, such as leaves, straw, or wood chips, are less consistent, and their nutrient content can vary widely. Rather than stressing about how much of which mineral you might be applying, I recommend applying these materials generously as mulch wherever they are needed. An annual test of your soil can highlight any long-term accumulation or net loss of nutrients, and you can adjust your inputs accordingly.

Once certain nutrient levels reach the top of recommended levels (often phosphorus is the first to do so), it may make sense to supply other nutrient needs by applying a custom blend of fertilizers, rather than more nutrient-rich compost. Below is a list of common organic amendments that can provide targeted

nitrogen, phosphorus, and potassium in the short term. But remember, soil biology and living plants are what create fertile conditions in the long run!

If adding fertilizer to a bed, it is important to mix it into the soil surface. Otherwise, once wet, the nitrogen content can volatize (evaporate) and be lost. Fertilizer can be incorporated with a light raking, or in the holes as seedlings are transplanted. Again, I use fertilizer as a final touch-up to address any deficiencies left after generous applications of compost and organic mulches; I do not see fertilizer as the basis of soil fertility.

For addressing micronutrient concerns, I am a fan of applying seaweed. Seaweed is a local and abundant resource for us here in Maine, and even for farms farther from the coast I think it is a valuable soil amendment. Farmers are more often culprits of sending nutrients downhill into the ocean, so to turn the tide and bring sea minerals back onto the land feels like a positive step. Seaweeds, such

Nutrient Content of Common Organic Fertilizers

	% Nitrogen	% Phosphorus	% Potassium	Availability	Notes
Alfalfa Meal	2–3	0.5	2–4	slow	
Bone Char	0	16	0	moderate	25% calcium
Blood Meal	12	0	0	rapid	
Cottonseed Meal	6	1–3	1	slow	
Feather Meal	12	0	0	moderate	
Fish Meal	6–12	3–7	2–5	rapid	
Langbeinite	0	0	22	moderate	11% magnesium, 23% sulfur
Peanut Meal	8	1	2	slow	
Potassium Sulfate	0	0	51	moderate	18% sulfur
Soybean Meal	7	1.5	3	slow	
Wood Ashes	0	1–2	3–7	rapid	raises pH; good trace minerals

as kelp meal, contain a broad spectrum of trace minerals needed by plants. These sea plants have also been shown to contain natural hormones that stimulate plant growth beyond their addition of micronutrients. To improve micronutrient deficiencies, apply kelp meal at a rate of 10 pounds per 1,000 square feet, but remember, generous compost applications and invigorated soil biology from mulches and diverse living plants will likely solve any issues with soil health.

Pests and Disease

Pests and disease are symptoms of ecological imbalance, and battling them directly can be counterproductive. Killing pests and obliterating disease in a biological context is like opening the refrigerator to cool the house; it masks the symptoms temporarily while perpetuating the root cause of the problem. Unwanted organisms are almost always signs of underlying issues with soil health, crop rotation, or biodiversity on the farm. You can use these signs to guide you in making improvements.

The first line of defense against pests and disease is the natural resistance that soil and plant health provide. Eliot Coleman advocates a "plant-positive" rather than "pest-negative" approach. Plants growing in soils brimming with microbial activity are less susceptible to pests. Roots tapped into undisturbed mycorrhizal networks fortify plants against disease. Rather than losing sleep over reduced yields, I choose to see pests and disease as explicit reminders to improve soil health and overall farm diversity.

Diversity above and below ground provides natural resistance to pests and disease.

To see an insect eating a crop and proceed to focus exclusively on killing that insect is reductionist, and ultimately self-defeating. Understanding living organisms as features within a pattern of ecological interactions enables us to address the root of pest problems without sinking into biocidal habits that exacerbate the underlying lack of life.

The hedgerows and beneficial plantings discussed earlier in this chapter provide pest control based on nature's model of diversity and balance. Natural solutions to pests and disease promote life rather than destroy it. Prolific populations of predatory and parasitic insects, encouraged through suitable habitat and a continuous supply of plant nectar and host species, help maintain a resilient system of checks and balances that prevent runaway pest infestations. Providing habitat for birds, snakes, amphibians, and other predatory vertebrates multiplies the stabilizing effect of diversity.

Low levels of pest populations are a healthy part of a stable ecosystem. When pesticide sprays eradicate insect species, their natural predators suffer. By eliminating their food source or host species, we unwittingly break the good guys' life cycles and leave the niche wide open for the bad guys to return. Common pests are usually able to bounce back much faster from these disturbances than the insects that keep them in check. Spraying poison on our food is not only disturbing from a health standpoint, it is ultimately counterproductive regarding its professed goal of pest control.

Row Cover for Short-Term Help

Transitory measures of pest control may be warranted for farms starting with poor soil health and low diversity. Physical exclusion, such as row covers (see box on page 91) or insect netting, can help tide us over until conditions of ecological stability are established. Over the years, I have found row cover helpful in protecting against populations of flea beetles, cucumber beetles, squash bugs, Colorado

Natural solutions to pests and disease promote life rather than destroy it.

Leaving crops like cilantro or mustard greens to flower is an easy way to feed beneficial insects as part of the crop plan.

potato beetles, and spinach leaf miners. I am convinced that the pressure from these pests is always linked to a lack of diversity within the farm organism, just as reactions to certain species within our own bodies are brought on by imbalances among our internal flora. With increased cover cropping, multicropping, beneficial plantings, and livestock integration, I have noticed reduced insect and disease pressure, and we are close to dispensing with row cover altogether.

A No-Spray Policy

Maintaining a strict no-pesticide policy can actually make management easier. Running a farm can be overwhelming, and the number of decisions to make and options to choose from can seem infinite. By eliminating entire categories of undesired practices from our tool kit, we can save time and avoid deliberation.

Adopting a no-spray policy is a case in point. When a flea beetle infestation wipes out an arugula bed, for instance, you won't waste time researching which organic pesticide to order, learning how to mix and apply it correctly, or confirming that the pesticide applicator license is up to date. You also don't have to worry about gathering your respirator and spray equipment. Instead, you can use the money you saved on spraying equipment to buy more compost to feed the plants so they can outgrow the beetles, to buy seeds of beneficial plantings to encourage natural predators, or to buy row cover to exclude the pests from the next planting.

Drawing boundaries on how we farm can help us stay true to our values and run a simpler and more focused operation.

FOLIAR DISEASES

Disease problems result not only from poor soil health, but also from crowded spacing, overirrigation, and lack of airflow. Three conditions are necessary for disease to thrive: a susceptible host, favorable conditions, and the presence of a pathogen. Chemical wisdom leads to focusing on eradicating the pathogen, while biological practices focus on bolstering plant immunity. While the soil life and root connections fortify a plant against infection, the plant also needs adequate space and airflow to make the most of its natural resistance. Increasing plant spacing, reducing irrigation, or replacing sprinklers with drip tape are easy ways to keep plant leaves dry and make conditions less favorable to foliar disease.

HARVEST AND HANDLING

Let food be thy medicine and medicine be thy food.
— HIPPOCRATES

Harvest is an exciting time on the farm. It is a celebration of our work and our interdependence with the land. Harvest festivals date back to the beginning of agriculture, honoring the miracles of life, death, soil, plant, air, water, and sun that sustain humanity. We don't have to throw a party with every bunch of kale we harvest, but let's take joy in the act of pulling sustenance from the earth. Harvesting also accounts for most of our labor through the height of the season. This chapter covers the ins and outs of harvesting and post-harvest handling, including efficient farm layout and workflow, keeping produce fresh and clean, appropriate harvest tools, and essential wash station infrastructure. The chapter ends with how we package, display, and deliver produce for our various markets.

Workflow and Efficiency

Permanent, raised no-till beds offer several inherent efficiencies. Crops from healthy, undisturbed soil have few blemishes from pests and disease and thus require little grading. Roots pull from the biological tilth of protected soils without forking or bed-lifting. Mulched paths and beds keep produce far cleaner than that grown on bare ground, and many crops need no washing at all. In light of all of these benefits, efficient harvesting begins with good soil care and field production practices.

More than half of our labor hours in a given year are spent harvesting, washing, and packing produce. We harvest four or five days a week from June through October, and even in the off-season we spend many hours sorting and packing storage crops. With so much time involved, developing a comfortable and efficient rhythm makes a big difference. The steps of our harvest and handling flow as follows:

1. Plan
2. Harvest
3. Transport to wash area
4. Unload
5. Wash — in one of four ways:
   - Leafy greens get dunked in a chill tank.
   - Roots with tops get sprayed by hand on a mesh table.
   - Roots without tops get tumble-sprayed in a barrel washer.
   - Fruiting crops usually require no cleaning but get wiped with a cloth if needed.
6. Drain/dry
7. Sort and pack
8. Store in walk-in cooler

The overall efficiency of this process can be maximized by focusing on smaller efficiencies within each step as well as the transitions between steps. The tools and infrastructure for each task largely determine how it is performed, so choosing the right array of basic equipment is a good place to start building efficiency. Throughout the harvest and wash process, the goal is always to maintain peak freshness and cleanliness. A big part of this effort involves minimizing handling, as harvested crops lose freshness with every extra minute they spend out in the warm air, and extra handling increases the risk of bruising or torn leaves.

The layout of the farm greatly influences harvest efficiency. Unnecessary movement is eliminated when the physical distance between each step is as short as possible. Close proximity of all tasks is somewhat inherent to the small farm, but there is almost always room for improvement. As discussed in chapter 3, colocating the wash station, walk-in cooler, customer pickup area, and storage for supplies in a single building at the center of the farm reduces travel distances on a daily basis.

Another way to shorten distances on a smaller scale is to optimize the spatial relationship between work and worker. Simple "micro-efficiencies" result from placing work as close as possible to the worker's hands, and at a height that ensures ergonomic motion. This is one of the first concepts I teach to new employees, as it is a very simple way to work smarter rather than harder.

The Harvest Plan

In addition to spatial efficiencies, effective harvesting and packing require a thorough and well-communicated plan. On Frith Farm, the order, quantity, and destination of crops to be harvested is determined the day before and summarized with the all-important Harvest Plan. This online document — available for any crew member to refer to — gets printed and posted in the wash station the night before harvest. The steps for how we compose the Harvest Plan are discussed in chapter 13. A sample harvest plan printout is shown at right.

The Harvest Plan is the central guide for all workers to refer to throughout the harvest. It communicates and records the following information:

- Order in which crops are to be harvested (top to bottom)
- Who is harvesting each crop (workers initial a line as they head to the field)
- Any issues to watch out for or notes on what bed to harvest from
- Total to be harvested of each crop
- How much of each crop is going where
- What orders have been packed (signified with a check mark)
- Overage harvested of each crop (written in; this amount gets deducted from the next harvest plan)

An organized plan keeps everyone on the same page and the harvest on track.

As the farm has grown, we created a position entitled "Wash and Pack Manager." This person runs the wash station during harvest and helps orchestrate overall workflow. Having the same person in charge each harvest day helps to establish comfortable rhythms and maintain consistent quality standards.

Freshness

The overarching theme of proper harvest and handling is "maximize freshness." If we were to follow nature's model, we would have our customers eat the vegetables right out of the field. The nutritional quality of living plants begins to diminish the moment they are severed from their connection with the soil. Aside from the spread of seeds, long-distance transportation and storage of living plant matter is not a natural phenomenon, but rather what humans have imposed in order to live far from their food sources. Our civilized world demands unnatural concessions, but we can hold onto the goal of minimizing time and distance from field to fork.

Freshness is a defining characteristic of good local food. It separates our vegetables with every bite from the industrially grown, homogenous produce shipped in to supermarkets from all over the world. An unwavering standard of quality is key to supporting the high prices and high praise of locally grown produce. Finding ways to maximize and preserve this freshness is a fundamental part of the harvest process.

A plant does not die with harvest. On the contrary, its leaves remain alive and photosynthesizing, actively losing moisture through transpiration. Decline begins the moment any part of a plant is removed from the earth and is hastened by high temperatures and low humidity. Therefore, the primary goal of harvest and handling is to get a crop to its optimal storage conditions as quickly as possible (see the table on page 161). For leafy greens and most root crops, this means storage conditions just above freezing and just shy of 100 percent humidity — approaching the conditions of natural dormancy. There are several common strategies that give legs to this journey:

Pre-irrigating. Irrigating leafy greens the day or night before harvest ensures they are at their perkiest. Drought-stressed plants will not keep well once separated from their root system.

Timing. Scheduling greens harvests for the early morning gets them out of the field before they soak up the heat of the day. The coldest hours of the day are typically just before dawn. The speed of harvest and length of transport can determine how long a crop is out of the ground before chilling. Market gardens have size to their advantage, as the distance from bed to wash station is often less than a couple

of hundred feet. Root crops and fruiting crops are less susceptible to wilting and can be harvested later in the day with minimal loss of freshness. We space out harvests over five mornings a week so that we are usually done by lunch and avoid handling crops during the heat of the day.

Shade. As a force of heat and desiccation, the sun's rays can rapidly reduce the freshness and quality of a harvest. I have seen totes of kale, chard, and lettuce reduced to mush when left in the sun for just a short time. This effect begins immediately when the sun hits a harvested leaf, and it should be avoided whenever possible. Keeping the harvest in the shade is a constant objective. Tall hedgerows, strategically located shade trees, and parasols on garden carts can all help this effort. Harvesting in small batches allows for more frequent transport to the wash station, and an extra trip partway through harvest may be worth the additional time.

Spraying with water. If a harvested leafy green crop has to sit before getting washed, spraying it with water will slow its evaporative losses. This spritzing has a minimal cooling effect, so it is only a stopgap measure prior to submerging the plants in cold water.

Submersion. To maximize freshness and storage life for leafy vegetables, the heat from the field must be removed as quickly as possible. The most common way to accomplish this is by submerging in cold water, as heat transfer is far faster in liquid than in air, and evaporative losses are halted underwater. A source of cold water is helpful here. Unless you're in an area with geothermal activity, the temperature of your well water will be very close to the annual average ambient temperature of your location. Here in southern Maine that's about 46°F (8°C), which keeps our well water cool enough to get most of the heat out of our greens before they go into the walk-in for further chilling.

Cold storage. A climate-controlled room is invaluable in preserving the fruits (and leaves and roots) of your labor. Getting a crop cold is one thing,

Ideal Storage Conditions and Approximate Storage Life of Common Vegetables

	Temperature (°F)	Humidity (%)	Approximate Storage Life
Leafy greens (chard, kale, lettuce, spinach, etc.)	32	95–100	about 10 days
Roots, topped (beet, carrot, celeriac, parsnip, rutabaga, storage radish, turnip)	32	95–100	up to 8 months
Storage Alliums (garlic, onion, shallot)	32	65–70	up to 8 months
Summer Fruiting Crops (cucumber, eggplant, pepper, tomato, summer squash)	50	90–95	about 10 days
Winter Squash	55–60	50–70	up to 6 months

but keeping it there for days is another matter entirely. I went my whole first season without a walk-in cooler, but if I could go back, I would give this piece of infrastructure higher priority from the start. The ability to extend the life of your food is well worth the investment. (See page 168 for a description of a walk-in cooler setup.)

Cleanliness

One of the most common pieces of customer feedback we receive is gratitude for the cleanliness of our vegetables. Clean vegetables not only look more appealing, they also reduce the time a consumer spends preparing them. This added value and visual appeal more than justify the work of washing. Methods to keep produce clean begin with production practices and continue right through storage and display. Here are a handful of strategies we employ to offer our customers the cleanest vegetables possible:

Keep the soil covered. When rain hits bare ground, it dislodges small soil particles that become suspended in the deflected drop. Low-growing leaves catch this dirtied water as it rebounds, and the fine dirt in the water clings to the leaves, which then require vigorous agitation in the wash tub to get clean. By contrast, when rain hits a cover of organic mulch, the soft plant material absorbs the impact like a sponge, and the water percolates gently down into the soil below. Thickly mulched paths also prevent shoes from kicking dirt up onto plants. Crops growing in well-mulched fields remain so clean they sometimes require no washing at all. In these ways, dirty produce is often a sign of inadequate soil coverage.

While no-till produce is rarely covered in dirt, it often contains some mulch debris and a variety of the benign insects that abound near the surface of healthy soil. We wash our produce partly to ensure we don't export too many earthworms, spiders, ladybugs, or centipedes off the farm.

Ensure proper plant spacing. Overcrowded plants invite disease. Overcrowding also results in slimy leaves and stunted roots, which must be picked out, slowing the harvest and reducing the crop yield. The solution is proper spacing (as described in chapter 5). We measure (rather than eyeball) transplant spacing, choose the right seeding plate or disc, and are ready to thin as needed. Staying on top of pruning and trellising of vining crops also helps.

Harvest cleanly. The best way to reduce the mulch debris entering the wash station is to train workers to harvest cleanly. A clean harvest is achieved by not letting hands or produce touch the ground, even if mulched. Smaller pieces of organic matter stick to wet surfaces and create more work for the washer. The extra care adds little time in the field and saves much time in the wash area.

Keep the water clean. Produce can only get as clean as the water it is washed in. An easy way to keep the chill tank water clean is to harvest and wash crops in order from cleanest to dirtiest. It so happens that the cleanest harvests are also the most tender and are harvested first thing each morning to take advantage of the cooler temperatures. For us, the order goes like this:

1. Baby greens (arugula, mustards, lettuce mix, spinach)
2. Full-size greens (Swiss chard, kale, collards)
3. Headed greens (celery, lettuce, bok choy, napa cabbage)

Roots get sprayed off or sent through the barrel washer, and fruit crops generally do not get washed.

Keep the wash area clean and organized. Our high standard of cleanliness for crops also applies to the wash station. Clean produce rarely comes from a dirty wash area. We make sure all washtubs, tables, and harvest containers are clean and in their place at the beginning and end of each day. It is the job of our wash and pack manager to oversee the harvest process and make sure the wash area is cleaned properly before the day ends.

Produce is cooled and cleaned by submersion in cold well water.

A pool skimmer is used between crops to remove floating debris.

A clean and tidy wash station sets the standard for clean produce.

Produce bags and closures are stored within arm's reach for easy packing.

Harvest implements (clockwise from top right): 1.75-bushel harvest lug, deep bulb crate, shallow bulb crate with harvest snips and knife, fruit-picking bag, 10-gallon Gorilla tub.

Harvest Implements

A basic set of tools enables a smooth and enjoyable harvest:

Knives. There are a plethora of specialized harvest knives designed for different crops. I have experimented with many of them and have found that it's best for every worker to carry a single multipurpose knife with them at all times. My favorite is the Victorinox serrated paring knife with a red handle and matching sheath. Inexpensive and extremely sharp, these knives work well for harvesting almost any crop. I give every worker a knife and sheath and make sure there are always extras on a magnetic holder in the wash area. There are few things more frustrating than time wasted searching for a knife on a busy harvest morning.

Snips. For harvesting flowers or thin-stemmed fruiting crops (tomatoes, eggplant, peppers, or cucumbers), I prefer a pair of snips, which are less likely than knives to cut fingers or damage adjacent fruit. We use the affordable long straight snip made by Corona.

Harvest crates and lugs. Some sort of vessel is required to transport crops in from the field. Where available, I recommend searching out used bulb crates. A byproduct of the flower bulb industry, these heavy-duty, UV-stabilized black crates are an amazing resource, and I have paid as little as $1 per crate at local nurseries. The demand for these crates has been increasing in recent years, however, and they are not always easy to find. Bulb crates come in two sizes; we use the deeper ones for root crops and the shallow ones for tomatoes.

In lieu of bulb crates, there are many types of harvest lugs that you can buy. My favorite is a green plastic, 1.75-bushel container with vent slits and drain holes. We use these for bulky greens like kale, chard, and lettuce heads. They're sold by most agriculture supply companies, and they can be nested when empty or stacked by rotating them 180 degrees. There is also a 1.22-bushel version that is a better size for heavier crops like roots or fruits.

Harvest tubs. We harvest the crops that might be damaged or soiled in vented crates, like salad greens, cherry tomatoes, or green beans, into solid Gorilla tubs. These flexible food-grade tubs have a handle on both sides and stand up to abuse remarkably well considering their light weight. With a rounded base and no drain holes, they can be dragged down the path without lifting. I find the large 10-gallon size to be the most useful.

Fruit picking bags. For harvesting trellised crops, like snap peas or cherry tomatoes, we sometimes use apple picking bags that hang on a shoulder and eliminate the need to bend over into a crate or tub. Both hands are free to pick, and the distance from vine to vessel is minimized. These bags can be emptied right out the bottom without removing them from your shoulder.

Garden carts. Transporting heavy crops from the field is best done on wheels. My preferred hand cart is the Large Garden Cart made by Carts Vermont. The large wheels roll smoothly over rough terrain, and the semipneumatic tires (available as an option) guarantee no flats. We use these carts extensively for all manner of farm tasks, not just harvesting.

Wheelbarrows. The wheelbarrow is one of my favorite farm tools. Making the most of gravity and the wheel, it facilitates — rather than replaces — human work. We use wheelbarrows for all manner of material spreading as well as for harvesting crops like onions and garlic. Harvesting right into a wheelbarrow cuts out the step of lifting crates and allows heavy loads to be wheeled down the paths rather than carried.

Lightweight tubs keep crops clean and portable.

Efficient transportation of produce requires the right containers and a good set of wheels.

Wash Infrastructure

It is easy to forget that a large percentage of the work of vegetable production happens post-harvest. Washing may not be as romantic as working with hands in soil and sun on skin, but the quality and marketability of produce depends on a significant amount of time washing, sorting, packing, and storing it properly. A basic setup of vegetable wash infrastructure allows us to perform these tasks efficiently and enjoyably.

Shelter. In our first season, we did all our washing in the shade of an apple tree, which worked well enough until the leaves began falling into the salad mix. To avoid similar challenges, and the discomfort of working in hot or wet weather, a wash station should be protected from the sun and rain. You can meet this need with a simple shed roof on posts. If you grow in a hot climate or are planning to do a lot of subfreezing winter production, an enclosed space with climate control, indoor plumbing, and floor drainage is a better, if more costly, way to go. I prefer

to take some downtime in the cold of winter, and in the other three seasons, our wash station benefits from the fresh air and natural light afforded by having no walls.

Drainage. Washing vegetables requires a lot of water, which must be able to drain away from the wash area to prevent creating a quagmire. Drainage can be provided simply by a thick layer of wood chips that elevates the work area above ground level. Local sawmills often sell chips made from debarked tree trunks (sometimes called "playground chips"), which are cleaner and take much longer to decompose since they contain no twigs, leaves, or bark. As the farm grows, surface drainage or a French drain (see page 43) may be necessary to steer water toward a lower point on the land.

Further along the spectrum is a concrete floor with integrated floor drains, which is necessary in an indoor, year-round wash station. I prefer the ergonomics of working on a soft bed of wood chips as opposed to a concrete floor, but for larger

Clean food makes customers happy.

A barrel root washer processes about 600 pounds of roots per hour.

operations, or to comply with food safety regulations, concrete might make sense. One benefit of solid floors is the ability to use wheels on them, such as with food-grade carts for transporting produce or with wash and pack equipment (on casters) to allow for a flexible wash station layout.

Plumbing. Water lines are needed to supply the spray table, root washer, and chill tanks. We use the same 1-inch polypipe that we use for our irrigation lines, and since we wash in an open-air structure, we leave the pipes exposed for easy access and draining. Plumbing a four-season wash area in our climate requires pipes to be buried below the frost line (4 feet deep, in our area) and the enclosure to be insulated and heated through the winter. We avoid these complications (and associated costs) with a seasonal harvest schedule.

Receiving area. Vegetables brought in from the fields need a place to be set down. Ideally, they might be unloaded right into the wash tub or root washer, but an intermediate resting place is often necessary. This area should be shaded, easy to spray down with a hose, and located immediately next to the wash tubs, spray table, or root washer. Receiving tables reduce the work of bending over to put down or pick up loaded crates.

Spray table. A mesh or slatted table makes spraying off crops quick and easy. A hose and simple spray nozzle make bunched roots like radishes, turnips, carrots, and beets glisten.

Root washer. In small quantities, roots can be spread in a single layer on a mesh table or in a crate and sprayed clean with a hose. For farms that regularly wash more than 100 pounds at a time, a barrel washer is a worthwhile investment that gets topped roots very clean. Grindstone Farm in upstate New York has been making barrel root washers for decades and is the go-to source for small farms in the United States.

Chill tanks. We use 100-gallon stock tanks as our chilling vessels. Many farms install electric air bubblers in their chill tanks to help remove dirt from leaves, but I find that greens harvested from undisturbed, mulched soil come with little dirt, and a gentle hand swishing in the tank is plenty to get them clean. The chill tank is also a washtub and headed greens like lettuce, celery, and bok choy get their bases cleaned in the same water as they chill.

Salad spinner. A significant portion of the work involved in producing salad greens is in washing and drying them. Dirt and excessive moisture in greens reduces their customer appeal and shelf life. We started out with hand-crank 5-gallon salad spinners

Stock tanks make inexpensive wash tubs.

A retrofitted washing machine gets greens drier than manual spinners can.

A drain valve allows for easy emptying.

that are affordable and perfectly adequate for small-scale beginnings. A competent worker can wash and dry 35 pounds of greens per hour with this tool. Upgrading to a larger electric spinner, however, saved us much time and resulted in drier salad greens.

I highly recommend a DIY spinner made with a washing machine and a retrofit kit (see Resources for a link to kits and detailed plans). This DIY spinner increases not only work efficiency but also the quality and storage life of the product. Fitted with a timer switch, the machine can be left to spin greens while you move to other tasks.

Pack tables and scales. Work surfaces near the chill tank, spray table, and root washer facilitate draining, weighing, and packing of produce. Any type of water-resistant table will do. I aim for at least one 8-foot table by each wash tub, spray table, and root washer.

Portable scales ensure accurate packing and enable recording of yields. The economical digital scale with a 40-pound capacity made by Torrey is the preferred model of many small-scale growers.

Storage totes. Reusable plastic storage totes are great for storing vegetables in the walk-in. Most produce stores best at high humidity, and the lids on these totes hold in moisture to maintain ideal conditions inside the tote even when the air is drier in the walk-in itself. We primarily use two sizes of attached-lid containers, sometimes called "flip-top totes." Made of rugged food-grade plastic, these are easy to clean and stand up to heavy abuse. The totes nest when empty and stack when the lids are closed. While on the pricey side, I believe they are well worth the investment (see table on page 171 for details on these containers).

We use removable painter's tape to label the contents of each tote as it is filled, and we restock our CSA and farmers' market displays directly from the totes.

Attached-lid containers preserve freshness and keep the walk-in cooler organized.

Frith Farm walk-in cooler, with shelving for attached-lid containers. Note the painter's tape on each container describing its contents.

Walk-in coolers. My first walk-in is still in use and is a homemade 8-foot cube, insulated with 4 inches of rigid foam on every face. This is a great size for a new market garden but is quickly outgrown by operations much larger than half an acre. I find a good rule of thumb is to have 100 square feet of walk-in space per acre of vegetable production. The space needed obviously depends on the types of crops you grow and the markets you sell to, but I find this to be a useful starting point.

After one season with the smaller walk-in, I purchased a second in the form of an insulated shipping container cut in half. This 8 × 20-foot box is lined with stainless steel on the inside and comes fully weatherproofed, apart from the two ends. For about the same cost of building a structure of the same size, an insulated shipping container requires very little work to get up and running. I installed an air conditioner on one end and a door on the other. I heartily recommend this approach to cold storage for any small farm. Unlike most stick-frame walk-ins, this cooler is portable and rodent-proof, and it depreciates very slowly. A little landscaping effort helps the exterior look less industrial and provides shade to reduce cooling costs. We also use the side of ours as a projection surface for crew movie nights.

We call it "the walk-in drive-in theatre." Stacking functions can extend beyond food production!

Having two coolers provides valuable versatility. We set our smaller cooler at 50°F (12.2°C) for the summer, which is the optimal storage temperature for tomatoes, peppers, eggplant, and cucumbers (see table on page 161). This significantly expands the time window to sell these crops and essentially eliminates the issue of fruit flies.

Each walk-in is cooled by a window air conditioner whose temperature sensor is heated to trick the unit into cooling below its factory-specified minimum of 60°F (15.5°C). The tiny heating element is controlled by a digital thermostat which can be set to lower temperatures. A simple, easy-to-use version of this "farm hack" setup is manufactured by CoolBot and can be purchased online (see Resources, page 225). CoolBot temperature controllers have revolutionized cold storage on the small farm, as they replace the high costs and complicated maintenance of conventional refrigeration with a cheap and easy DIY alternative.

Controlling an air conditioner with a CoolBot is very straightforward and largely free of maintenance. I find setting the walk-in temperature in the high 30s F° (2–4°C) strikes a good balance between

A CoolBot module overrides the factory settings on a standard air conditioner, allowing it to cool down to 35 degrees F.

Onions prefer lower humidity than other crops and are stored in mesh bags to allow proper ventilation.

energy use and storage life. Air conditioner fins seem much more prone to accumulating ice if set to cool below 35°F (2°C).

The shelving and layout of our walk-in coolers is designed around the dimensions of our storage totes. This allows easy access to every tote in the cooler from a central aisle. Totes are labeled with their contents and the date packed, so looking inside a tote to discover what's there is never necessary. Overhead LED lighting is controlled by a motion sensor, freeing up both hands for carrying totes and ensuring lights are never left on by mistake.

Presentation and Delivery

The presentation of our produce is an opportunity to showcase the fruits of our labor and demonstrate the same level of care with which they were grown. Organization and attention to detail in our CSA or farmers' market display communicates to customers the quality of our vegetables. Appropriate packaging and transportation keep products fresh and easy for wholesale customers to inventory and display.

Keeping produce fresh while on display for farmers' market or CSA pickup can be problematic, especially when temperatures are high or humidity is low. Here are some basic techniques to help keep veggies from wilting while they are out in the open air:

Shade. Direct sunlight is one of the fastest ways to reduce freshness in most vegetables. Pop-up tents or other shade structures are a crucial part of any vegetable display.

Pre-bagged greens. Greens in bags do not dry out, and remain fresher than bulk greens open to warm or dry air. Excessive moisture in bags causes sliminess and reduced shelf life, however, so care should be taken to dry greens adequately before bagging.

Bunched greens in water. We treat bunched greens just like flower bouquets, and give the stems a fresh cut immediately before placing them in pans of water. This display allows the greens to take up water through their stems and remain fresher than if stacked in a dry pile.

Wet burlap. Covering greens in wet burlap or other absorbent material insulates them from the heat and maintains humidity to prevent wilting. The burlap can be rewetted as necessary.

Mist. Keeping a spray bottle of water handy for regular misting can help prevent wilting on dry days.

The care that goes into a market display tells a story about the care that went into growing the food.

Stack 'em high. It may feel counterintuitive to stack produce high during hot or dry weather, but the mass of larger piles actually helps retain moisture, and the outer layer of produce insulates the bulk of the pile from the heat. It is also a well-accepted phenomenon that the more bountiful a display is, the faster it sells. "Stack 'em high and watch 'em fly" is a common farmers' market refrain.

Packaging

A benefit of engaging in community supported agriculture is that packing time is minimized and much packaging material is avoided. For CSA pick-ups, we display produce loose in wooden crates and let members count and weigh out their selections. We provide rolls of 11 × 17-inch produce bags but encourage members to bring their own reusable containers to collect their share. Packing for whole-sale or farmers' market, on the other hand, often requires more time and packaging to facilitate transportation and sales.

I find that certain produce sells better at farmers' market when it is pre-bagged. While I dislike the extra packaging, the customers in my area seem to appreciate a "grab and go" shopping experience. Making them select individual carrots or tong salad greens into a bag reduces our sales. So we prepack carrots and salad greens into small bags of uniform weight. This also facilitates the checkout process, which is important since long lines can turn shoppers away. Wholesale orders from natural food stores get packed in larger bags. All packaging is stored on shelves directly above the pack tables and is labeled with its size and the correct weight of greens or roots that go in each. We use color-coded twist ties to designate which bags are going to which resale customer.

Produce Container Details

Container	Size	Empty Weight (lb)	Capacity — Roots (lb)	Capacity — Greens (lb)	Source
Harvest Tubs					
Medium	7-gallon	1.5	—	3–4	Red Gorilla USA
Large	10-gallon	2	—	5–8	
Black Bulb Crates	(inches)				
Shallow	22 × 15 × 7	~3	25	—	Local nurseries
Deep	22 × 15 × 9	~3.5	40	—	
Flip-Top Totes	(inches)				
12-gallon	22 × 15 × 12.5	6	50	6–8	Buckhorn
17-gallon	27 × 17 × 12.5	8.5	80	10–12	
Gusseted Poly Bags	(inches)				
Small	4 × 2 × 12, 1-mm	<0.01	1	—	Interplas
Medium	6 × 3 × 15, 1-mm	<0.01	3	⅓	
Large	10 × 6 × 20, 1-mm	0.02	10	2	
Extra-Large	12 × 8 × 30, 1.5-mm	0.05	25	6	
Mesh Bags	(inches)				
13" open top	—	<0.01	2	—	Harris Seed
¼-bushel	11 × 19	0.05	10	—	
½-bushel	15 × 25	0.08	25	—	
1-bushel	18 × 32	0.11	50	—	

An efficient delivery vehicle is no larger than necessary.

Waxed boxes are the container of choice to deliver bulky greens and fruiting crops. We label each box with its contents and destination. Tomatoes get their own special 10- or 15-pound cardboard flats, and cherry tomatoes are sold in pulp pint boxes that fit 12 to a flat. We encourage our customers to save all these boxes for us to reuse.

Onions, garlic, and shallots get stored in half-bushel mesh sacks, which comfortably hold 25 pounds each. Sometimes we retail smaller 2-pound mesh bags of onions, or we fill them with 1 pound of garlic and trim the top of the bag to a more attractive length.

Keeping packaging materials simple and consistent has helped us maintain efficiency in the wash and pack process (see table on page 171).

Maintaining freshness during delivery requires protection from wind, sun, and extreme temperatures. The open bed of a pickup truck on a hot sunny day (or a subfreezing winter day) is not ideal, but a refrigerated box truck is overkill for most very small farms (see The Hidden Costs of Scaling Up on page 187). We use a Toyota Prius to deliver all our vegetables. Tightly packed, it fits about $1,500 worth of produce, which matches our typical orders nicely. Fuel costs are less than 1 percent of the delivered value, and navigating and parking on city streets is easy. With the air conditioner turned up and some strategic cardboard blocking the sun though the back windows, the Prius keeps produce fresh throughout our relatively short delivery runs.

Whatever infrastructure and processes you develop for harvesting, washing, packing, and delivering, remember that freshness and cleanliness are what set the small local farm apart, and the quest is never over for new strategies to improve the quality and presentation of our food.

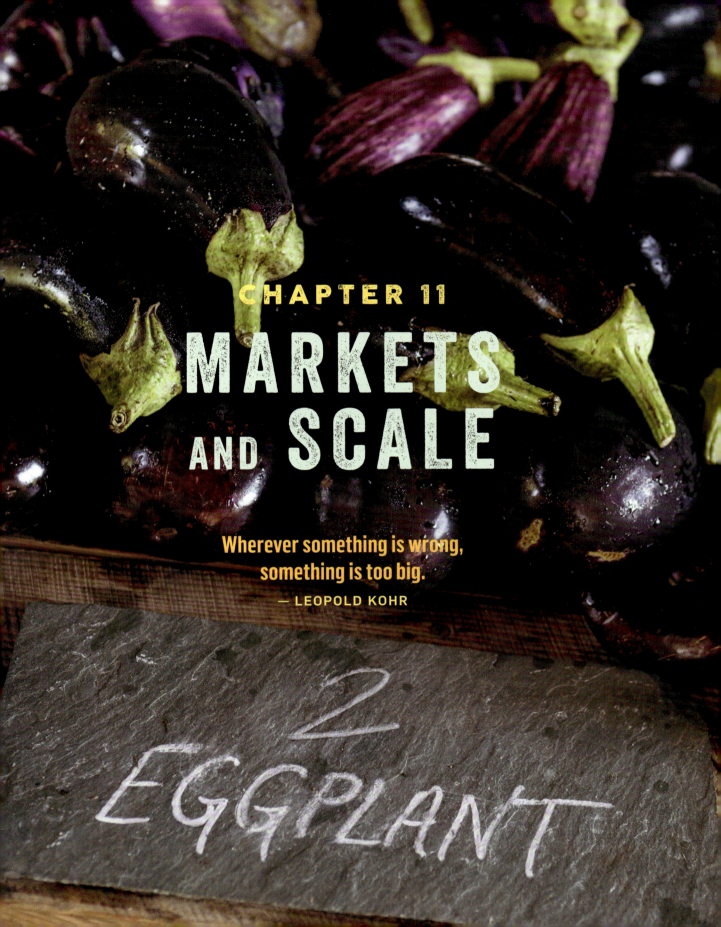

CHAPTER 11
MARKETS AND SCALE

*Wherever something is wrong,
something is too big.*
— LEOPOLD KOHR

2
EGGPLANT

Selling what you grow is the final step in the process of earning a living from farming. The quality and quantity of vegetables you produce matter little if nobody buys them. This chapter lays out ideas for establishing the farm as a vibrant local business and a source of something more than consumable goods.

Location Is Everything

Choosing the right location to farm is the first and most important step toward selling what you grow. There are many other factors (acreage, cost, taxes, building codes, privacy, etc.) that may tempt you away from populated areas, but the economic viability of market farming depends on its proximity to customers. As discussed in chapter 3, I recommend aiming to be within 10 minutes of a population center of at least 20,000 people. This single decision at the outset of starting a farm will affect marketing, employment, efficiency, and profitability for the life of the farm. It is certainly possible to succeed in more rural locations, but connecting with customers and workers will be more difficult, and driving will become a more significant part of the day-to-day operations. In the context of market farming, I believe the benefits of growing within a dense community outweigh the perks of being out in the country.

Food with Context

Markets for the no-till farmer can be about so much more than supply and demand. The value offered extends beyond traditional economic metrics. The farm offers nourishment and health; it produces food that is untainted by environmental abuse or social exploitation; it offers space for customers to bring family and friends to form relationships with the source of their sustenance; it fosters community in a time when this word is increasingly losing its tangible meaning.

In the early stages, successful marketing for the direct-market farm is as much about convincing local community members to invest in the idea of the farm as it is about trading products for their money. And who doesn't like fresh food or small local business? Every person eats, and most of us care at least somewhat about what we put in our bodies. The appeal of localized agriculture is universal and need not correlate with politics or demographics. Indeed, I love the mixing of different values, incomes, ages, and interests that happens on the farm. This little piece of land becomes a sort of common ground — a safe place for people to enjoy the agricultural connection that we all share. I believe the sense of place the farm offers is worth as much as the food it sells. Sharing the farm and its values with customers is as important as extolling the quality and freshness of its products. This is why we only offer on-farm pickup for our CSA (more on this later).

I have faith that we are slowly entering an era of ethical food consumption. More and more consumers want food that has a clean history — and are willing to pay for it. For many eaters, the taste of factory-raised meat is tainted by the suffering of animals and the pollution caused by concentrated feed lots. The flavor of out-of-season tomatoes cannot be separated from the exploitation of workers and the emission of greenhouse gases. Food is the very substance we are made of, and it is harder and harder to stomach the ills of society with every meal. The direct-market farm offers a clean-conscience alternative to the dubious and anonymous produce at the big-box supermarket. If you offer consumers a personal and honest food experience, they will not only pledge their loyalty; they will spread the word to friends, family, and coworkers.

DIVERSIFICATION

Adding new enterprises is one way to increase the customer appeal of the farm and its offerings. A wider variety of products attracts a wider customer base. Pick-your-own flowers and fruit are summer crowd-pleasers and bring people to the farm who would otherwise pass it by. Baby animals are perhaps the best marketing tool there is; people come from afar to point at the sheep, catch a glimpse of the baby pigs, or hold a day-old chick and often leave with vegetables or other purchased products.

The marketing value that diversification adds to the farm is difficult to calculate, but that makes it no less real. Certain enterprises have more value than shows up on a financial statement, as acknowledged with the concept of a "loss leader." Diversification also offers a number of other benefits:

- Diffused economic risk
- Stacking of enterprises to make better use of land, labor, and markets
- Ecosystem benefits of increased biodiversity
- Perspective to focus on enterprises with highest demand
- Potential for cyclical farm systems and symbiotic relationships among enterprises
- Attractiveness of farm to employees
- Refreshing nature of varied work

While pursuing diverse enterprises can add synergies to the farm as a whole, it is wise to avoid the pitfalls of hyperdiversifying, especially when starting out. As a beginning farmer I wanted to learn and try everything, and I overextended myself and the farm's budget my first year. Especially when starting at the bottom of various learning curves, I find it savvy to begin small and focused, then add new endeavors as time, money, and energy allow.

The human-scale no-till farm creates an environment that people find attractive. The noise, fumes, and dust of large machinery do not clog the air, and crew members are always around to answer questions or explain our work. Backyard gardeners understand and relate to how we grow, and they often learn new methods to apply at their scale. Paths and fields are sized for humans and carts and encourage self-guided touring of the farm. A rich diversity of flowering plants further entices visitors to explore. Trees and hedgerows offer shade on sunny days and support a vibrant community of buzzing insects, birds, and other wildlife for people to enjoy. Children play on swings and climb leaf piles, and families picnic in the courtyards. Many of our customers work full-time indoor jobs or live in neighborhoods with limited plant diversity and soil life, so this access to nature has real value. A healthy context for living and working is its own form of marketing.

The Local Market Trifecta

Direct-to-consumer sales form the foundation of market farming. Direct sales earn the full value of a product, whereas wholesaling through a distributor hands over much of the profit margin to a third party. I was able to grow Frith Farm using a common mix of overlapping markets — what I call the trifecta of local marketing:

1. Community supported agriculture (CSA)
2. Farmers' market
3. Local grocers and restaurants

There are synergies that arise from engaging all three of these markets. Farmers' markets get the farm's name out into the community and help attract new CSA members. For some people, a CSA share is too much of a commitment, while a farmers' market offers more flexibility. Local grocers and restaurants are a great catchall for surpluses that won't sell at CSA or market. These outlets are also forms of free advertising and can direct new customers to the farm.

Often our products at local grocers will inspire people to come to the farmers' market, where they get to know us for a season or two and then sign on as CSA members. The varied markets do our marketing for us, and after the first couple of seasons, very little additional advertising has been needed.

Community Supported Agriculture (CSA)

The CSA model is ideally suited to the direct-market farm. Through CSA, customers pay up front for a subscription to the farm — a regular "share" of its harvests for a season. Unlike many farms, we do not pre-box or deliver CSA shares but instead require members to come pick up weekly at the farm. Connecting customers to the place where their food is grown is a major part of our marketing and our mission. With the right location, getting CSA members to the farm adds more value to their experience than inconvenience.

The positive qualities of CSA are significant:

Guaranteed market. Since CSA members sign up and pay before the season begins, the farmer knows precisely how much produce has been sold before seeds are planted. If CSA membership is lower than desired, this too is valuable information, and alternative markets can be found or crop plans adjusted before the season gets under way.

Cash flow. The pay-up-front nature of the CSA model supplies the farmer with valuable cash during the lean off-season. If money is tight, this can save the time and cost of securing a loan or the challenges of making do without needed supplies.

Discounted price. CSA shares typically cost less than the same amount of produce sold at a farmers' market or in a retail store. By buying into the CSA, customers enjoy the freshest possible produce at discounted prices.

CSA members get to pick as many herbs and flowers as they please throughout the season (left).
An "Extras" table offers cosmetically imperfect produce that members can take for free (right).

Freedom from transactions. Once the initial CSA payment is made, no further exchange of money takes place for the rest of the season. Customers can focus on enjoying the beauty of the farm and the quality of its food without the distraction of transactions. The purpose of being on the farm becomes nourishment rather than commerce, pleasure rather than business, and sharing bounty rather than buying and selling products.

Member loyalty. On-farm CSA creates a connection between farm and customer that cannot be replicated by farmers' markets or restaurant sales. Members come to the farm each week, see the farmers working in all weather, watch the crops grow and die back, and experience the sights, sounds, and smells that shift with the season. The food they take home is laden with experience as well as nutrition. For some, this connection to the farm is reason enough to come back each year, regardless of the food they take home. A member is more than a customer. I encourage a sense of ownership for our CSA members and want them to feel that the farm is their own — and, in many ways, it is, for without them it would not exist.

Harvest flexibility. In a certain sense, CSA members are a captive audience. They pay up front and trust the farmer to grow food to their liking. This provides valuable flexibility for the farmer. If the kale is not looking good, Swiss chard can be offered instead, and no sales are lost. Unfortunately, this flexibility is often abused by CSA farms. Other markets are given priority, while CSA members are left with the motley assortment of produce that couldn't be sold elsewhere. Members soon catch on and don't sign up again the next season. The farmer points at the declining membership as a sign that the "fad" of CSA is passing.

To run a successful CSA, it is important to resist the temptation to slough off second-rate produce on members while taking advantage of the flexibility with which vegetables are offered each week. We have an "extras table" for produce that doesn't meet our quality standards, and CSA members help themselves to these veggies without counting them toward their regular share items.

Shared risk. By paying up front, the customer shares in the farmer's risk of variable yields. This concept can scare some CSA members away,

A sign-in sheet helps us keep track of who has picked up.

however, and for me it is not a primary reason to engage in CSA. If it came down to it, I would rather refund customers than leave them feeling unsatisfied.

Pick-your-own flowers and herbs. With a regular flow of CSA customers to a farm comes the opportunity to offer herbs and flowers as pick-your-own (PYO) additions to the weekly share. We advertise that CSA members get to pick all the herbs and flowers they please throughout the season, and I have a feeling that many of our members sign up primarily for this perk.

CSA WITH CHOICE

Surveys tend to agree that the most common reason members drop out of a CSA is that it gives them too much of the wrong vegetables. Nothing

We put the same effort into our CSA display as into our presentation at farmers' market.

disheartens a principled consumer more than throwing out good food. To address this concern, we developed a system of CSA that offers choice, and our members say they love it. It prevents them from taking home what they don't want, and it offers us valuable feedback on what to grow more or less of. The CSA pickup works as follows.

Customers arrive at the farm and initial next to their name on the sign-in sheet. Vegetables are displayed in the barn like they are at farmers' market, but without prices. Instead, pieces of slate list how much of each vegetable counts as an "item" in the CSA share. Full-share members get to choose any 12 items; half-share members get 6. An "item" might be a pound of carrots, two onions, or a bunch of kale. If a member loves kale, they could take 12 bunches home as their entire share, or they can mix and match as they please from all the offerings.

We usually display between 15 and 20 different items to choose from at each pickup. The flexibility this offers has several significant benefits for both the farmer and the consumer:

Freedom to choose. A pre-boxed CSA share is bound to disappoint a fraction of members, as not everyone likes the same vegetables. Giving customers the freedom to make their own selections ensures nobody will be stuck eating (or discarding) food they don't like. This system offers the appeal of a farmers' market shopping experience within the structure and sense of ownership of an on-farm CSA.

Less waste. Farmers tend to like predetermined CSA boxes because harvest numbers are known in advance, with no uncertainty. The lack of waste on the part of the farm, however, means that CSA members end up throwing away or forcing down vegetables they don't want. Letting members choose what they take home limits consumer waste, and at the end of the day it is the farmer who deals with (and learns from) the unwanted vegetables.

Outlet for small quantities. It is difficult to incorporate small quantities of a vegetable in a predetermined CSA share. What if you have 50 CSA members, but only 30 heads of broccoli are ready? Within our system of choice, those broccoli heads are simply added to the offerings. It is fine if they run out because there are 15 or 20 other items to choose from. And we often save one or two enticing items with limited quantity for the last few hours of the pickup window, so that the late birds can get their worm, too.

Built-in feedback. The varieties and quantities of vegetables left after a CSA pickup provide information more valuable than any survey data. Take note: this is the produce that customers want less of. By recording the total harvest and the quantities left over, the farmer sees a precise picture of customer demand and can modify future offerings accordingly.

Offering CSA members choice presents some challenges. Deciding how much to harvest can be difficult at first. Plan on overharvesting for the first several pickups as members' preferences become clear, or be ready to go out and harvest more when popular items run out. The success of the system relies on not letting too many vegetable offerings run out during pickup. Latecomers should get to choose from as nice a spread as the early birds.

CSA is often associated with a lack of choice, and the imposed selection of vegetables can turn away would-be members. I initially wanted to offer CSA members *unlimited* free choice, meaning each member could take as much of every item as they wanted each week. Share prices would be based on the number of children and adults in the household. The response I got from customers was immediate and clear: they wanted a more clearly defined system. Individuals who ate a lot of vegetables didn't want to feel bashful about loading up each week, while larger families that normally bought a half share didn't want to feel like they were overpaying. Even with a sliding scale payment system, people wanted to know exactly how much they were buying when they signed up.

We adopted our current system of choice five years ago and have received incredibly positive feedback since. It defines the number of items in a whole or half share, but it gives complete freedom of choice within these limits. One of the best parts of any system of choice is the valuable guidance it offers to adjust what we grow according to the quantities and varieties that our members choose to take home.

Farmers' Market

Farmers' market adds valuable market diversity, and it's a whole lot of fun. There is a spirit of festivity that comes with setting up tents and arranging displays alongside fellow farmers and artisans. Live music, tasty samples, and multigenerational crowds add to the convivial atmosphere. While setting up, stocking, and breaking down can be exhausting, the market is a public celebration of the farm and its offerings. It is a venue for people to meet their farmer, learn about their food, and offer feedback and gratitude in a community setting.

While I consider us primarily a CSA farm, I see farmers' market as a natural pairing. Some customers are curious about CSA but are not ready to shell out for a season's worth of vegetables right off the bat. Farmers' market is a place for them to get to know us and our food before committing to a CSA share. It's also a way to meet new customers. All manner of people come to market who might have never heard of the farm. The advertising of the market works on the farm's behalf. And for some customers, the flexibility of shopping at market fits their lifestyle better than a weekly CSA share.

The one off-farm market we attend is our local town market, a few miles down the road, and we have shown up rain or shine since I started the farm nine years ago. At my first market, I made $83 and was thrilled. This was the farm's very first revenue and it was as if I had pulled it right out of the ground. Since then, we have grown our customer base and improved our selection and presentation every season. Nine years later, we regularly bring in between $2,000 and $3,000 each market from the same corner of the town hall parking lot.

Over the years, I have picked up the following tips for running a successful stand at market:

Presentation. The care that goes into presentation should be on par with the quality of the showcased vegetables. The market display is an opportunity for the farmer to communicate the level of care that defines the farm and its products. A sloppy, sparse display tells a story about how the food was grown, as does a clean and abundant one. Good food engages all the senses, and an aesthetically pleasing presentation is the first part of a delicious experience.

Socializing. Many customers attend farmers' markets for more than the food. They value a relationship with their farmer, and they appreciate when market interactions involve more than a rushed transaction. When possible, we bring an extra person to market to allow us to spend some time conversing, answering questions, and offering cooking advice while attending to the lines and restocking. I see these interactions as part of the value we offer at market and an important part of our job while there. Selling our produce need not keep us from being friendly.

Pragmatic pricing. Completing transactions can have a limiting effect on market sales. Every shopper has a limit for how long of a line they will join to check out. Pricing produce pragmatically is an easy way to simplify the checkout process. Consistent, round numbers make addition easy and reduce errors. We assign the same price to as many vegetables as possible. I find the $3 mark is ideal for many crops. Lettuce heads, kale bunches, and one-pound carrot bags are all $3 each. Squash and zucchini are two for $3, and roots are $3 a bunch. We even select market onions for size and sell them two for $3. Crops sold by the weight are similarly grouped with the same per-pound price. Whatever your pricing, keeping it rounded and uniform will simplify math

THE ON-FARM MARKET

Driving products off the farm creates a degree of separation between the consumer and the source of their food, and there is no reason why you can't set up your own farmers' market right on the farm. The roadside farmstand is a time-tested way to draw in neighbors and passersby. An on-farm market can be as simple as a few vegetables sold on the honor system or as a developed as a fully staffed farm store and cafe with value-added products and goods from other farms.

We used to load our entire market setup into a pickup truck.

A dedicated market trailer eliminates unnecessary loading and unloading of tents, tables, etc.

and free up mental space to respond to a friendly comment or question while checking someone out.

When setting prices, focus on what you need to make for the farm to remain viable. In my experience, almost all customers trust the farmer to set a fair price. I suspect that the few people who consistently question our pricing may prefer the selection and prices at a supermarket box store, and their expectations need not drive prices down. While I believe making our food accessible is a moral obligation for farmers, there are ways to do so that do not threaten our livelihood (see Food Access on page 214).

Shopping baskets. After watching market shoppers juggle and drop vegetables for many seasons, I finally invested in shopping baskets. I realized that many customers were limiting their purchases to

what they could physically carry. Now we have an attractive set of nesting wicker baskets with washable linen liners. These baskets improve the customer experience and facilitate larger purchases.

Dedicated trailer or vehicle. This is certainly not necessary at first, but as your market display and sales grow, a dedicated trailer or van for all the pieces of market setup will save much time and hassle. Unloading tents, tables, signs, and crates back at the farm is tiring and unnecessary. It also increases the risk of forgetting to repack vital items for the next market. Even with checklists and reminders, I regularly had to turn around for a crucial forgotten item like a scale or water bucket. A dedicated trailer greatly reduces the work and stress of market day.

ON FRITH FARM
KEEPING IT LOCAL

While we sell a lot of vegetables to nearby grocers, driving vegetables around town is not a practice I'm looking to expand, and I continually turn down potential accounts. Transportation of food is a defining part of our industrial ag system — and one that community-based farms can largely avoid. Driving does not enhance freshness or quality, and it uses more energy in the form of fossil fuels than is likely contained in the transported vegetables.

When I started looking for land to farm, I knew I did not want to spend more than a couple of hours a week driving. I settled on a smaller-than-planned property in a largish town. Nine years later, I am still happy with the decision, as all of the food we grow is sold within a 15-mile radius. The location of a farm largely determines customers' willingness to travel to it as well as the extent to which sales rely on deliveries.

Frith Farm Bulk Price List

ITEM	UNIT	PRICE IN DOLLARS	MIN. ORDER	ITEM	UNIT	PRICE IN DOLLARS	MIN. ORDER
Arugula	lb	9.00	2	Tomatoes, Cherry	pint	4.00	12
Beans, Green	lb	4.00	10	Tomatoes, Heirloom	lb	3.25	15
Beets	lb	2.00	25	Turmeric, Baby	lb	15.00	2
Brussels Sprouts	lb	6.00	10	Turnips, Purple-Top	lb	1.75	10
Cabbage, 1–2 lb each	lb	2.00	25	Herbs, fresh	bunch	2.50	none
Cabbage, 2–4 lb each	lb	1.50	25	Anise Hyssop			
Carrots	lb	2.00	25	Basil, Italian			
Celeriac	lb	2.00	10	Basil, Specialty			
Collards	bunch	2.00	12	Burnet			
Cucumbers	lb	2.00	15	Chives			
Eggplant	lb	3.25	10	Cilantro			
Garlic	lb	10.00	5	Dill			
Garlic Scapes	lb	6.00	2	Fernleaf Fennel			
Ginger, Baby	lb	13.50	2	Garlic Chives			
Kale	bunch	2.00	12	Garlic Scapes			
Kohlrabi	lb	2.00	10	Lemon Balm			
Lettuce Heads	head	2.00	12	Lovage			
Mesclun	lb	9.00	2	Mint			
Onions	lb	2.00	25	Oregano			
Parsnips	lb	2.00	25	Parsley, Curly			
Peas, Sugarsnap	lb	5.00	10	Parsley, Italian			
Peppers, Sweet	lb	3.25	10	Sage			
Radishes	bunch	2.00	12	Savory			
Radishes	lb	2.00	10	Shiso			
Rutabagas	lb	1.75	10	Thyme			
Shallots	lb	4.00	10				

ITEM	UNIT	PRICE PER	MIN. ORDER
Spinach (lb, 9.00, 2)			
Eggs	dozen	$5.25	12
Chicken, whole	lb	$5.25	none
Turkey, whole	lb	$6.50	none

ITEM	UNIT	PRICE IN DOLLARS	MIN. ORDER
Spinach	lb	9.00	2
Squash, Summer	lb	2.00	15
Squash, Winter	lb	1.75	25
Swiss Chard	bunch	2.00	12

All products are certified organic.

For farmers' market or farmstand sales, we multiply these prices by about 1.5 and have no minimum order.

Sales records. Knowing what sells and what doesn't is vital to shaping the growth of the farm. While a farmer gets a good sense of demand through simple observation, there is no substitute for quantitative sales records when it comes to crop planning and ordering seeds for the next season. To avoid the hassle of recording each transaction, we simply record how much of each vegetable is packed for market and how much returns to the farm. The difference is what sold, and we reconcile the calculated total with what comes home in the cash box. This recordkeeping adds little time to the day and provides valuable information that helps us continually improve our offerings.

Local Grocers and Restaurants

While not exactly direct-to-consumer, sales to local food co-ops, natural grocers, and farm-to-table restaurants are often included in the category, since no wholesaler or distributor takes a cut of the transaction. These sales can provide a valuable safety net to absorb potential overproduction. They also attract new customers to the farm when grocers or restaurants feature the farm's name in their marketing.

A roadside farm sign is a valuable first impression for passersby.

We first entered these markets by accident when we had unsold produce at the end of a farmers' market. We drove it to the local natural food store and asked if they wanted any. Nine years later, we are close friends with the owner and produce manager, and they are our top retail customer, buying almost $50,000 worth of vegetables each year. We have since developed similar relationships with several other establishments.

The cost of delivery increases with distance, but the value of the delivered product remains the same. The customer experiences no more value if you drove an hour to them than if you drove two minutes. This is a strong argument for selling within as tight a radius as possible, or for increasing prices for more distant customers. We make the most of delivery trips by setting minimum orders ($100) and by driving an appropriately sized, fuel-efficient vehicle (a Prius).

Our relationship with local natural food stores, in combination with our CSA and farmers' market, enables us to sell nearly every last vegetable we grow. What isn't sold at market gets snatched up at the next CSA pickup. When a bumper crop overwhelms CSA and farmers' market, natural food stores absorb the extra. This trifecta of overlapping markets provides flexibility and resilience and helps us keep our prices where we want them.

Spreading the Word

With the right location and mixture of markets, active advertising is largely unnecessary. Farmers' market brings the farm into the community and attracts new customers. Local grocers and restaurants help spread the farm's name and ideals. CSA members tell their neighbors, coworkers, and friends about their experience. Once the farm has a critical mass of customers, word-of-mouth can provide all the marketing needed. A recommendation from a trusted friend wins over a customer faster than any form of paid advertising. That said, spreading awareness of the farm takes some initial effort. These are

MAINTAINING AN ONLINE PRESENCE

Establishing an active internet presence can broaden a farm's community in remarkable ways. At a minimum, I recommend maintaining an up-to-date website with a summary of the farm's mission, history, practices, products, and markets. Beyond that, Instagram, Facebook, Youtube, mass E-mails, blogs, and forums are just some of the other ways to bring the farm online.

Few vocations are as photogenic as farming, and sharing photos and captions that depict our work is a great way to spawn interest and establish relationships that go beyond traditional marketing. Here are some tips for creating a successful presence on social media:

- Choose a profile name and image that are recognizable and specific to your farm.
- Write a one-sentence bio that includes the farm name, location, and what makes it special.
- Make a post at least twice a week.
- Focus your posts on what you are passionate about.
- Engage your audience by asking questions and tagging other users.
- Be honest and sincere, but don't use your posts to vent or complain.
- Link your online social media accounts so that each post shows up on all platforms automatically.

Even as you spread the farm's image and ideals online, keep in mind that social media is designed to be addictive. Creating firm boundaries around time spent online can help keep you rooted in the off-line world where food is actually grown.

the simple, low-cost techniques I employed to help build up a self-sustaining customer base:

Farm sign. A large, attractive sign by the road projects the desired image of the farm and its products to precisely the people who make the best customers: your neighbors.

Website. A detailed, up-to-date website portrays the farm at its best and provides relevant information regarding farm practices, products, history, employment opportunities, and more.

Social media. In this age of online networking, an active social media presence is an effective way to share what the farm is all about in an easily digested format.

Local news. Why not have local outlets do your advertising for you? A new farm in town makes a great local news story and should be an easy sell to newspapers, radio clubs, food bloggers, and the like. Almost half of my first year's CSA members signed up after reading a cover story about the farm in the free local paper.

Word of mouth. Word of mouth is a powerful advertising phenomenon that happens naturally all by itself. But it can also be encouraged. In the early years, I asked CSA members to help spread the word and even offered a "refer-a-friend" discount. Your core customers can be your biggest allies; they want the farm to succeed almost as much as you do. Giving them permission to evangelize on the farm's behalf can make them feel even more connected.

Third-party advertising. I see third-party advertising as a last resort, though perhaps necessary for more rural farms. Paying someone else to place an ad is more expensive and generally less effective than direct word of mouth, so I suggest making the most of the previous strategies before turning to paid advertising. That said, building an initial customer base may require a mix of all available marketing resources.

Market-Based Growth

The demand of local markets should determine what, when, and how much to grow. These limits are difficult to know when you're starting out; thus, the importance of starting small and responding to demand rather than pushing to increase it. The worst kind of waste is the unsold finished product.

Market-based growth is guaranteed within the CSA model. Customer demand is established (and paid in full) before the season begins, and production is planned accordingly. We offer an early-bird discount if members sign up by January 1, giving us an early sense of what to expect for the season. (This time frame also takes advantage of the holiday spirit, and we suggest that CSA shares make wonderful gifts!) Our choice-based system of CSA described earlier lets us zero in on specific demand for each crop and variety and to adjust our crop plan to suit.

A farmers' market functions similarly: whatever produce is sold out (or left over) at the end of the day provides valuable information that guides our growth. Farmers' market sales are far from guaranteed, however, so for us, attending market is as much about attracting new CSA members as it is about adding a revenue stream.

Building a CSA membership takes time, which works out well since building a farm does, too. I found that the rate at which I could establish beds and refine production methods synced up nicely with the rate of new CSA interest. With the few key advertising efforts described earlier, I was able to attract 40 CSA members my first year. From there, the CSA has grown organically with the farm, almost entirely by word of mouth. These numbers will vary widely with location and marketing, but as a reference, here is the trajectory of our CSA membership over the first six years:

- Year 1: 40 CSA families
- Year 2: 75
- Year 3: 87
- Year 4: 92
- Year 5: 103
- Year 6: 124
- Year 7: 144
- Year 8: 144
- Year 9: 156
- Year 10: 190

A farm's CSA growth rate is largely determined by proximity to population centers and their local food culture. We are located in a township of roughly 20,000 people and are 15 minutes from another town of 60,000. Farms in more urban areas will likely attract members quickly, while farms in rural locations might find that very few families are willing to pick up at the farm at all, so may have to depend on other forms of marketing.

By starting small and minimizing capital expenses, a farm can grow with demand rather than in spite of it. Market-based growth minimizes debt and overhead costs, along with the associated anxiety. Farming within known market limits assures products can be sold at full value with little waste. It is generally more enjoyable (and profitable) to feel relaxed and confident about sales outlets than to scramble to push overproduction on a reluctant market.

Whatever scale you farm at and however you market your products, I encourage you to see the exchange of food with customers as more than an economic transaction. Farms have the distinct potential to address environmental, social, and economic issues with a single holistic solution. The attitude with which we approach marketing and the growth of our business determines the extent to which we either perpetuate an extractive consumer culture or help create an alternate path. As idealistic as these thoughts may be, I believe farmers are uniquely positioned to lead the way toward durable localized economies and a sustainable future.

Frith Farm's very first CSA pickup

THE HIDDEN COSTS OF SCALING UP

Contrary to the gospel of economics, the profitability of market farming can actually decrease with scale. There are a number of risks and complications that arise as a farm grows, and the associated costs can outpace the increase in revenue. With new infrastructure and equipment come various built-in expenses that can saddle the farm with increasing overhead. I call these the hidden costs of scaling up, and they accumulate with each new piece of equipment or infrastructure:

- Depreciation
- Loan interest
- Maintenance and repairs
- Downtime for maintenance and repairs
- Additional storage space needed
- Additional training of workers to use equipment
- Increased liability and worker's compensation
- Decrease in worker satisfaction due to noise, fumes, dust, and safety concerns
- Less-efficient spacing to accommodate equipment
- Decrease in quality of work performed
- Additional marketing required to sell product
- Reduced price of products in order to move greater volume

Reduced overhead is but one reason to stay small. As described in chapter 1, farming at a human scale grounds us in community and leads to a degree of satisfaction and a level of care that are diluted as size increases.

Human beings are the only animals who have to work. . . .
Other animals make their livings by living.

— MASANOBU FUKUOKA

CHAPTER 12
LABOR

Vegetable production is one of the most labor-intensive forms of agriculture, and often labor is the least resilient aspect of a farm operation. Attracting, hiring, training, and retaining employees is no small endeavor and yet it largely determines how well a farm will run. This chapter presents the value of a healthy work environment, the pros and cons of different labor models, and the management tools we use at Frith to make the most of the farm's human resources.

Labor as an Asset, Not an Input

An asset is something of ongoing worth, while inputs are consumable. Assets are valued, protected, and invested in, while effort is made to reduce the need for inputs, and to pay as little as possible for them. What if we viewed the people who work the farm as social assets rather than labor inputs? What if we sought to maximize the farm's human engagement instead of seeing employment as an obstacle to profit that should be minimized? Mechanization has led to fewer and fewer people involved in agriculture, with far-reaching consequences. But there is an alternative approach to efficiency that celebrates the role of humans in the growing of food. Productivity and resilience can result from investing time, energy, and money in the farm's human resources.

I see a strong argument for saving labor — that is, upholding the value of human work — instead of investing in "labor-saving" technology and equipment. In a fully mechanized world, what is left for us to do? Is the human ideal to simply sit around and consume? We are biological creatures and require physical activity to stay healthy. Farming at a human scale with a minimum of machinery repairs the connection between growing food and burning calories. Humans are also much more adaptable and resilient than machines. Growing many crops in a small area is ideally suited to the ingenuity and versatility of the human mind and body.

Why make payments on equipment rather than work alongside our fellow humans? The money paid for machinery typically leaves the local community and supports an industrial system of mining, fabrication, marketing, and shipping that is fraught with environmental and social issues. Wages paid to employees stay in the community — and actually help create community through communal work. Personally, I find working with other humans to be more interesting than sitting on a tractor (though I know many farmers love their tractors). When farming on a human scale, work becomes social, and the lines between business and pleasure are blurred. The work itself becomes the purpose, instead of merely the means to an end.

The productivity of any system is restricted by its most limited resource. This is a useful notion in the context of plant ecology as well as labor. Workers are an intrinsic part of the whole farm system and are often its limiting resource. Even the best agricultural methods are of little value if there are insufficient hands to implement them. I find that the more people I employ, the more productive the farm becomes. Instead of looking for ways to eliminate labor, I try to find reasons to hire more. The joy of working with an energetic group of farmers goes hand in hand with the productivity and innovation that is inspired by this critical mass of human minds.

The scale and intensity of a market garden will largely determine the size of its labor force. By choosing to work by hand instead of by machine, the no-till farm increases the ratio of humans to acres. I've seen enough examples of success to state with confidence that two people can make a decent living from less than an acre of intensive vegetable production. I have chosen to scale up without adding machinery, and grow on 2½ acres with a dynamic community of workers. Energy and ideas coalesce when humans join forces in pursuit of common goals. In some ways, labor is the most vital living part of the farm. Abundance and diversity of life leads to increased productivity and resilience, and humans are a critical living element of the farm ecosystem.

There is arguably no other path toward sustainability than the integration of humans into biologically productive landscapes.

The Right Work Environment

Efficient work comes from a healthy community of workers just as good yields come from a healthy soil community. Efforts to create a fulfilling workplace are more effective than treating symptoms of poor work performance. Many farmers love to complain about employees, and we all have stories involving gates left open, seed packets left out in the rain, tomato plants decapitated in the name of pruning, or similar horrors of inexperience and poor training. Whenever I get frustrated with some such blunder, I remind myself that ultimately it is the farm's work environment that is at fault. As employers, we have the opportunity and responsibility to foster a

A healthy work environment allows for a degree of creative freedom.

Here Cricka loves carrots so much he dresses up like one to wash them.

positive, productive environment that inspires good work and employee satisfaction.

These are the elements of a rewarding work environment that we try to create on the farm:

A common culture. As humans, we need a sense of belonging in order to feel secure and comfortable in our work. This confidence comes from shared values and a common culture. A primary concern of ours when hiring is to ensure a degree of commonality among all employees. We encourage diversity while looking for applicants who share the core values we are working to uphold as part of our mission. If a prospective employee is not interested in eating local food, for instance, chances are they will not be happy at the farm and may even cause discord in the community.

A sense of purpose. Without understanding the big-picture trajectory of their work, people can wonder why they are doing what they're doing, and whether it matters at all. Work becomes relevant when we know the reasons behind each task and how it contributes, at least in some tiny way, to a better world. A good employer ensures each worker understands the context of their work and the value of their contribution. Without understanding our zero seed rain approach to weeding, for example, pulling small weeds from underneath a crop might feel pointless and tedious.

A structure of creative freedom. Few workers thrive on an assembly line. Humans have amazing creative ability, which is stifled when tasks are dictated too rigidly. On the other hand, a lack of organization or definition can leave workers frustrated or confused. We aim to provide a structure of well-defined tasks and expectations while allowing workers to figure out the best way to accomplish each job with minimal oversight. For example, I dictate that eggs are to be collected every day after work (and suggest an efficient manner of doing so), but I leave it up to the person on layer chores to figure out the time and techniques that ultimately work best for them. This freedom prevents micromanagement and opens the way for innovation.

Team spirit. Work is generally more enjoyable when it is tackled as part of a team. Humans evolved in tribes working toward common goals, and the camaraderie that comes from a group effort is irreplaceable. With this in mind, we always tackle larger tasks in groups, as the pace and the mood stay on track when a critical mass of workers takes on a laborious job. Even when working on individual tasks, a sense of team spirit inspires productivity and upholds morale. We encourage this sense of cooperation with a shared plan for the week (discussed in chapter 13) and by having each worker report back to the crew about individual progress.

Respect and recognition. Few workers will give their all if they are not respected and recognized for their efforts. Fair compensation is essential, but money is not enough on its own. Respect cannot be purchased. For the employer, listening and empathizing are as important as instructing and correcting. To ensure the scales are tipped toward appreciation, I aim to offer employees at least two pieces of positive feedback for each constructive critique. I think of this as a relational bank account to which every compliment deposits good will and from which every correction or request makes a withdrawal. A job well done deserves praise and gratitude, and proper acknowledgement builds the credit that pays off when improvements need to be made. A comment in passing or a one-line e-mail or text go a long way toward affirming the value of someone's efforts.

It is commonly understood that employees will choose a job in a positive work environment even

A brief morning meeting starts the day with a sense of team.

if it pays less than other, less favorable work. Any small-scale farm will likely pay workers less than they could earn elsewhere. And yet, many young people with high earning potential are applying to work on small farms because the compensation offered is largely in the form of meaningful work and a high quality of life.

Communication

Good communication is the lifeblood of a working community and brings the attributes of a positive work environment to life. A lack of clear and frequent communication leads to disorganization, frustration, and apathy. Below are some communication strategies we employ to foster self-sufficiency, increase productivity, encourage feedback, and keep morale high on the farm.

Clear expectations. We strive for transparency in all aspects of the farm, but especially in the hiring and training of employees. The clearer and more detailed we are about expectations around issues like punctuality, vacation days, sick time, and quality and pace of work, the easier it is for our crew to meet or exceed them. In my experience, clearly communicated high standards inspire quality work.

A shared plan. We create a written plan for the week every Sunday and share it with all crew members. Getting everyone on the same page facilitates workflow and eliminates miscommunication from the whisper-down-the-lane effect of needless repetition.

Scheduled check-ins. A schedule of regular one-on-one check-ins is set and shared with the crew before the season begins. This time I have with each employee allows a valuable exchange of feedback and ideas. I ask workers to come up with at least one suggestion for improvement for each meeting, and I make it clear that constructive criticism should go both ways.

Social time. All work and no play makes for a dull existence. Regularly scheduled group social times, such as community dinners, happy hour drinks, or movie nights, are not only fun but also create an informal context for checking in and getting a feel for how everyone is doing.

Work alongside. There is an endless to-do list that can distract the farm owner from getting out into the fields. Even with a solid crew of self-sufficient workers, I find there is no better way to strengthen the team mentality than to work alongside everyone regularly and in all manner of work and weather. This effort shows that we are all in it together and provides a less structured context in which to ask questions and express concerns.

Labor Models

The way labor is structured on a farm can vary greatly. There is no single right way to employ people, as the model that works best will depend on a host of factors particular to a given farm, its location, and the personality of its owners or managers. Following are some labor models that have worked well for us at our intensive human scale.

Apprenticeships are a mix of education, community living, and hard work.

FRITH FARM APPRENTICESHIP

These are intense, physically demanding positions that cover the full spectrum of life on the farm.

What We Look For
- Enthusiasm, open-mindedness, and a highly positive attitude
- Attention to detail and ability to follow directions closely
- At least six months of outdoor physical work experience, such as farming, trail crew, landscaping, or similar
- Demonstrated interest in organic agriculture and community engagement

What We Offer
- Experience living as part of a diversified farm
- Veggies, eggs, and meat from the farm
- Accommodations in the renovated 200-year-old farmhouse
- Regular lectures and discussions on relevant farm topics
- Hands-on experience and training in all aspects of farm practices, including:
  - soil husbandry
  - seed propagation and transplanting
  - no-till vegetable production
  - crop rotation
  - cover cropping
  - irrigation
  - harvesting and post-harvest handling
  - pastured poultry
  - meat/poultry processing
  - firewood harvesting and splitting
  - direct marketing and customer relations
- A monthly stipend commensurate with experience

Work is highly physical, averages about 45 hours per week, and is performed in all weather. We require a commitment for the full season, April to Thanksgiving.

Apprenticeships

I believe the apprenticeship model is an ideal labor format for the no-till market farm. Live-in apprenticeships create a dynamic farm community, foster the exchange of skills and ideas, reduce costs for both the apprentice and the farmer, and potentially spread the farm's ideals and practices to new places. Mixing labor with education helps establish the kind of positive work environment described earlier. Performance improves when work is contextualized, and curiosity stimulates innovation.

With a network of social ties that has grown over the last nine years, the farm now connects with new apprentices largely through word of mouth. We also advertise our apprenticeships on our website and through the Maine Organic Farmers and Gardeners Association (MOFGA). In Maine, we are fortunate to have MOFGA as an active supporter of local agriculture. They are the oldest and largest state organic organization in the country, and they help organic farmers in many ways, including the coordination of apprenticeship opportunities.

There are any number of ways to structure a farm apprenticeship. The version we have developed over the years is advertised on our website and described on the facing page.

Work-for-Shares and Volunteers

We offer work-for-share opportunities for anyone interested, regardless of experience or level of commitment. Any person can come on a CSA harvest day and help out for the morning in exchange for a share of vegetables. This openness connects the farm to the community, and new faces and extra hands make harvest that much more pleasant. Those who want to volunteer more can accrue a credit that they can spend at farmers' market or in our on-farm store. Whenever possible, we try to compensate volunteers for their time without money changing hands. Monetizing our shared labor and its fruits can cheapen the exchange.

Our farm is always open to volunteers. I gained much of my initial farming knowledge from simply showing up and asking to help out on different farms. We try to compensate those who can't make it on a CSA harvest day with whatever extra vegetables we have on hand, but mostly volunteers simply want the time outdoors surrounded by the natural beauty of the farm.

Before settling down, I traveled and volunteered on a number of farms through the organization called World Wide Opportunities on Organic Farms (WWOOF). I love the WWOOF model and joined the list of participating farms my first couple years. While I hosted some wonderful, hard-working WWOOFers, in the end I left the program because I found most traveling volunteers came with a transient attitude that conflicted with the groundedness I wanted for the farm community. For the right farm, however, WWOOF can be a valuable way to connect with worldly volunteers.

Hourly Workers

For workers who want to live off the farm, or if on-farm housing is limited, a labor structure of hourly pay is common. While we have had hourly workers for years now, this is my least favorite labor model. I find that when time is equated to money, its true value is diminished. Just knowing that the clock is being punched changes my mentality, both as an employee back in the day, and now as an employer. It's as if the song "Money" by Pink Floyd is playing in the background of all hourly work. I acknowledge that paying by the hour is perhaps the simplest way to compensate fairly on a mixed vegetable farm, but I prefer other options when possible.

A piecework labor model is a great way to weaken the rule of the clock. Placing the value of labor on the work itself shifts the focus in a positive and productive direction. If I know I can comfortably mix the soil and make the blocks for 20 greenhouse trays in an hour, then paying $1 per tray for someone to make soil blocks puts the power of earning in their hands. If they want to work up a sweat and block 30 trays an hour, more power to them. If they'd rather relax and listen to a podcast while blocking at a rate of 10 trays an hour, that's fine, too. Piecework pay relieves the employer of time-related stress and empowers employees to choose their own pace. Unfortunately, paying by piecework for the vast array of tasks performed in a market garden operation is complicated to the point of being impractical.

Offering workers a salary also shifts the focus away from the clock (though it does not incentivize pace the way piecework pay does). Offering a stable salary to workers is a goal of mine. Currently, the seasonal nature of our work makes this difficult, since we essentially take four months off each winter. We are building additional business enterprises around a commercial kitchen and retail farm store, largely to help fill the employment gap of winter. I look forward to one day offering salaries to our core crew and not worrying as much about the hours and pace of the day-to-day.

Managers

As the farm has grown, our labor structure has expanded to include managers. These are typically apprentices who want to stay on the farm beyond their initial season. This sequence benefits both the farm and the employee. By hiring from within, the farm is guaranteed a good fit and a fully trained manager from day one. The manager knows exactly what they're signing up for and solidifies their education by turning around and training the next round of apprentices. My goal in developing a resilient labor structure is to remove myself as a linchpin from as many farm processes as possible, and this progressive pattern of employment effectively helps me do just that. I am freed up to play a support role, stay on top of planning and paperwork, and make sure we do not lose sight of the big picture.

Our daily management decisions are currently divided among our four management positions:

Field Manager. The field manager is in charge of implementing the crop plan and oversees all aspects of vegetable production on the farm. Their job is also to train, support, and work with the other crew members to ensure efficiency, quality, and enjoyment of work in the field.

Wash and Pack Manager. The wash and pack manager is in charge of implementing the harvest plan and runs the wash station during every harvest. This person oversees post-harvest handling, quality control, and distribution of farm produce. They also train and support other crew members to help out and have fun in the wash station.

Livestock Manager. The livestock manager is in charge of all livestock on the farm. This person often works independently but also trains and supports other crew members to ensure daily livestock chores are completed appropriately and enjoyably.

Farm Manager. I act as the general farm manager and try to stay on top of customer relations, ordering, infrastructure maintenance, planning and recordkeeping, finances, and other administrative duties. My job is also to train and educate crew members, support other managers, and foster a positive work environment for all.

Great Expectations

Regardless of labor structure, a well-defined and clearly communicated set of expectations assures that everyone is on the same page. We have a simple yet comprehensive document that spells out expectations for the season, and we ask each employee to initial it as part of accepting a job on the farm. This document gives us something to lean on when there is miscommunication or when duties are not being fulfilled. It also keeps me honest in my role as an employer, as the expectations go both ways.

Attracting and Retaining Employees

Proximity to population centers is a primary factor in attracting employees. Word-of-mouth connections are proportional to the flow of people visiting the farm, and (as with marketing) this form of employment advertising is more valuable and effective than any other. We make most of our hires through the network of people who visit or work on the farm. Attracting and retaining employees is all about demonstrating and ensuring that the farm is a positive working environment, as described earlier.

If we fail to provide a sense of belonging and purpose, space for creative growth, a positive team spirit, and appropriate respect and appreciation, we cannot expect our fellow human beings to devote their time and energy to our cause, regardless of how much we pay them. Here are some specific efforts we make at Frith Farm to create an attractive place to work:

Get organized. A chaotic and disorganized workplace often drives away good workers. Few people want to devote time and energy to poorly defined tasks, murky expectations, and a messy farmstead. Cleaning up our act is often the first step toward attracting better employees.

Spell out (and hold to) high standards. I find that the best employees are attracted to high expectations that are clearly communicated. Serious workers want to know that all members of the crew are held to the same high standards. We try to address any shortcomings immediately in a kind and constructive way so that everyone knows their work is important. Bad habits are much harder to correct than an initial mistake.

Provide a social experience. We offer a package deal for apprentices and managers who live on the farm. This is not a nine-to-five day job; it is a communal way of life. Housing is in a beautiful old timber-frame house that is worthy of being called "home." Shared use of farm vehicles enables employees to avoid the expense of a car. Food is provided from the farm. Up to nine people live on the farm during the season, with many more who come and go as part of a wider community. Tapping into a social network of kindred spirits is more important for many young farmers than a fat paycheck. It certainly is for me.

Show care and camaraderie. Working as part of a supportive team is more attractive than punching the clock in a hierarchical workplace defined by power dynamics. If someone is struggling, we seek to support, not chastise, and try to understand and empathize before critiquing and correcting. This is not always easy, but it is worth the effort. When employees are supported in a team effort, productivity and self-improvement happen naturally without enforcement.

Train adequately. Most mistakes made on the farm boil down to inadequate training. Carelessness is too often blamed when poor training is the real culprit. We can't expect employees to do a job well

EMPLOYEE OWNERSHIP

In his book *Companies We Keep*, John Abrams describes the cornerstones of a sustainable business and makes a strong case for employee ownership. I am not there yet with my farm, but I feel inspired to move in that direction, and I believe every business owner should consider what Abrams describes as "a path to a more democratic, more responsible, more permanent kind of company."

We are not just hiring a pair of hands to meet our labor needs; we are inviting someone into our community, our family, and our home.

The Hiring Process

Shaping the farm and its systems into an alluring work environment will attract potential employees, but a solid vetting process is still needed to ensure a good fit. Here are the steps of our hiring process in a nutshell:

1. **Advertising.** Once the farm is established, word of mouth becomes a primary mode of attracting new employees, but other useful avenues include:
   - Agricultural organizations, like MOFGA, ATTRA, PASA, Acres USA, etc.
   - Employment websites, such as goodfoodjobs .com and craigslist.org
   - A farm website or blog
   - Social media platforms, like Facebook, Instagram, etc.
   - Fliers in local businesses, schools, and libraries
   - Local job fairs

2. **Application.** I find the best way to weed out ambivalent applicants is to require a written application, complete with a resume and three reference contacts. If someone doesn't have the inclination to complete these steps, chances are they aren't superexcited about working with us. I use the application that MOFGA developed for their apprenticeship program, which consists of a dozen or so short-answer questions that give a good sense of an applicant's goals, experience, and expectations.

3. **Phone interview.** For nonlocal applicants, we conduct a phone interview or online video chat to make sure a trip to the farm will be worth everyone's time. These calls usually last about 20 minutes, and we cover the gamut of experience, interests, goals for the season, and an overview of the farm and its work. We look as much for a good community fit as we do for a skilled farm worker.

unless we show them how to do it, in a way that they understand. I find there is no substitute for working alongside new crew members, even after a task has been thoroughly explained with words, writing, or pictures. Employees who have been around a year or two also do a lot of the training. This process makes the seasoned worker think carefully about their process and hopefully feel like more of an expert. It also spreads the task of training among the crew so it doesn't all fall on me.

Compensate fairly. Workers are seldom happy if they feel they are not fairly compensated. Compensation can take a variety of forms; the value of housing, utilities, food, education, monetary pay, and other services provided to employees should add up to an equitable compensation for the work they perform. Whatever numbers you attach to these values, ultimately fairness is more a feeling than a formula. If employer or employee ever feels like compensation is unfair, something needs to change.

4. **Reference checks.** The value of references can vary greatly. I find there is no better reason for hiring an applicant than a positive reference from another commercial farmer. An applicant without a farmer reference is more of a wild card, but we interview anyone with solid outdoor work experience and a demonstrated interest in agriculture.

5. **In-person interview.** The on-farm interview is the final step before making a job offer. Ideally, a candidate comes for a half-day of paid work alongside the crew, followed by a one-on-one conversation about expectations, compensation, and how the job will further the candidate's goals.

6. **Job offer.** We send the job offer by e-mail so there is a record of our agreement if they accept. The e-mail spells out the previously discussed expectations and compensation. We are almost always thrilled with the people to whom we offer employment and make sure to express our excitement as part of our job offer.

Task Times

The human element of a small farm is perhaps its biggest unknown variable each season — even more than the weather. The people we hire and the experience and personalities they bring to the farm impact our work and crew dynamic every day of the season. One way to grapple with the varying nature of human work is to create goals around pace and efficiency.

I find new workers appreciate a baseline reference for the speed with which they complete a task, keeping in mind the importance of the pace being realistic for a beginner; it is better for the worker's morale to exceed the expectation than to work hard and continually come up short. The time it takes to complete farm tasks varies with such factors as the weather, field conditions, crop spacing, weed and disease pressure, and how much coffee workers have consumed, so I recommend each farm develop its own set of realistic and clearly communicated expectations around work pace.

I suppose all rules of thumb are by definition "handy," but a farming friend shared an especially useful one with me regarding the work pace of harvesting. He suggested that a single person should be able to harvest, wash, and pack about $80 worth of produce each hour. Much less than that and the operation would benefit from an efficiency overhaul. I find this number helpful when determining if a marginal crop is worth picking or when assessing the work pace of a harvest morning. If, for instance, the harvest takes five people 4 hours, that's 20 hours of work. At $80 an hour, the value of produce harvested and packed should be about $1,600. This basic math is a quick and easy way to gauge the efficiency of a harvest and pack operation.

It is easy to develop tunnel vision when it comes to efficiency, especially when numbers and dollar signs get involved. I constantly remind myself that I did not start a farm to create a seamlessly efficient assembly line of vegetable production. In one sense, I started a farm to get away from the reductionist obsession with the bottom line. Profitability is key to the survival of any business, but to endlessly maximize efficiency and profit at the expense of other values is not the basis of good farming or a sustainable world. There is satisfaction in working

THE RATIO OF HUMANS TO LAND

In my experience, you need no fewer than two full-time workers per acre to achieve the full potential of intensive human-scale vegetable production.

Hand carts and harvest crates highlight the farm's human scale.

efficiently, yet there is joy in slowing down to take in and appreciate the rich soil, the fresh air, the energy-giving sun, and the billions of fellow life forms that make up the farmer's workplace. As long as the farm remains economically viable and compensates its employees fairly, I prefer to focus on more pleasant aspects of agriculture than time sheets and financial statements.

STREAMLINING

The extra activity around the edges of each task — the time for assembling tools, carts, and supplies, and walking to and from the fields — can easily add up and erode a farm's efficiency. Keeping tools and supplies organized and located as close as possible to the work reduces extra motion and wasted time.

CHAPTER 13

PLANNING AND RECORDKEEPING

Success always leaves footprints.
— BOOKER T. WASHINGTON

Recordkeeping is many farmers' least favorite task, but it doesn't need to be drudgery or busywork. In fact, farm records can follow directly from pragmatic planning. This chapter describes how to focus plans and records on what matters, and covers the systems we use at Frith Farm to streamline planning and recordkeeping so that we can spend more time out on the farm, not in the office.

The Whole-Farm Organism

Successful planning for any farm operation begins with recognizing that an efficient farm functions as an integrated whole. Planning one area of the farm without considering how these intentions impact other aspects of the farm can lead to counterproductivity. Allan Savory developed a powerful holistic planning framework that he details in his book *Holistic Management*. He shows how working within this framework ensures that our efforts move in a direction that is approximately right, rather than precisely wrong. I highly recommend reading Savory's book (or consulting with someone who has) and going through the process he lays out for developing a holistic farm plan.

Savory's framework may seem daunting for the beginning farmer. When I was new to farming, I was so excited to start growing food that a book on mission statements and management frameworks might not have held my attention. While going through the entire holistic management process is not necessary to start a successful farm, I would suggest, at a bare minimum, crafting a mission statement as a summary of what the farm is all about. Without this description of "true north," farmers can all too easily lose their way amidst the long hours, growing to-do list, and endless weeds of the day-to-day.

I find a very simplified approach to holistic planning is a useful check as I plan the next day, week, or season on the farm. A coherent plan starts with the broad purpose of the farm as an organism (or organization, if you prefer) and supports this purpose through daily, weekly, and monthly tasks. The process has three simple steps:

1. **Define the farm's purpose.** Begin with a mission statement, or statement of purpose, that describes the big picture: What is the purpose of the farm? What are you ultimately working toward? The answers to these questions become the compass that guides the direction of farm decisions. Every journey is simply a series of steps, and unless we know where we are headed in the long run, there is no way to know the best next spot to place our foot each day.

2. **Plan the season.** With a defined statement of purpose, the farmer can then plan the season ahead so that work moves in a compatible direction. For a mixed vegetable farm, a plan for the season is mostly encapsulated in the crop plan, which describes which crops are grown where and when (see chapter 5), along with a plan for any major projects or infrastructure improvements. It is important to examine this seasonal plan to make sure it works in accordance with the ideals spelled out in the farm's statement of purpose.

3. **Plan the week.** The plan for each week of the season (see page 205) should work directly toward the plan for the whole season. This sequential inspection of our efforts is like checking the alignment of a car — the goal is to make sure all parts of the farm are working smoothly and intentionally in the same direction. The plan for a given day is contained within the plan for

the week and works directly toward the week's objectives (which pushes toward the goals of the season, which align with the farm's long-term mission). In this way, the work of every day fits into a larger context of intention. Each completed task is a step toward fulfilling the defined purpose of the farm. Without this assurance, it can be easy to lose heart when work is daunting or its relevance is unclear.

Here is an example of how these steps might look: Our mission at Frith Farm is to build soil, increase biodiversity, and strengthen community through the growing of wholesome food. Our crop plan prioritizes soil health and diversity with cover crops and interplantings and focuses on the varieties our local customers have asked for. Our plan for the season also includes projects such as perennial plantings for increased diversity and a new greenhouse space to host community events. The plan for each week or day becomes a logistical arrangement of tasks that lead toward our goals for the season. Whether we are pounding posts for our new greenhouse or splitting wood to provide a communal source of heat for next winter, each item on the to-do list fits into a larger vision for the farm's trajectory.

Recordkeeping Strategies

As we go about following the plan and accomplishing tasks, we're faced with the question of recordkeeping: What should we keep track of, and in how much detail? Recordkeeping can be the bane of a farmer's existence, adding stress and interfering with the actual growing of food. Here are some strategies that help to streamline the recording process and keep information concise and relevant:

Keep it simple. Good farming does not require hourly temperature data or yield records accurate to the nearest pound. Remember the concept of significant figures from high school science class? The records we keep are only as accurate as their least accurate component. Keeping track of what is done when or how much is grown where is hardly like balancing a checkbook. I take generous liberties with rounding numbers, both financial and production, and simply ignore data that feels redundant or irrelevant. For example, I track individual sales to the nearest dollar and aggregate sales to the nearest hundred, and I keep planting and harvest records by the week, not the day. I do not record transplant dates, since this information is already accounted for indirectly with the greenhouse seeding schedule.

Record only what will be useful. Maybe this is obvious, but it is amazing in the current age of information how much data can be recorded that will never be looked at again. If I don't see a direct purpose for recording information, I simply don't bother. Like physical clutter lying around the farm, excessive records take up valuable mental bandwidth and can distract us from our farming mission.

Let the plan become the record. A well-formed, closely followed plan simply becomes the record. I think of this approach as "plankeeping" instead of recordkeeping, and I devote time each winter to dial in our crop plan and greenhouse seeding schedule to the point that few, if any, adjustments are needed during the growing season. This allows us to focus on the work itself and not worry about planning or recordkeeping in these areas during the busiest times of the year. At the end of the season, the plan is the record.

Integrate recordkeeping with dynamic planning. Some plans inevitably have to change. For our weekly task list, we have developed a system of updating plans on a real-time, collaborative basis. This ever-evolving plan organizes daily priorities and becomes an accurate record of completed tasks (see The Plan for the Week on page 205).

Record in aggregate. Keeping track of aggregate data and then calculating individual records, such as revenue per bed or time per task, requires less work and provides more accuracy than trying to record every individual movement on the farm. For example, we weigh or count everything that is harvested for CSA or farmers' market, then we tally up what is left over at the end of the day to determine what was sold. At the end of the season, we add up all our sales for each crop and divide by the number of beds to calculate the revenue per bed as well as the associated yield for each crop. Having standardized bed dimensions makes this easy. This process is far less work than trying to weigh each crate as it is harvested or record each customer transaction.

Piggyback farm records on other recordkeeping processes. We have to create invoices for every wholesale order, so it makes sense to use these invoices as our sales records. And since we maintain consistent pricing throughout the season, the sales records are easily translated into production data. Another similar efficiency comes from using a bank card for all farm purchases: transactions are recorded automatically, and expense data is available through online banking records. Tapping into preexisting recordkeeping processes eliminates data entry and redundant records.

A single place to record important lessons. Taking notes on separate lists, notebooks, and scraps of paper reduces the likelihood that observations will be incorporated into future plans. Experiments, successes, and failures are useful tools of learning only if we can recall how they went down. I have a single spreadsheet titled "Notes for Next Season" that is a catchall for important observations and lessons. Whatever form it takes, keeping a concise record of what worked and what didn't is an important step on the path of continuous improvement.

Collaborative Spreadsheets

My preferred planning and recordkeeping tool is the web-based spreadsheet, and I use Google Sheets for all farm documents (online spreadsheets are free). There are an increasing number of apps and software packages designed to make farm planning and recordkeeping easier, but I prefer the old-fashioned manual spreadsheet to the extra features and unknown programming decisions of third-party software. The benefits of using online spreadsheets include:

Cost. Online spreadsheets are entirely free, while most apps and recordkeeping software come with up-front costs or monthly fees.

Access. Cloud-based spreadsheets can be accessed and edited from any device, and the risk of data loss is minimized.

Transparency. Online spreadsheets are easily shared with employees, customers, and the wider community.

Collaboration. Web-based spreadsheets facilitate simultaneous editing and collaboration among managers and crew.

Communication. Exchange of information occurs in one place. Everyone is always on the same page, literally. Employees can look at plans and records on their own time and at their own pace.

The collaborative spreadsheet enables us to integrate planning and recordkeeping into a single dynamic and transparent process. And, with careful monitoring or real-time editing, the crop plan seamlessly becomes the crop record (what was planted where, and when). Farm recordkeeping need not be onerous or time-consuming. In fact, oftentimes it need not be a task at all. Why create separate records when the relevant information can be integrated into the planning process? Following are some examples of how we streamline planning and recordkeeping.

The Plan for the Week

The Plan for the Week is a continually edited online spreadsheet that guides our daily activity. The spreadsheet has a column for each day of the week, with tasks for the day listed in rows below them. Every crew member has access to the cloud-based document, and there is a farm laptop in the barn to enable easy referencing and updating throughout the day. With this planning format, there's no need to erase information (as you do with a whiteboard), and there's no need to transcribe information (as when multiple people are working off of handwritten lists).

Our process of writing and updating the Plan for the Week goes like this:

1. **Walk the farm.** At the beginning of each week, we take a stroll around the farm to determine the priorities for the week.
2. **Make the plan.** I create the plan by duplicating the previous week's plan and deleting all of the completed tasks. Then, I reorganize the remaining tasks, along with the priorities from the farm walk, to form the new plan for the week.
3. **Execute the plan.** Each day, as tasks are completed, they are crossed off (using a strikethrough font), and any notes or observations are added to the spreadsheet.
4. **Assess and reprioritize.** At the end of each day, the plan is viewed to see what was completed and what still needs to happen. Based on what was done and the notes included, tasks are reprioritized for the remaining days in the week.

This system has worked well for us over the years, enabling a detailed yet adaptable level of organization and communication around daily work. And with no additional effort, the plan becomes a digital diary of what was accomplished every single day of the season. The plan's usefulness as a detailed, searchable record is worth almost as much as its primary purpose as a planning and labor management tool.

A shared online spreadsheet details the plan for the week and becomes a record of each day of the season. Note the tabs at the bottom for each week.

Here are some tips to make the plan work smoothly and enjoyably:

Strike-through font. Crew members strike out tasks as they are completed so everyone can see what has been done and what task to tackle next. I encourage employees to revel in the satisfaction of crossing off a job well done.

Crew initials for specific tasks. If a particular task should be completed by a specific crew member based on experience, I put their initials in front of it. This fosters transparency among the crew, as everyone sees what their teammates are up to throughout the day.

Just enough tasks for the day. I make an effort to fill each day only with a manageable number of tasks, even when we are behind. Morale is bolstered by getting something done from tomorrow's list, but it can suffer when only a small fraction of the current day's list was crossed off.

Catchall "Future" column. A farmer can always think of more to do than fits in a week. Rather than having unfinished tasks pile up on the plan, I create an eighth column entitled "Future" that serves as a catchall for longer-term tasks. This column can be added to and pulled from as needed to balance out the week.

New tab for each week. We take care to never delete or overwrite information. By creating a new tab for each week, the spreadsheet becomes a diary of the entire season with no extra recordkeeping.

Searchable records. A simple search query can answer questions about what was done and when in previous years. For example, each year our organic certifier wants to know the date we moved the laying hens out of the high tunnel in the spring, and a quick search for "layers high tunnel" reveals the information in less than a second. I can think of few other recordkeeping formats that are as comprehensive or as easy to extract information from. And the beauty of the system is that it is simply a by-product of our planning process.

The Crop Plan

A crop plan requires a good amount of work in the fall and winter, but it saves a lot of time when it counts most — during the busy growing season. During our first couple of seasons, we had to make some on-the-fly changes to our initial plan, but once I got a sense of our land, climate, markets, and growing practices, I was able to design a crop plan that could be followed realistically and required little adjustment throughout the season. The crop plan contains three main components: crop rotation, greenhouse schedule, and seed order.

CROP ROTATION

This describes the overall plan: the placement of each crop in both time and space. In other words, what goes where and when, for this season and beyond. This part of the crop plan is described in more detail in chapter 5. The crop rotation document is shared digitally with the whole crew, and an easy-to-read copy is printed and tacked to a board in the barn for quick reference throughout the season.

GREENHOUSE SCHEDULE

The greenhouse schedule includes the dates and quantities for each plant variety that is to be

A printout of the crop rotation plan is tacked to a board and referred to throughout the season. When followed closely, this plan becomes the record.

propagated in the greenhouse, listed in order of seeding date. A printed copy of the greenhouse schedule document lives on a clipboard storage box that is used to transport seeds to and from the greenhouse, and each line gets checked off as it is completed. The schedule for the entire year is printed before the first seeding so there's no need to spend additional time on propagation planning during the season.

SEED ORDER

Once the greenhouse schedule is complete, calculating the correct amount of seed to order is greatly simplified. Having standardized 100-foot beds makes the math easy. For direct-seeded crops, seed companies generally offer values for seeds needed per 100 row-feet, but actual seeding rates can be measured by weighing a seed packet before and after seeding a bed. Keep in mind that these numbers will vary with the size and shape of the seed as well as with the settings of the seeder. (I like to order 20 percent more seed than I think I will need, just to be safe. Not having enough seed when you need it costs far more than having a little extra at the end of the season.) A well-calculated seed order saves money, and reusing calculated seeding rates from year to year saves planning time. The seed order also provides insight

if seeds are wasted or misplaced, and it is a required part of the annual inspection process for Certified Organic farms.

The Harvest Plan

Each harvest day is planned according to a combination of two factors: what is ready to harvest and what customers want. In an ideal world these are one and the same, but often the quantities and timing do not line up perfectly. While our overlapping markets (described in chapter 11) help us smooth out these discrepancies, harvest decisions have to be made on a daily basis.

The harvest plan summarizes the objectives for each harvest to ensure a smooth and consistent operation. It tells the crew how much of each vegetable to harvest (and in what order) as well as where the product is going.

Our harvest planning process starts a couple of days before each harvest and includes four main steps:

1. **Walk the fields.** A lap around the farm with pencil and paper provides notes on what is ready for harvest.
2. **E-mail customers.** An availability list is sent to retail customers (who then submit their order by

the evening before harvest), and a preview of what to expect in shares is sent out to CSA members.

3. **Make the harvest plan.** Each harvest day is a new tab on a single online spreadsheet. Each row lists, in order, the vegetable variety to harvest, and each column tells how much is going to a given outlet (CSA, market, or a particular wholesale customer).

4. **Print and post.** The harvest plan document gets printed and posted in the wash area the night before the harvest to prevent any delays from morning challenges (wake-up alarms not going off, printers failing, etc.).

During the following day's harvest, each crew member initials next to a line on the harvest plan, starting at the top of the plan and working our way down. When a worker finishes harvesting a crop, they go initial by the next unclaimed task on the plan. The wash station manager checks off each item as it is washed, packed, and stored in the walk-in cooler. If we are short or if quantities need to be adjusted, this is noted on the printed harvest sheet. Wholesale invoices get adjusted as needed, and the harvest list becomes the record of what was offered to CSA, or what got taken to market. Then, when the leftovers of CSA and market are tallied, the total of each product sold is calculated by subtraction.

Recordkeeping remains straightforward and painless when integrated with the regular planning and operations of each harvest.

Production Records

We record vegetable yields indirectly through their sales. We sell through four different outlets (CSA, farmers' market, grocers and restaurants, and a farm store) and keep track of sales in a few different ways. For CSA and farmers' market, as described earlier, we record what is offered and what is left over, then calculate the difference to determine

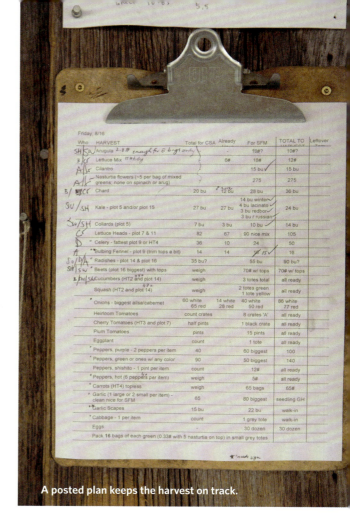

A posted plan keeps the harvest on track.

how much is sold of each crop. For invoiced sales to grocers and restaurants, we use the invoices as the sales record, and we go back through each invoice during the off-season to tally totals for each vegetable. (Software like Quickbooks performs this step for you.) Our farm store sales function on the honor system: customers write what they buy on a clipboard and leave cash or a check in a box. When the clipboard paper fills up, we tally the sales amount for each product sold.

By selling everything we grow and maintaining consistent pricing, our sales data translates readily into yield data. Dividing by the number of 100-foot beds of a given crop (easily determined from the crop plan) we can calculate our revenue and yield per bed. Taking the analysis a step further, we look at the fraction of the season that each crop is in the ground (also from the crop plan), and divide the crop's revenue by this fraction to determine the revenue per bed *per season*. This number is a good indication of the profitability of a given crop, since it takes into account both the time and space required to grow the product. A more complete analysis would also consider the labor required for each crop, which we do not explicitly record.

To follow an example through this process, let's consider kale. We sell kale wholesale for $2 per bunch and retail for $3 per bunch. For 2018:

- Total kale sales = $9,400 ($3,400 wholesale and $6,000 retail)
- Total yield = 3,700 bunches
- Kale beds planted: 14
- Yield per bed: 264 bunches (3,700 ÷ 14)
- Revenue per bed: $671 ($9,400 ÷ 14)

Since we leave the kale plants in the ground for about half the growing season, we divide the per-bed revenue by 0.5 to determine that the kale revenue per bed per season is $1,343.

The table below lists our production data, obtained through this same process, for the highest-earning vegetables at Frith Farm in a recent year.

Revenue Data for Top-Earning Vegetables

Vegetable	Revenue	Beds Planted	Revenue per 100-ft Bed	Fraction of Season	Revenue per Bed-Season
Carrots	$29,787	44	$677	0.5	$1,354
Tomatoes	$26,085	15	$1,739	1	$1,739
Garlic	$21,062	24	$878	0.5	$1,755
Lettuce Heads	$19,040	28	$680	0.33	$2,061
Lettuce Mix	$17,094	26	$657	0.33	$1,992
Onions	$14,797	21	$705	0.67	$1,052
Spinach	$11,684	26	$449	0.33	$1,362
Kale	$9,317	15	$621	0.5	$1,242
Arugula	$9,280	12	$773	0.33	$2,343
Squash, Summer	$8,248	8	$1,031	0.5	$2,062
Beets	$7,912	15	$527	0.5	$1,055
Peppers	$7,398	4	$1,850	1	$1,850
Cucumbers	$6,917	6	$1,153	0.5	$2,306
Celery	$5,016	6	$836	0.6	$1,393
Ginger	$4,883	2	$2,442	1	$2,442
Radishes, Fresh	$4,234	13	$326	0.33	$987
. . . (45 other crops)					
Total Veg Revenue:	$256,223			Average:	$1,250

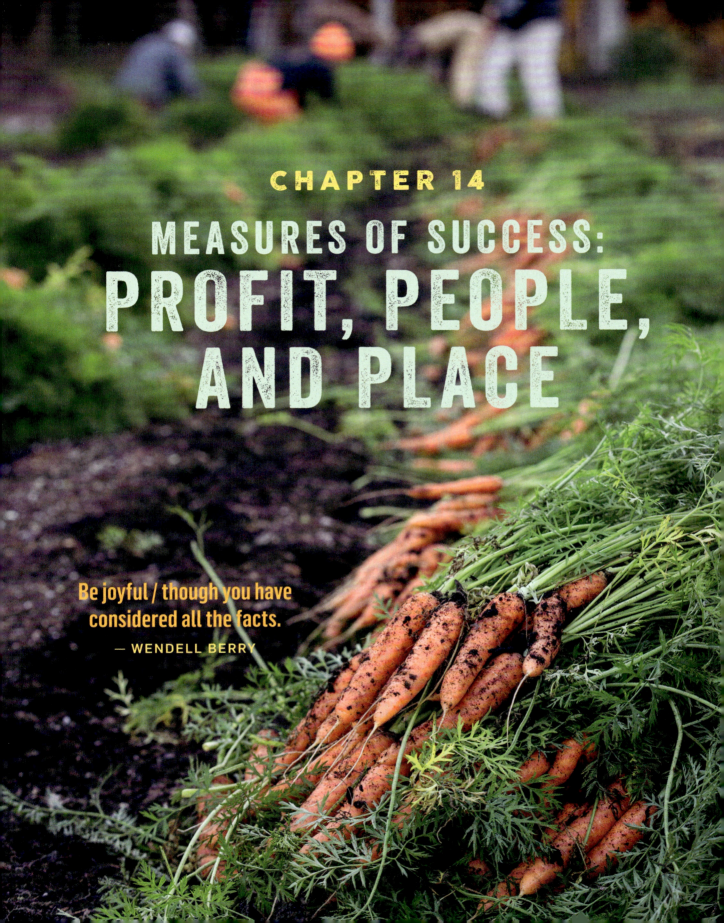

CHAPTER 14

MEASURES OF SUCCESS:
PROFIT, PEOPLE, AND PLACE

Be joyful / though you have
considered all the facts.
— WENDELL BERRY

"Success" is an elusive concept that all too often gets reduced to a monetary bottom line. This chapter presents a more holistic set of metrics to evaluate our success as farmers, and explores the aspects of farming that lead to a quality life.

Reinvestment

Profitability is an espoused requisite of sustainability. The three legs of the proverbial stool are social well-being, environmental health, and economic viability — often shortened to "people, the planet, and profit." But where those profits go after they are made is a rarer discussion, even though this extra money can easily undo the sustainability of the way it was generated. The very word "profit" can invoke a mentality of extraction. By definition, profits are financial gain — what is left over after all expenses have been paid — and are thus free to be removed and spent off-farm without responsibility or guilt. In nature there are no surpluses; whatever is produced is reinvested in the land and its living community. If a tree has a particularly good year, its wealth is reinvested in the fungal network that supports its roots and the earthworms that feed on its fallen leaves. With nature as our model, the concept of profit can be replaced by that of reinvestment.

From the time I started out, I have reinvested the farm's profits back into the land, its infrastructure, and its community. While the cost of labor and organic matter are usually tallied as farm inputs, I choose to see them as a reinvestment of resources in the people and land who help generate them, just as the tree reinvests in the life that enables its productivity. When the money paid to workers is seen as an investment rather than an input expense, the whole attitude toward labor shifts. No longer is labor a dirty word or an expense to be minimized. When compost and organic mulches are lumped in the same category as industrial fertilizers, their long-term value to the land is overlooked. Healthy soil generates its own natural dividends, and the interest compounds continually. An investment is something that pays

off over time in proportion to the amount invested. I believe resources devoted to the farm's workers and soils function the same way, and they pay off in the strength and resilience of the agroecological community that makes the farm productive.

The table below shows where the farm's revenue went in 2018. The expense categories that I see as regenerative are reinvestment in people and in place. Those to minimize are inputs, equipment,

Following the Money: Where 2018 Farm Revenue Went

People	
Farm crew	$120,000
Loan payments to family	$11,000
Land	
Local biomass	$28,000
Local seed and perennial plants	$8,000
Permanent infrastructure	$56,000
Away	
Nonlocal inputs (fertilizer, feed, supplies, energy)	$32,000
Manufactured tools and equipment	$14,000
Overhead (taxes, insurance, fees)	$45,000
TOTAL	$314,000

Profitability is an insufficient measure of sustainability unless we address where the profits end up.

and overhead. While to some degree they are necessary in the context of an industrialized economy, these latter expenses support linear processes that essentially convert resources into pollution. When we buy products like synthetic mulches, product packaging, fossil fuels, and manufactured equipment, we are helping fund the destruction of the planet's natural capital. This sacrifice may be warranted at times, but let's not kid ourselves about the role we as farmers play in the consumptive economy.

Overhead is a more amorphous concept. It is a catchall category that encompasses all expenses that are not used directly for labor or materials. These include taxes, insurance, loan interest, marketing, and regulatory fees. These expenses do not always add tangible value to the food we produce, the community we build, or the local economy we support. In a perfect world, most of the money coming into the farm would come from — and stay in — the community. Let's work to reinvest as much of our revenue as possible back into the place and the people that generate it.

The concept of economic success is familiar to all of us, as its pursuit is the driving force behind decision making in almost all areas of modern society. In the context of holistic farming, however, economic considerations are not separate from environmental concerns or social ideals. It is precisely the symbiotic union of ecological stewardship and community involvement that gives rise to honest economic returns, which are sustained and multiplied when they are reinvested in the ecology and community of the farm.

Agriculture-Supported Community

Community supported agriculture (CSA) is a well-known concept, but what if we reversed the direction of support and thought of the arrangement as agriculture-supported community? Like the health of soil and the plants that grow in it, the success of local farms and the health of the surrounding community are one and the same; neither can thrive without the other. By extending its roots out into the community in the form of employment opportunities, education, and improved access to healthy food, the farm nourishes the very resource base it depends on.

No-till human-scale farming is inherently based in — and focused on — community. On the other end of the spectrum from commodity agriculture, no-till market farming is personal and subjective and produces unique products custom-tailored to the needs and desires of the community. The social connections of the no-till farm simultaneously define it as community supported agriculture and as agriculture-supported community.

Education

Education is an inherent part of community, and so the community-based farm is naturally involved in education. Everything we do as farmers and employers is teaching some kind of lesson, whether we intend it to or not. The flavor of the produce we sell teaches the consumer about freshness, nutrition, and soil health. The way we train our crew spreads valuable skills and information to potential farmers. The social success of the farm can be defined by the sense of connection fostered between community members, and education helps establish and spread these connections.

To the extent we can maximize our agro-educational impact, our communities will strengthen and our farms will flourish. Indeed, our very survival depends on a societal understanding of what sustains us. As Eliot Coleman writes, "If we wish to teach reverence for the earth, we need to insist that practical time spent on the soils of a farm is just as valuable in training citizens for the 21st century as intellectual time spent in the halls of academe." Farmers play a critical role in spreading the knowledge and survival

Pick-your-own flower gardens draw CSA members out into the fields.

skills that enable human civilization to persist. This task is monumental in aggregate but occurs naturally as part of the daily operations of any human-scale farm.

There are many ways to enhance the educational impact of the farm:

Apprenticeships. Any type of employment is a form of education, but designing labor around an apprenticeship model (see Apprenticeships on page 195) places explicit value on the educational component of compensation.

Volunteers. Providing access to the farm and its methods through volunteer opportunities opens the door for anyone looking to learn (see Work-for-Shares and Volunteers on page 195).

Mentorship. Sharing lessons and advice freely with other farmers is a critical form of collaborative education. This open-source exchange of ideas benefits everyone and overcomes the self-serving economic concepts of proprietary information and trade secrets.

Workshops. On-farm workshops are a great way to acknowledge the educational role of the farm in community and to introduce people to new ideas, nutritious food, and a sustainable approach to agriculture.

Events. Just getting people to the farm is educational in and of itself. Enticing people with concerts, bonfires, or other events exposes them to a farmscape that will likely widen their perspective of agriculture.

Farm tours. Scheduled farm tours are a low-stakes way for customers and neighbors to meet their farmer and get a sense of how their food is grown.

Newsletters, blogs, and social media. Regular communication helps develop and maintain a relationship with customers and other followers. Many lessons are embedded even in simple descriptions of farm happenings.

Farmers' market. Education happens with every customer interaction. Offering samples and describing how vegetables are grown gives meaning to market-goers' purchases and often inspires curiosity and further learning.

Youth education. Perhaps the most important people to educate about farming are children. Young people have yet to form firm conceptions of the world and thus are fertile ground for agricultural ideals to grow and blossom. From inviting school groups to tour the farm to hosting a summer farm camp, there are many ways to engage local youth, and there is arguably no better social investment a farm can make.

Farmer-to-farmer trainings. Exchange of methods and insights among farmers allows us all to farm better. Hosting classes or intensives geared toward growers is a great way to spread ideas and help others benefit from lessons learned. Contact your local agricultural organizations or cooperative extension office or get active on social media to connect with other farmers. I believe agricultural knowledge should be open-source and actively disseminated, as we all benefit collectively from the health of individual farms.

Food Access

Organic farming is often criticized for its expensive prices and its inaccessibility to certain demographics, and often for good reason. It is not enough for farmers starting with relative privilege to shrug off these critiques and mutter something about the true cost of food. Certainly farmers deserve a fair price for the fruits of their labor, but we also have the unique power, and thus the responsibility, to get healthy food to those in our communities who would otherwise go without. These are some strategies for taking an active role in expanding local access to quality food:

SNAP and WIC. One of the first steps toward improving the public's access to our food is to make sure the farm is set up to accept Supplemental Nutrition Assistance Program (SNAP) and Women, Infants, and Children (WIC) food benefits. Formerly called food stamps, SNAP benefits are currently

dispersed through an electronic benefits transfer (EBT) card. The terms *SNAP*, *EBT*, and *food stamps* are often used interchangeably. The recipients have gone through a lengthy and sometimes demeaning application process, so at least we farmers can fill out the paperwork to become an authorized vendor. Information on how to accept WIC and SNAP payments is available online at fns.usda.gov.

At the time of writing, there is a national program that subsidizes SNAP shares so that customers receive a two-for-one deal on all produce — all the more reason to get involved.

Donations. The most direct way to get healthy food to those who need it may be to donate to your local food pantry or soup kitchen. A quick internet search can reveal your closest options, and any connections you make can likely recommend additional places to donate. Food pantries are often run entirely by volunteers — some of the most committed and generous people I've ever met — and I find their excitement over receiving quality local produce to be worth as much as any paycheck.

Gleaning. Gleaning is the gathering of food that remains in a field after it has been commercially

Members of a gleaning club harvest salad greens from overgrown beds. Their harvests get donated to local food pantries and soup kitchens.

harvested. It is an age-old practice that dates back to Biblical times and was a legal entitlement of the poor in Europe until the late 1700s. Farmers were actually required to leave a fraction of their harvest on the plant for those in need. Though gleaning has shed much of its legal and religious significance, it remains an effective way to connect to the community and offer free food to anyone willing to pick it. In some areas there are even gleaning clubs — groups of volunteers who will come to a farm and glean, then take the gleanings to a local food pantry or soup kitchen. Partnering with ally organizations can greatly facilitate our ability to increase food access.

Sliding-scale pricing. A simple way to lower financial barriers to food access is to offer sliding-scale pricing for CSA memberships. We let our customers determine the price that is affordable to them, all the way down to zero, and we accept whatever sum they decide on with no questions asked. This has worked well for us, and I trust our customers to know their own level of need. There is far too much stigma and indignity surrounding economic hardship; we as farmers have the opportunity to offer affordable food to our community members in a courteous and respectful manner.

Work trades and barter. Despite our encouragement, I find many customers are uncomfortable paying less than full price for their vegetables. Often they prefer to pay in other ways, so we accept all forms of barter, and offer work-for-CSA-share opportunities.

Ride shares. All of our CSA pickups are on the farm, which essentially requires customers to own a vehicle and have the time to make the trip out to us. We recognize that this prevents some potential customers from accessing the food we grow as part of our CSA. We have aspirations of organizing volunteers (ideally other CSA members) who can either drop off CSA shares or offer rides to those who want to visit the farm and pick their own herbs and flowers as they pick up their share.

Training the next generation

Advertising. It means little to offer easy access to food if the word does not get out that these offerings exist. The word-of-mouth advertising that we rely on so heavily does not always reach all corners of the community. Handing out fliers at local food pantries, posting clear descriptions of accepted forms of payment at farmers' markets, and soliciting articles about the farm's payment options in local news outlets are great ways to communicate the availability of the farm's food in an inclusive manner.

Measures of Social Impact

The social impact of a farm is difficult to quantify and, as a result, is easily downplayed or ignored. The social success of a farm, however, is observable and inseparable from its overall success as a business and its value as an ecological resource. Indeed, the social influence a farm inspires through employment, education, food access, and providing a place for community to gather is intertwined with its ecological and economic impacts, and each feeds the other three.

Though many human benefits of the farm cannot be calculated, there are several measures by which

Our annual "community carrot harvest" attracts pickers of all ages.

a farm can evaluate and track its social efforts in quantifiable terms:

Payroll. As with any local business, investing in the people who run the farm feeds the cycles of localized economy just as healthy farmland supports the natural cycles of its ecosystem.

Employee retention. Employees who keep coming back are a sign of the social health of the farm.

Customer retention. Customers returning year after year are the result of more than a sound business model; they are a sign of the farm's value to the community.

Number of farm alumni. Every apprentice trained and farmhand inspired creates a ripple effect, spreading the values and practices of the farm into the wider community.

Visitors to the farm. The number of people coming to the farm is not only a measure of local interest and value but also of the farm's useful function as a community gathering place and a source of education.

Diversity of customers and employees. By serving and teaching diverse populations, a farm can work toward breaking down prejudice and healing injustice in a food system with plenty of both.

Pounds of food donated. Channeling nutritious food into places of scarcity has an immediate and direct effect on community health.

Number of underserved served. Finding ways to reach those who cannot get to the farm or afford its products heals broken connections within the community and nourishes relationships as well as individuals.

Number of generations on the farm. Farming can be a way of life for all ages. Restoring multi-generational agriculture ensures the inheritance of knowledge and the survival of ancestral growing practices.

Spaceship Earth

In his 1968 book *Operating Manual for Spaceship Earth*, Buckminster Fuller likens our planet to a small spaceship in the vast emptiness of space. If some astronauts were alone aboard a craft hurtling through the depths of outer space, there would be little doubt that they would work together to maintain the vessel's life support systems. Their intellects would clearly comprehend that survival demanded it. Likewise, it is time for our species to recognize that we are on just such a spaceship, and our future is at risk. There is no place to land this ship and no other ship to board — this vessel is all we have. It is meticulously designed to support us and is equipped with a vast and extensive life support system that is powered entirely by the sun. If maintained properly, this support system generates all the resources we need to prosper. As Buckminster Fuller puts it, "Spaceship Earth was so extraordinarily well invented and designed that to our knowledge humans have been on board it for two million years not even knowing that they were on board a ship."

We evolved as part of the very systems that are supposed to maintain this spaceship. Somewhere along the way we stepped outside of our role as ecosystem participants and began leveraging our sizeable intellect in order to extract and accumulate material wealth from our surroundings.

The advent of agriculture enabled this planetary shift in the focus of human activity. As hunters and gatherers, we fit into the cycles of the natural world, characterized by borderless terrain, complete renewability, zero waste, and expanding life and diversity. Our movement of material and accumulation of wealth was limited to what we could carry, as foraging and hunting necessitated a nomadic lifestyle. Humans' function on the landscape was not unlike other animals of the wild.

With the first domesticated livestock and the first saved seed, we started on a trajectory of extracting more wealth from the land than we returned to it. For the first time in history, we could take more than we had to give back. This enabled the concept of ownership and the accumulation of wealth that led to all sorts of extracurricular activities, both benevolent and pernicious. The increase in food production per person allowed humans to focus on pursuits beyond sustenance, and thus began the development of culture and the dawn of civilization. The technology of agriculture gave humans the time and energy to make art, develop science, and exploit the earth's natural resources.

Agriculture is at the prehistoric root of our current predicament as a fast-growing population on a finite planet. Conventional agricultural practices continue to exacerbate our problems by cashing in our soil resources for a short-term boost in food production. We are engaged in what Wes Jackson calls "deficit spending" of our natural capital. In a short-sighted effort to meet the desires of the present, we are destroying the very resource base that enables our future.

Regenerating Our Life Support

While agriculture is largely responsible for the reduction of the planet's natural capital throughout human history, I believe it can also reconnect us to our ecological roots and help transform our role as a species from parasitic consumer to symbiotic producer. The key to our survival lies in how we relate to the land and coax it into providing our energy, purifying our air and water, and sustaining our health without diminishing its ability to continue doing these things into the future.

In an economic analysis that accounts for all the usual externalities, a farm's natural capital is worth as much as its economic capital. Good farming makes continual deposits to our species' communal savings account in the bank of ecological resources. A diverse and prolific web of life is the basis of health in soil, plants, and animals, and this ecological health forms the land-based component of our planet's life support system. By feeding and protecting the soil-plant food web through farming according to nature's model, we regenerate the essential resource that sustains us as a terrestrial species.

When we keep the soil undisturbed and covered in a diversity of living plants, we enhance rather than disrupt natural cycles of fertility and productivity. This is the mechanism of regeneration and prosperity that has been refined and perfected over the last 470 million years. It is unlikely that we, a very new addition to Earth's manifest, are capable of reengineering our spaceship's life support system to function better. The choice is clear enough: either we get on board with nature's blueprint for prosperity, or we jump ship and gamble our existence on the sci-fi dream of terraforming Mars. As a realist and a patriotic Earthling, I vote for the former.

Carbon Farming and Climate Change

Agriculture has the unique ability to solve two of our most far-reaching global problems with a single commonsense solution. These problems are widespread soil degradation and excessive carbon in our atmosphere. The solution is carbon sequestration in the form of humus and living organisms in and on our agricultural soils. Through no-till farming practices we can build soil organic matter and reduce atmospheric carbon in the process.

According to the World Bank, there are 12 billion acres of agricultural land on our planet. A one percent increase in organic matter in the top 10 inches of an acre of soil removes roughly 8.5 tons of carbon from the atmosphere. If we made such an increase to all our agricultural soils, we would transform 100 billion tons of polluting atmospheric carbon into life-giving soil organic matter.

This translates to a reduction of 48 parts per million (ppm) of carbon dioxide in our atmosphere. We are currently at 410 ppm, and climbing. To get back to our pre-fossil-fuel level of 280 ppm, we need to increase the organic matter of our planet's agricultural soils by an average of less than three percent. Imagine how fertile a world that would be!

While the calculations are simple, the practicalities of such monumental shifts are obviously more complicated. Nevertheless, the potential of no-till carbon farming to rejuvenate our soils and mitigate climate change should give us both hope and purpose. Every increase in soil organic matter we accomplish on our farm contributes, however slightly, to a better world.

Building soil organic matter is a win-win. Not only is this effort part of a worldwide solution to climate change, it also increases the productivity and resilience of our land, and thus the economic health of our farms.

Measures of Ecological Health

Though the full value a farm adds to its ecosystem is impossible to quantify, there are certain contributions we can measure to evaluate and improve the farm's ecological health:

Photosynthesis. While we can't easily measure the farm's carbon capture directly, we can estimate how much of our land is thickly covered in a diversity of living plants at any time throughout the season. These snapshot evaluations of the state of our fields can give a sobering indication of our room for further growth as harvesters of the sun.

Precipitation retained. In most climates, the healthier the farm ecosystem, the less water will run off of it. Healthy soil and a productive landscape function as a giant sponge that soaks up precipitation and holds it right where it's needed. Though difficult to measure, water visibly running off the farm is an indication of

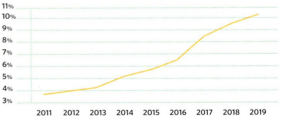

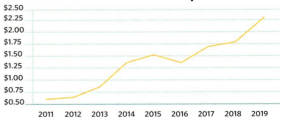

Economic health and soil health go hand in hand.

the need for more plant life and soil organic matter, and a more absorbent landscape.

Quality of water running through and off the farm. When water *does* run through or off an ecologically healthy farm, it remains clear of sediment and nutrients. Silt and leachate not only lead to potential pollution, they also represent a loss of soil and fertility through erosion.

Soil organic matter. The organic matter in the soil provides food and habitat for microorganisms, improves soil texture and water-holding capacity, and provides reaction sites for biochemical soil processes. And every bit of carbon in the soil is that much less in the atmosphere. What better place to store our excess carbon than in the life of the soil that sustains us?

Soil biological activity. Soil organic matter does not necessarily guarantee healthy biological activity. In severely compacted or waterlogged soils, organic matter is often very high. A peat bog is an extreme example. There are a number of soil tests that measure biological activity, and these results can help track the farm's progress toward ecological health below ground.

Earthworm counts. One low-tech biological soil test is to dig up a given volume of soil and count the number of earthworms present. The noble earthworm is one of the best indicators of fertile soil. High worm populations go hand in hand with ecological health.

Money spent on inputs and overhead. In the commodity economy of manufactured fertilizers and agricultural supplies, every dollar spent represents environmental harm and reduction of our planet's natural capital. Even if we choose our sources carefully, the very framework of our industrial system — from the mining and processing of materials to the construction of roads and the manufacture of trucks to transport the goods to our farm — comes with significant environmental costs. We add to the damage of this extractive economy with each input we purchase.

The cost of overhead supports a similar scaffolding of industrialized society. Some of these expenses are inevitable given the world we live in, but we would do well to acknowledge their role in the greater ecological health of our planet.

Quality of Life

What matters most in this world? What defines our success? What are the underlying characteristics of a good life, well lived? How we answer these questions determines how we engage the world and what legacy we leave behind for future generations. Unfortunately, industrial society answers these questions almost exclusively in monetary terms, alienating us from the values and emotions that define us as human.

The growth-based consumptive economy of the current era has affected all aspects of society — polluting our environment, uprooting our communities, eroding our rural landscapes, corrupting our politics, and isolating each of us as individual units of labor and consumption in an economic machine that siphons money from the many engaged in hands-on work to the few engaged in monetary manipulation. Breaking out of this progression toward ecological and cultural exhaustion is no small task, but it is the grave responsibility of each and every one of us if we are to thrive as a species. It requires only basic math to understand that indefinite growth on a finite planet is unsustainable.

The first step may well be to recognize the true ingredients of a satisfying, fulfilling life. If we can focus our efforts as farmers and as humans on what actually matters to us, perhaps we can avert the destructive course of growth for growth's sake. In his book *Holistic Management: A Commonsense Revolution to Restore Our Environment*, Allan Savory instructs the reader how to craft a quality-of-life statement. What defines a high quality of life is obviously subjective and unique to each person, but Savory suggests four categories to consider in evaluating what gives life meaning. I have borrowed some of his ideas here, and added my own interpretation.

Physical Health, Comfort, and Safety

Perhaps the most obvious aspects of a quality life relate to the practical concerns of survival. Every organism on this planet seeks good food, hospitable shelter, comfortable temperatures, and physical security. Without meeting these basic needs, the enjoyment of life will be limited. Satisfying these needs requires a minimum level of financial resources, and until this level is reached, priorities naturally focus on economic concerns.

Starting a farm is no different; economic viability is a basic need on which the farm's other accomplishments depend. Once basic standards of living are achieved, however, studies show that there is no further correlation between more money and a more fulfilling life. Clearly there is more value to life than accumulating material means, and there is more value to farming than profitability. While no-till farming can be highly profitable, I believe there is a greater contribution toward quality of life that comes from reinvesting excess profits in the other areas that give life meaning.

Meaningful Relationships

Humans are social creatures who require interpersonal connection to thrive. We seek a sense of belonging — to relate to how others act and feel, and to have our own actions and feelings understood and respected. Human-scale farming maximizes human relationships, both on the farm and in the surrounding community. Non-mechanized work requires many hands working in unison. Direct-to-consumer marketing depends on community connections and interpersonal word-of-mouth recommendation. The community-supported farm becomes a place for people to join together to celebrate our natural role in nurturing life, creating food, and nourishing each other.

Personal Growth

The human mind and body need to be challenged to unleash their creative potential. Operating a lever on an assembly line does not foster personal growth. To engage our enormous brains and the roughly 800 muscle groups that make up our bodies, we need a variety of tasks that combine the mental and the physical and that encourage creativity and innovation.

Throughout human history, farming has provided us with physical work, mental challenges, and the personal growth that results. Human-scale farming by definition seeks to celebrate the human body and mind through creative and fulfilling work. The variety of tasks and lack of mechanization on a no-till market farm keep the body fluid and the mind engaged.

In agriculture, growth on a personal level may well correspond to the health and diversity of living growth on the landscape. The fruits of our labor are both internal and literal. As Masanobu Fukuoka puts it, "The ultimate goal of farming is not the growing of crops, but the cultivation and perfection of human beings."

Societal Contribution

Fulfillment often comes from a feeling that we serve something greater than ourselves. Without this sense of purpose, our efforts can lack meaning. Many of us want to feel like we play an important role in our community, our society, and the world. Engaging in human-scale regenerative agriculture is a way to make a difference both locally and globally. From job creation and nutritional health to regeneration of natural capital and reduction of atmospheric carbon, no-till farming can work toward improving the quality of life not just for the farmer and their community but for the entire planet.

There has never been a better time to start farming.

ACKNOWLEDGMENTS

I could not have embarked on my farming journey without the moral and financial support of family and friends. I am forever indebted to Mary, James, Stuart, Dot, Gene, Owen, Rebecca, Anna, Anne, Judy, Denis, and everyone who helped me take my first steps as a farmer.

I owe my education and growth as a farmer to the curiosity, passion, and generosity of the individuals who helped build and run the farm over the last nine years. You all know who you are. Listed roughly in chronological order, these are the people who made Frith Farm what it is today: Stuart, Robbie, Hillary, Jack, Courtney, Jeff, Kirsten, Dawn, Joseph, Will, Josh, Cricka, Sarah, Wester, Naomi, Andrew, Alex, Katy, Jack, Damaris, Isabel, Ryan, Leslie, Laura, Daniel, Shon, Katie, John, Kate, Sarah, Caroline, Becca, Hannah, Becky, Richard, Karen, Katia, Liz, Livy, Elyse, Seneth, Sophia, Ana, Diane, Chase, David, Molly, Dennis, Kate, Ana María, Anna, and the many volunteers who invested their time and energy in this place.

Lastly, but far from least, I am grateful to Sarah for her patience and compassion, and to Ellis for being the most wonderful distraction anyone could ask for.

I have learned a lot since I first started writing this book. My awareness of my privilege as a white American man is incomplete but increasing. My growing understanding of colonialism and the history of US agriculture is opening my eyes to the racial and cultural biases that shape our society. This self-education is ongoing, so it is difficult to incorporate into the static format of a book. Re-reading the text before its second printing, I cringe at the blindspots it shows.

Blatantly absent from the book is the discussion of land justice to address the fact that US farming is based on land stolen from Native Americans and wealth accumulated from enslaved Africans and their descendants. Also missing is the idea of making reparations to help heal the trauma of slavery, genocide, cultural erasure, and racism throughout US history. My omissions highlight the comfortable ignorance that allows these injustices to continue to this day.

True holistic thinking includes the history of the land and its inhabitants. Humans are of the soil; exploitation of land and exploitation of people go hand in hand. We cannot solve our ecological problems without addressing the social injustices that create them.

I farm on Wabanaki land. Whose land are you on? Find out at https://native-land.ca/

RESOURCES

Recommended Tools and Supplies

These are some of the inputs and suppliers that I've found most useful and reliable over the last 10 years. This list is not comprehensive and depending on your location there may be better sourcing options locally.

Seeds

When available, I recommend buying from local seed companies that sell varieties particularly suited to your climate.

Johnny's Selected Seeds
www.johnnyseeds.com

Fedco
www.fedcoseeds.com

High Mowing
www.highmowingseeds.com

Fruition Seeds
www.fruitionseeds.com

Hawaii Clean Seed
www.hawaiianorganicginger.com

Wood Prairie Farm
www.woodprairie.com

Greenhouse Supplies

Greenhouse structure, heater, automatic roll-up sides, and other components
Rimol Greenhouse Systems
www.rimolgreenhouses.com

Potting Soil

Vermont Compost Fort Vee
Vermont Compost Company
www.vermontcompost.com

Soil Blockers

Stand-up 35 soil blocker (1-inch blocks), stand-up 20 soil blocker (1.5-inch blocks), stand-up 12 soil blocker (2-inch blocks), stand-up 6 soil blocker (3-inch blocks)
Johnny's Selected Seeds
www.johnnyseeds.com

Heat Mats & Controller

Hydrofarm seedling heat mat, 20" × 48" (107 Watts), Hydrofarm single outlet thermostat controller
Johnny's Selected Seeds
www.johnnyseeds.com

Seedling Trays and Pots

Heavy duty 1020 trays, traditional inserts for 1020 trays (for seedling sales), square pot carrying trays (insert for 1020 tray that holds 18 coir pots), 3⅞" × 4" coir pots
Greenhouse Megastore
www.greenhousemegastore.com

Rolling Dibbler

For marking transplant spacing

Infinite Dibbler
Two Bad Cats, LLC
www.twobadcatsllc.com

Push Seeder

For all direct seeding.

Earthway 1001-B Precision Garden Seeder
Earthway
www.earthway.com

Irrigation

Wonder Waterer Wand (for greenhouse seedlings), Xcel Wobbler Sprinklers with riser assembly and push-connect fittings, drip tape, fittings, pumps, and more
Rain-Flo Irrigation
www.rainfloirrigation.com

Black polyethylene pipe (Polypipe) for main lines and laterals
Local plumbing supply store

Bed Preparation and Weeding

Organic mulches (compost, leaves, hay, straw, wood chips)
Local farmers, landscapers, nurseries, transfer stations, and waste management companies

Soil amendments and fertilizers
Organic Growers Supply
www.fedcoseeds.com/ogs

North Country Organics
www.norganics.com

Wheelbarrow, 6-cubic-foot poly
Local hardware store or garden center

Broadfork, collinear hoe, stirrup hoe, wire hoe, hand hoe, bed preparation rake, silage tarps, 24' × 100' × 5mil
Johnny's Selected Seeds
www.johnnyseeds.com

Digging fork (for root crops and perennial weeds)
Local hardware store or garden center

Trellising

T-posts, 8-foot
Local farm supply or hardware store (sometimes requires special order)

Electric metallic conduit (EMT), ¾' × 10', with setscrew couplings
Local hardware store

Steel brace bands, 1⅜" (for securing metal tubing to T-posts)
Any greenhouse supply company

Sisal twine (for hanging tomato and cucumber plants), Hortonova netting (secured vertically for peas; horizontally for peppers and cut flowers)
Johnny's Selected Seeds
www.johnnyseeds.com

High Tunnels

Rimol Nor'Easter with extended ground posts and automatic roll-up sides
Rimol Greenhouse Systems
www.rimolgreenhouses.com

Row Cover & Stakes

Spunbound row cover, 19 grams per square meter (0.56 oz/ sq yd), 8" anchor pegs (3 prongs for good grip even in mulched pathways)
Rain-Flo Irrigation
www.rainfloirrigation.com

Wire Hoops for Row Cover

9-gauge galvanized steel wire
Local farm supply or hardware store

Power Equipment

BCS walk-behind Tractor with rotary plow and flail mower
Earth Tools
www.earthtools.com

Compact utility tractor (30+ horsepower) with front-end loader
Local used sales from private parties or dealers

Riding mower, chainsaw, weed whacker
Local equipment dealer

Harvesting

Large garden cart
Carts Vermont
www.cartsvermont.com

Harvest Knife and Sheath

Victorinox Wavy paring knife with red handle

Victorinox paring knife pouch
Katom Restaurant Supply
www.katom.com

Harvest Snips

Corona long straight snips
Corona
www.coronatoolsusa.com

Harvest Bags

Wells & Wade fruit picking harvest bucket or bag
Agricultural Solutions
www.agriculturesolutions.com

Harvest Tubs

Gorilla tubs, 10-gallon
Red Gorilla USA
www.redgorillausa.com

Harvest Lugs

Stackable/nestable container, 1.75-bushel (for bulky greens), stackable/nestable container, 1.22-bushel (for roots)
Nolt's Produce Supplies, LLC
www.noltsproducesupplies.net

Used bulb crates
Local plant nurseries

Washing and Packing

Wash Basin

Rubbermaid stock tank, 100-gallon
Local farm supply store

Greens Spinner

DIY washing machine conversion
Tutorial for sale at
www.dryyourgreens.com

Packing Supplies

Polyethylene produce bags
International Plastics
www.interplas.com

Colored twist ties (a different color for each wholesale customer)
Webstaurant Store
www.webstaurantstore.com

Sisal twine (for closing root bags)
Johnny's Selected Seeds
www.johnnyseeds.com

Mesh bags (for storing allium crops)
Harris Seeds
www.harrisseeds.com

Wax boxes (for delivering produce)
Find used from local natural grocers

Note: Check with your organic certifier before reusing produce packaging. I make sure to reuse only boxes labeled "Organic" to eliminate risk of contamination. Wax boxes are expensive to buy new but can be purchased in bulk from: Packaging Corporation of America www.packagingcorp.com.

Wooden display crates
Homemade from local rough-sawn lumber

Retail Pulp Boxes

Molded paper berry boxes, half pints, pints, and quarts
Organic Growers Supply
www.fedcoseeds.com/ogs

Produce Scales

Tor-Rey digital scale, 40-lb or 80-lb capacity
Webstaurant Store
www.webstaurantstore.com

Cold Storage

Insulated Shipping Container, Used, 8' × 20' or 8' × 40'
Local supplier or distributor (an internet search for "shipping container" can help locate closest source)

CoolBot (module for overriding temperature setting on a standard air conditioner unit)
Store It Cold, LLC
www.storeitcold.com

Thermostat
(for space heater in winter to prevent walk-in cooler from freezing)

DuroStat portable waterproof prewired thermostat
FarmTek
www.farmtek.com

Poultry Production

Day-Old chicks and poults

Freedom Ranger Hatchery
www.freedomrangerhatchery.com

Cackle Hatchery
www.cacklehatchery.com

Meyer Hatchery
www.meyerhatchery.com

Mt. Healthy Hatchery
www.mthealthy.com

Murray McMurray Hatchery
www.mcmurrayhatchery.com

Portable Grain Bins

Versa-Tote feed trailer, 3,000-pound, 5,000-pound, and 6,500-pound models
L-H Manufacturing
www.lhmfg.com

Poultry Processing Equipment

Kill cones, scalder, plucker, transport crates, and more
Featherman Equipment
www.feathermanequipment.com

Fencing Supplies

Electronet fences, chargers, insulators, posts, and more
Premier 1 Supplies
www.premier1supplies.com

Kencove Farm Fence Supplies
www.kencove.com

Work Apparel

Double-front work pants, knee pad inserts for work pants, waterproof bib overalls
Carhartt
www.carhartt.com

Rubber boots
Xtratuf
www.xtratuf.com

Slip-On leather boots
Blundstone
www.blundstone.com

SELECTED BIBLIOGRAPHY

Chapter 1: Farming at a Human Scale

Abbey, Edward. *One Life at a Time, Please.* Henry Holt and Company, 1978.

Alexander, Christopher. *A Pattern Language: Towns, Buildings, Construction.* Oxford University Press, 1977.

Berry, Wendell. *It All Turns on Affection: The Jefferson Lecture & Other Essays.* Counterpoint Press, 2012.

Coleman, Eliot. *The New Organic Grower: A Master's Manual of Tools and Techniques for the Home and Market Gardener.* Chelsea Green, 1995.

Fukuoka, Masanobu. *The One-Straw Revolution.* New York Review of Books, 1978.

Jackson, Wes. *Consulting the Genius of the Place: An Ecological Approach to a New Agriculture.* Counterpoint Press, 2011.

Kimmerer, Robin Wall. *Braiding Sweetgrass: Indigenous Wisdom, Scientific Knowledge and the Teachings of Plants.* Milkweed Editions, 2015.

McKibben, Bill. *Deep Economy: The Wealth of Communities and the Durable Future.* Henry Holt and Company, 2007.

Montgomery, David R. *Dirt: The Erosion of Civilizations.* University of California Press, 2008.

Salatin, Joel. *Folks, This Ain't Normal.* Center Street, 2011.

Savory, Allan. *Holistic Management: A Commonsense Revolution to Restore Our Environment.* Island Press, 2016.

Schumacher, E. F. *Small Is Beautiful: Economics as if People Mattered.* Harper & Row, 1975.

Steiner, Rudolf. *Agriculture Course: The Birth of the Biodynamic Method.* Rudolf Steiner Press, 2004.

Wessels, Tom. *Reading the Forested Landscape: A Natural History of New England.* Countryman Press, 1999.

Chapter 2: Ecological Agriculture

Alexander, Christopher. *The Timeless Way of Building.* Oxford University Press, 1979.

Chapman H. W., Gleason L. S., Loomis W. E. "The carbon dioxide content of field air." *Plant Physiology* 29, 6, (1954): 500-503.

Faulkner, Edward H. *Plowman's Folly.* University of Oklahoma Press, 1943.

Howard, Sir Albert. *An Agricultural Testament.* Oxford University Press, 1940.

Ingham, Elaine. *"Building Soil Health."* Online Presentation PVP096.

Jackson, Wes. *Consulting the Genius of the Place: An Ecological Approach to a New Agriculture.* Counterpoint Press, 2011.

Jones, Christine. "Liquid Carbon Pathway." Australian Farm Journal Edition 338, (July 3, 2008).

Lowenfels, Jeff. *Teaming with Fungi: The Organic Grower's Guide to Mycorrhizae.* Timber Press, 2017.

Mann, Charles C. *1491: New Revelations of the Americas Before Columbus.* Vintage Books, 2006.

Phillips, Michael. *Mycorrhizal Planet.* Chelsea Green, 2017.

Savory, Allan. *Holistic Management: A Commonsense Revolution to Restore Our Environment.* Island Press, 2016.

Shepard, Mark. *Restoration Agriculture: Real-World Permaculture for Farmers.* Acres USA, 2014.

Steiner, Rudolf. *Agriculture Course: The Birth of the Biodynamic Method.* Rudolf Steiner Press, 2004.

For a complete list of various botanical families less common to vegetable production, see mycorrhizas.info/nmplants.html.

Chapter 3: Getting Started

Coleman, Eliot. *The New Organic Grower: A Master's Manual of Tools and Techniques for the Home and Market Gardener.* Chelsea Green Publishing, 1995.

Donahue, Brian. *Reclaiming the Commons: Community Farms and Forests in a New England Town.* Yale University, 1999.

Hartman, Ben. *The Lean Farm Guide to Growing Vegetables: More In-Depth Lean Techniques for Efficient Organic Production.* Chelsea Green, 2017.

Hubka, Thomas C., *Big House, Little House, Back House, Barn: The Connected Farm Buildings of New England.* University Press of New England, 2004.

Minnesota Institute for Sustainable Agriculture. *Building a Sustainable Business: A Guide to Developing a Business Plan for Farms and Rural Businesses.* 2003

National Young Farmers Coalition. www.youngfarmers.org

Penniman, Leah. *Farming While Black: Soul Fire Farm's Practical Guide to Liberation on the Land.* Chelsea Green, 2018.

Salatin, Joel. *You Can Farm: The Entrepreneur's Guide to Start and Succeed in a Farming Enterprise.* Polyface, 1998.

Schumacher, E. F. *Small Is Beautiful: Economics as if People Mattered.* Harper & Row, 1975.

United States Department of Agriculture, Census of Agriculture, 2012.

Wiswall, Richard. *The Organic Farmer's Business Handbook: A Complete Guide to Managing Finances, Crops and Staff — and Making a Profit.* Chelsea Green, 2009.

Chapter 4: Establishing Beds

Fortier, Jean-Martin. *The Market Gardener: A Successful Grower's Handbook for Small-Scale Organic Farming.* New Society, 2014.

Lee, Andy and Foreman, Patricia. *Backyard Market Gardening: The Entrepreneur's Guide to Selling What You Grow.* Good Earth Publications, 1993.

Phillips, Michael. *Mycorrhizal Planet.* Chelsea Green, 2017.

Chapter 5: Planting

Hanson, Beth. "Soil Solarization," *Rodale's Organic Life.* March 5, 2003.

Fortier, Jean-Martin. *The Market Gardener: A Successful Grower's Handbook for Small-Scale Organic Farming.* New Society, 2014.

Faulkner, Edward H. *Plowman's Folly.* University of Oklahoma Press, 1943.

Chapter 6: Irrigation

Maynard, Donald N. and Hochmuth, George J. *Knott's Handbook for Vegetable Growers.* John Wiley & Sons, 2007.

Chapter 7: Weeds

Coleman, Eliot. *The New Organic Grower: A Master's Manual of Tools and Techniques for the Home and Market Gardener.* Chelsea Green Publishing, 1995.

Jackson, Wes. *Consulting the Genius of the Place: An Ecological Approach to a New Agriculture.* Counterpoint Press, 2011.

Jenkins, Joseph. *The Humanure Handbook: A Guide to Composting Human Manure.* Joseph Jenkins, Inc., 2005.

King, F. H. *Farmers of Forty Centuries: Organic Farming in China, Korea, and Japan.* Dover Publications, 2004.

Kroeck, Seth. *Crop Rotation and Cover Cropping: Soil Resiliency and Health on the Organic Farm.* Chelsea Green, 2011.

The Xerces Society. *Farming with Native Beneficial Insects: Ecological Pest Control Solutions.* Storey Publishing, 2014.

Chapter 8: Methods of No-Till Disturbance

Environmental Fact Sheet "Recommended Minimum Water Supply Capacity for Private Wells," New Hampshire Department of Environmental Services, 2010.

Chapter 9: Natural Soil Care in Action

Ingham, Elaine. "Building Soil Health." Online Presentation PVP096, www.soilfoodweb.com.

Phillips, Michael. *The Holistic Orchard: Tree Fruits and Berries the Biological Way.* Chelsea Green, 2011.

Chapter 10: Harvest and Handling

Bubel, Mike and Bubel, Nancy. *Root Cellaring: Natural Cold Storage of Fruits and Vegetables.* Storey Publishing, 1991.

Maynard, Donald N. and Hochmuth, George J. *Knott's Handbook for Vegetable Growers.* John Wiley & Sons, 2007.

Chapter 12: Labor

Abrams, John. *Companies We Keep: Employee Ownership and the Business of Community and Place.* Chelsea Green, 2005.

Salatin, Joel. *Fields of Farmers: Interning, Mentoring, Partnering, Germinating.* Polyface, 2013

Chapter 14: Measures of Success: Profit, People, and Place

Fuller, R. Buckminster. *Operating Manual for Spaceship Earth.* Southern Illinois University Press, 1969.

Savory, Allan. *Holistic Management: A Commonsense Revolution to Restore Our Environment.* Island Press, 2016.

Salatin, Joel. *Fields of Farmers: Interning, Mentoring, Partnering, Germinating.* Polyface, 2013

For more information on how to accept SNAP and WIC payments, see fns.usda.gov.

Metric Conversion Charts

TEMPERATURE CONVERSION

To convert	to	
Fahrenheit	Celsius	subtract 32 from Fahrenheit temperature, multiply by 5, then divide by 9.

EASY-TO-REMEMBER EQUIVALENTS

0°C = 32°F

10°C = 50°F

20°C = 68°F

30°C = 86°F

40°C = 104°F

Every 10°C = 18°F

LENGTH EQUIVALENTS

U.S.	Metric
1 inch	2.54 centimeters
1 foot (12 inches)	0.305 meters
1 yard (3 feet)	0.914 meters
1 mile (5,280 feet)	1.61 kilometers

AREA EQUIVALENTS

U.S.	Metric
1 square foot	0.093 square meters
1 acre (43,560 square feet)	0.405 hectares
1 square mile (640 acres)	2.59 square kilometers

WEIGHT EQUIVALENTS

U.S.	Metric
1 ounce	28.4 grams
1 pound (16 ounces)	0.454 kilograms
1 ton (2000 pounds)	0.907 metric tons

VOLUME EQUIVALENTS

U.S.	Metric
1 cup	237 milliliters
1 pint (2 cups)	0.473 liters
1 quart (2 pints)	0.946 liters
1 gallon (4 quarts)	3.79 liters
1 cubic foot (7.48 gallons)	28.3 liters
1 cubic yard (27 cubic feet)	0.765 cubic meters
1 acre-inch (27,154 gallons)	103 cubic meters

INDEX

Page references in *italic* indicate illustrations; **bold** page references indicate charts.

GET FIRSTHAND FARMING ADVICE
WITH MORE BOOKS FROM STOREY

Compact Farms by Josh Volk
Design a profitable farming enterprise on 5 acres or less.
Detailed plans from 15 real farms across North America
show how to maximize productivity and avoid difficulties,
regardless of whether your plot is rural or urban.

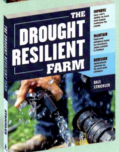

The Drought-Resilient Farm by Dale Strickler
Protect your farm and your future with these innovative
strategies from a successful sixth-generation Kansas
farmer. You'll learn how to get more water into your soil,
keep it there, and help your plants and livestock access it.

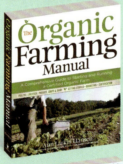

The Organic Farming Manual by Ann Larkin Hansen
This comprehensive guide to starting or transitioning to
an organic farm equips you with the information you need
to grow, certify, and market organic produce, grains, meat,
and dairy.

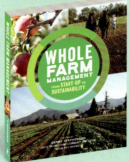

Whole-Farm Management Edited by Garry Stephenson
Whether you're dreaming of starting a farm or already operating one, this invaluable handbook developed by Oregon
University's Small Farms Program holds the keys to making
smart, strategic business decisions to ensure lasting success.